Teaching English, Language and Literacy

Are you looking for one book that covers every aspect of the teaching of English at primary level?

Now fully updated, this third edition of *Teaching English, Language and Literacy* includes brand new chapters on children's literature and reading comprehension. Rooted in research evidence and multidisciplinary theory, this book is an essential introduction for anyone learning to teach English from the early years to primary school level.

The authors draw on their research, scholarship and practice to offer advice on:

- developing reading, including choosing texts, and phonics teaching
- improving writing, including grammar and punctuation
- language and speaking and listening
- planning and assessing
- working effectively with multilingual pupils
- understanding historical developments in the subject
- the latest thinking in educational policy and practice
- the use of multimedia
- maintaining good home-school links
- gender and the teaching of English language and literacy

All the chapters include clear examples of practice, coverage of key issues, analysis of research, and reflections on national policy to encourage the best possible response to the demands of national curricula. Each chapter also has a glossary to explain terms and gives suggestions for further reading.

This book is for all who want to improve teaching English, language and literacy. Designed to help inform the practice of students on teacher training courses, but also of great use to those teachers wanting to keep pace with the latest developments in their specialist subject, this book covers the theory and practice of teaching English, language and literacy.

Dominic Wyse is Professor of Early Childhood and Primary Education at the Institute of Education (IoE) at the University of London.

Russell Jones is Senior Lecturer in Education and Childhood Studies at Manchester Metropolitan University.

Helen Bradford is an Affiliated Lecturer at the Faculty of Education, University of Cambridge.

Mary Anne Wolpert is an Affiliated Lecturer at the Faculty of Education, University of Cambridge.

Teaching English, Language and Literacy

Third Edition

Dominic Wyse, Russell Jones,
Helen Bradford and
Mary Anne Wolpert

Routledge
Taylor & Francis Group

LONDON AND NEW YORK

First edition published 2001
Second edition published 2008
This third edition published 2013
by Routledge
2 Park Square, Milton Park, Abingdon, Oxon OX14 4RN

Simultaneously published in the USA and Canada
by Routledge
711 Third Avenue, New York, NY 10017

Routledge is an imprint of the Taylor & Francis Group, an informa business

© 2013 Dominic Wyse, Russell Jones, Helen Bradford and Mary Anne
Wolpert

British Library Cataloguing in Publication Data
A catalogue record for this book is available from the British Library

Library of Congress Cataloging-in-Publication Data
Teaching English, language and literacy / edited by Dominic Wyse . . .
[et al.]. — 3rd ed.
  p. cm.
  Prev. ed. main entry under Wyse, Dominic.
  1. Language arts (Elementary) I. Wyse, Dominic, 1964–
LB1576.W99 2013
372.6—dc23

                                          2012027487

ISBN: 978–0–415–66997–9 (hbk)
ISBN: 978–0–415–66998–6 (pbk)
ISBN: 978–0–203–07352–0 (ebk)

Typeset in Bembo
by RefineCatch Limited, Bungay, Suffolk

Printed and bound by CPI Group (UK) Ltd, Croydon, CR0 4YY

Contents

Figures

Tables

Preface

This third edition of our book is the most significant rewrite since its inception, and a fitting way to mark the tenth anniversary (plus a bit more) of *Teaching English, Language and Literacy*. When Dominic and Russell had the idea for the book, they were new lecturers in Liverpool searching for a comprehensive introduction to their subject. When they discovered that such a book didn't exist, they put forward a proposal to Jude Bowen who was then a commissioning editor for Routledge. Reviews were very favourable so the rest, as they say, is history.

The most significant change for this edition of the book is the addition of two new authors, Helen Bradford and Mary Anne Wolpert. Their experience leading the outstanding PGCE English course at the University of Cambridge, and their complementary practical teaching experience and academic interests, have brought vital fresh perspectives.

The overall structure of the book has changed. This resulted in two entirely new chapters, including one on reading comprehension written by Helen. The other new chapter is the extended one on children's literature written with new material from Mary Anne who also brought together sections on texts for children which were in different places in the second edition. Another part of the structural changes is a stronger signal about the place of language in relation to literacy, hence the language chapters now appear earlier in the book. Dominic's work in the years since the last edition included the development of new theory on the teaching of English, language and literacy (Wyse, Andrews and Hoffman, 2010; Wyse, 2011[1]) which has resulted in major revision of the theoretical framing of the book that is explicit in Chapter 2, 'Learning and language'.

Every chapter has been updated and many have had substantial changes to reflect new research, new theory, new practice and rapidly changing

---

1 Wyse, D., Andrews, R. and Hoffman, J. (eds) (2010) *The Routledge International Handbook of English, Language and Literacy Teaching*. London: Routledge.
   Wyse, D. (ed.) (2011) *Literacy Teaching and Education: SAGE Library of Educational Thought and Practice*. London: Sage.

government policies. The longer chapters of the book are the most obvious examples but every other chapter includes new material of some kind.

English is one of the most fascinating, controversial and challenging subjects of the school curriculum. The fact that English is the language we speak also makes it a subject that is closely linked with our identities, which is one of the reasons that it often engenders passionate views. Another reason that it is important is that all teachers have to be teachers of English because learning takes place through talking, reading and writing. In the early years and primary curriculum, great stress is put on English because it is a bridge to all other learning.

This book is a comprehensive introduction to the ideas, concepts and knowledge that are part of the study of English teaching. *Teaching English, Language and Literacy* is written for trainee teachers, their tutors, for more experienced teachers and for other students of education. The partnerships between providers of teacher education and schools have maintained the need for a book that offers a comprehensive overview of the subject to enable teacher mentors to update their professional knowledge in specific areas when appropriate. It is designed as a reader that will enhance and consolidate the learning in early years and primary English programmes and as an essential guide to the teaching of English. The book's hallmarks have always been that it is:

- aimed at teachers with a view to **informing their thinking and practice**;
- **a comprehensive** account of teaching English, language *and* literacy;
- **critically evaluative** in style, e.g. in relation to government policy;
- built on an **explicit theoretical framework**;
- rooted in **research evidence** and multidisciplinary theory.

The book is divided into five parts: I. 'Introduction'; II. 'Language'; III. 'Reading'; IV. 'Writing'; and V. 'General issues'. The bulk of the book consists of short chapters that cover the variety of aspects that make up the English curriculum. All of these chapters include clear examples of practice, coverage of key issues, analysis of research and reflections on national policy. The short chapters are complemented by five longer ones. The first of these addresses the important subject of the history of English and English teaching. The second signals our appreciation of the importance of texts for children. The other three look at children's development in language, reading and writing, and relate this development to teaching approaches. The structure of the longer chapters allowed us to tackle some of the most important aspects of the English curriculum in depth and at a higher level. Part V is made up of issues that tend to be applicable to all three areas of language, reading and writing. The exception to this structure is 'Learning and language', which is located in the introduction because this theoretical chapter frames our thinking throughout the book.

One of the important features of the book is its comprehensive scope. The subject of English is an area that boasts an impressive array of scholarship and practice. While there are many books that have addressed the modes of reading, writing and speaking and listening separately, there are very few which address the complete subject area. By doing this we have accepted that inevitably some parts of the subject are touched on only briefly. In recognition of this, you will find more than 100 descriptions of recommended books and papers for further reading which appear in the 'annotated bibliographies' for every chapter. A novel feature of these bibliographies is a system of coding which allows you to judge the reading level and the balance between theory and practice:

★   Mainly focused on classroom practice
★★   Close balance between theory and practice
★★★ Research- and theory-based

L1   Introductory reading
L2   Intermediate reading
L3   Advanced reading

We are fully in support of the idea that teaching should be an evidence-informed activity, and so each chapter in the book is underpinned by our reading of research. In addition to our references to papers, books and official publications, we also make reference to a range of websites. This is always a tricky business. This revision of the book took many months to complete and in that time information and communications technology (ICT) has continued to develop. In the light of this we have chosen sites that we hope will stand the test of time.

The most important part of reading a book like this is that it will enable you to become a better teacher. No book can offer a magic solution to becoming an effective teacher. Learning to teach – like most learning – requires practical engagement with the subject in partnership with experienced people. However, in order to establish direct and explicit links with practice we use case studies, analysis of resources, reflections on children's work, teachers' thoughts, examples of teaching, and each chapter concludes with 'practice points' which have been written to focus attention on some of the most important practical ideas of which you should be aware.

This book covers a wide range of essential knowledge. If we consider technical vocabulary alone, there are many definitions supplied in the 'glossaries' that are a feature of every chapter. So if you are unsure about the meaning of a particular word as you are reading, you do not need to reach for a dictionary because most of the key words are defined for you at the end of the chapter. Another aspect of knowledge that has been played down in recent years is the knowledge of issues. This is, we feel, vital to both effective teaching and success in the education profession. In order to maintain the tradition of English as a vibrant subject, we hope teachers will continue to fully engage with the issues and ideas that are explored in this book.

Note

Throughout this book the following icons are used to assist the reader:

→   Recommends the reader looks at another chapter in the book.
☞   These words are included in the glossaries at the end of each chapter.

Acknowledgements

Dominic and Russell would like to thank the many students, teachers and colleagues who have shown appreciation for their work critically reflecting on government policy on the teaching of English, language and literacy. They would also like to acknowledge the contribution of Charles Sarland and Roger Bainbridge to the first edition.

We would also like to thank all the Routledge staff who have been involved in making the book such a success, including Alison Foyle who commissioned the third edition.

Finally, we would like to record our appreciation for the outstanding reflections from the reviewers who commented on the second edition. Most of their recommendations have been acted on as we worked to refine the book.

Part I

Introduction

Chapter 1

The history of English, language and literacy

One of the important aspects of historical knowledge is that it enables us to better understand the present. This chapter briefly examines three significant historical angles: the history of English as a language; the history of the teaching of English; and the history of national initiatives to improve the teaching of English. We conclude in the present by looking at the National Curriculum and the phonics screening check.

The three words 'English', 'Language' and 'Literacy' in the title of this book are significant because they are central to many of the debates that have raged about the teaching of English in primary schools. During the 1970s and 1980s, the teaching of 'language' was the focus. The job of primary schools was to foster the development of children's language through reading, writing and, to a lesser extent, talking. This focus included the need to support multilingual children's development in English and other languages. The teachers who coordinated the subject were known as 'language coordinators'. The teaching of language in primary schools was seen as different in many respects from the teaching of English conducted in secondary schools.

With the coming of the Education Reform Act 1988, 'English' was re-established as the main focus for primary education. The subject was, however, still to be concerned with the teaching of the three language modes of reading, writing and talk. 'Speaking and Listening' became of equal importance to Reading and Writing for the first time, and this was prescribed by the National Curriculum. Coordinators were now to be called 'English' coordinators. The advent of the National Literacy Strategy (NLS) ☞ in 1997 resulted in a heavy focus on 'Literacy'. You will probably have guessed that subject leaders were renamed 'literacy coordinators'.

The first part of this chapter looks at some of the historical aspects of the subject that have shaped its development. It is important that all teachers have a historical perspective on their work; at the very least, this can give you a means to critically examine modern initiatives and to check how 'new' they really are.

We start with a brief look at some of the significant moments in the development of the English language and reflect on their continuing relevance to classroom teaching. This is followed by reflections on the history of the *teaching* of English. We conclude with an outline of some of the major national projects that have been undertaken and finish right up to date with a look at the phonics screening check.

The English language

English, like all languages, is constantly changing. When the editor of the *Oxford English Dictionary* was interviewed in 1998, he commented on the fact that 'phwoarr' had just been included in the dictionary, defined as an exclamation of sexual attraction. Each time publishers produce new editions of dictionaries, new words – and new meanings for old words – are added in recognition of the constant evolution of language. The *Oxford English Dictionary* has a large team of people who are constantly searching for new uses and new additions to the language. The online version of the dictionary is a spectacular resource. As well as recording language change, dictionaries play a major role in the standardisation of the language. It is interesting to note that American Standard English is represented by specific dictionaries such as those published by Merriam-Webster but British Standard English is, for example, represented by the *Oxford English Dictionary* or *Chambers Dictionary*. The significant influence of publishing has also resulted in standard reference works that lay down particular conventions. So if you have ever wondered how to reference properly using the 'Author–Date' method, try *The American Psychological Association (APA) Style Guide* (or for a simplified version, try *The Good Writing Guide for Education Students* (Wyse, 2012). For teachers, the idea that language is always changing is an important one. If we place too heavy an emphasis on absolute and fixed 'rules', we may be teaching in a linguistically inaccurate or inappropriate way (→ Chapter 21). Effective teaching needs to be built on an understanding of those features of the language that are stable and those that are subject to constant change.

This process of change is by no means a recent phenomenon. Human beings' creation of alphabetic written language was a highly significant development. All alphabets were originally derived from the Semitic syllabaries of the second millennium. The developments from both Greek script and the Roman alphabet can be seen in the use of the Latinised form of the first two letters of the Greek alphabet in the word itself, 'alphabet'. 'Alpha' was derived from the Semitic 'aleph' and 'beta' from 'beth' (Goody and Watt, 1963). Historically, the alphabet has been at the heart of some of the most enduring debates about the development of written communication, for example whether the alphabet simply emerged from logographic or pictographic forms. In Harris' (1986) examination of the origins of writing, he called this particular idea of emergence an evolutionary fallacy, arguing that the alphabet was 'the great invention' because its graphic signs have almost no limitations for human communication, unlike logos or pictographs. The continuing development of writing, for example through internet and electronic text forms, is further testament to written language's extraordinary capacity to adapt to, and be part of, cultural change.

It was during the fifth century that the Anglo-Saxons settled in England and, as always happens when people colonise, they brought changes to the language, a process that resulted in 'Old English' being established. The few texts that have survived from this period are in four main dialects ☞: West Saxon, Kentish, Mercian and Northumbrian. The last two are sometimes grouped together and called Anglian. West Saxon became the standard dialect at the time but is not the direct ancestor of modern Standard English ☞, which is mainly derived from an Anglian dialect (Barber, 1993). If you take the modern word 'cold' as an example, the Anglian 'cald' is a stronger influence than the West Saxon version, 'ceald'.

In the ninth century, the Vikings brought further changes to the language. Place names were affected: 'Grimsby' meant 'Grim's village' and 'Micklethwaite' meant 'large clearing'. The pronunciation of English speech was also affected, and it is possible to recognise some Scandinavian-influenced words because of their phonological form. It is suggested that 'awe' is a Scandinavian word and that this came from changes of pronunciation to the Old English word 'ege'. One of the most interesting things about Scandinavian loanwords ☞ is that they are so commonly used: sister, leg, neck, bag, cake, dirt, fellow, fog, knife, skill, skin, sky, window, flat, loose, call, drag and even 'they' and 'them' (Barber, 1993).

In more recent times, words from a range of countries have been borrowed. Here are a small selection of examples: French – elite, liaison, menu, plateau; Spanish and Portuguese – alligator, chocolate, cannibal, embargo, potato; Italian – concerto, balcony, casino, cartoon; Indian languages – bangle, cot, juggernaut, loot, pyjamas, shampoo; African languages – banjo, zombie, rumba, tote. However, for many of these words it is difficult to attribute them to one original country. To illustrate the complexities, consider the word 'chess':

'Chess' was borrowed from Middle French in the fourteenth century. The French word was, in turn, borrowed from Arabic, which had earlier borrowed it from Persian 'shah' 'king'. Thus the etymology ☞ of the word reaches from Persian, through Arabic and Middle French, but its ultimate source (as far back as we can trace its history) is Persian. Similarly, the etymon of 'chess', that is, the word from which it has been derived, is immediately 'esches' and ultimately 'shah'. Loanwords have, as it were, a life of their own that cuts across the boundaries between languages.

(Pyles and Algeo, 1993: 286)

The influence of loanwords is one of the factors that has resulted in some of the irregularities of English spelling. David Crystal (1997) lists some of the other major factors. Above we referred to the Anglo-Saxon period; at that time there were only 24 graphemes (letter symbols) to represent 40 phonemes (sounds). Later 'i' and 'j', 'u' and 'v' were changed from being interchangeable to having distinct functions and 'w' was added, but many sounds still had to be signalled by combinations of letters.

After the Norman conquest, French scribes – who had responsibility for publishing texts – respelled a great deal of the language. They introduced new conventions such as 'qu' for 'cw' (queen), 'gh' for 'h' (night) and 'c' before 'e' or 'i' in words such as 'circle' and 'cell'. Once printing became better established in the West, this added further complications. William Caxton (1422–92) is often credited with the 'invention' of the printing press but that is not accurate. During the seventh century the Chinese printed the earliest known book, *The Diamond Sutra*, using inked wooden relief blocks. By the beginning of the fifteenth century the process had developed in Korea to the extent that printers were manufacturing bronze type sets of 100,000 pieces. In the West, Johannes Gutenberg (1390s–1468) is credited with the development of moveable metal type in association with a hand-operated printing press.

Many of the early printers working in England were foreign (many came from Holland in particular) and they used their own spelling conventions. Also, until the sixteenth century, line justification ☞ was achieved by changing words rather than by adding spaces. Once printing became established, the written language did not keep pace with the considerable alterations to the way words were spoken, resulting in weaker links between sound and symbol.

Samuel Johnson's dictionary, published in 1755, was another important factor in relation to English spelling. His work resulted in dictionaries becoming more authoritarian and used as the basis for 'correct' usage. Noah Webster, the first person to write a major account of American English, compared Johnson's contribution to Isaac Newton's in mathematics. Johnson's dictionary was significant for a number of reasons. Unlike dictionaries of the past that tended to concentrate on 'hard words', Johnson wanted a scholarly record of the whole language. It was based on words in use and introduced a literary dimension, drawing heavily on writers such as Dryden, Milton, Addison, Bacon, Pope and Shakespeare (Crystal, 1997: 109). Shakespeare's remarkable influence on the English language is not confined to the artistic significance of his work; many of the words and phrases of his plays are still commonly used today:

> He coined some 2,000 words – an astonishing number – and gave us countless phrases. As a phrasemaker there has never been anyone to match him. Among his inventions: one fell swoop, in my mind's eye, more in sorrow than in anger, to be in a pickle, bag and baggage, vanish into thin air, budge an inch, play fast and loose, go down the primrose path, the milk

of human kindness, remembrance of things past, the sound and fury, to thine own self be true, to be or not to be, cold comfort, to beggar all description, salad days, flesh and blood, foul play, tower of strength, to be cruel to be kind, and on and on and on and on. And on. He was so wildly prolific that he could put two in one sentence, as in Hamlet's observation: 'Though I am native here and to the manner born, it is custom more honoured in the breach than the observance.' He could even mix metaphors and get away with it, as when he wrote: 'Or to take arms against a sea of troubles.'

(Bryson, 1990: 57)

Crystal (2004) makes the point that although spelling is an area where there is more agreement about what is correct than in other areas of language, there's still considerable variation. Greenbaum's (1986) research looked at all the words beginning with 'A' in a medium-sized desk dictionary which were spelled in more than one way; he found 296. When extrapolating this to the dictionary as a whole, he estimated 5,000 variants altogether, which is 5.6 per cent. If this were to be done with a dictionary as complete as the *Oxford English Dictionary*, it would mean many thousands of words where the spelling has not been definitively agreed. Crystal gives some examples including: accessory/accessary; acclimatize/acclimatise; adrenalin/adrenaline; aga/agha; ageing/aging; all right/alright.

Many of Greenbaum's words were pairs but there were some triplets: for example, aerie/aery/eyrie. And there were even quadruplets: anaesthetize/anaesthetise/anesthetize/anesthetise. Names translated from a foreign language compound the problems, particularly for music students: Tschaikovsky/Tchaikovsky/Tschaikofsky/Tchaikofsky/Tshaikovski.

The teaching of English

The establishment of state education as we know it can be conveniently traced back to the 1870 Elementary Education Act. Prior to that, the education of working-class children in the United Kingdom was largely in the hands of the voluntary sector: church schools, factory schools and, in the earlier part of the nineteenth century, schools run by the oppositional Chartist and Owenite Co-operative movements. The 1870 Act led to the establishment of free educational provision in elementary schools for all children from the age of five up to the age of 12. Education up to the age of ten was compulsory, but if children had met the standards required they could be exempted from schooling for the final years. State schools and voluntary sector schools existed side-by-side from that date, a distinction that is still found today. Class differences were firmly established: the elementary and voluntary schools were schools for the labouring classes and the poor. The middle and upper classes expected to pay for the education of their children; secondary education in the form of the grammar and public schools was not available to the bulk of the population.

The curriculum in the voluntary schools and later in the elementary schools was extremely limited. Writing meant copying or dictation (DES, 1967: 5601). Oral work involved such things as the children learning by heart from the *Book of Common Prayer*, which included: 'To order myself lowly and reverently to all my betters' and 'to do my duty in that state of life, unto which it shall please God to call me' (Williamson, 1981: 79).

The elementary schools emerged at a time when the government exerted considerable control over the curriculum through the 'Revised Code' established in 1862 (→ Chapter 11), better known as 'payment by results'. This was administered through frequent tests in reading, writing and arithmetic – the three Rs. If the children failed to meet the required standards, the grant was withdrawn and the teachers did not get paid. Under such conditions curriculum development was impossible because schools had to focus so much on the tests in order to get paid (Lawson and Silver, 1973).

Though the code was abolished in 1895, and the statutory control of the curriculum relinquished in 1902, the effects lasted well into the twentieth century, leading one inspector to comment that 30 years of 'code despotism' meant that 'teaching remained as mechanical and routine ridden as ever' (Holmes, 1922). Despite these criticisms, however, the introduction of universal compulsory education meant that literacy rates climbed steadily.

'English' as a subject, 1900–39

At the start of the twentieth century, the term 'English' referred to grammar only; reading and writing were not even seen as part of the same subject. A major landmark in the development of the subject was the Newbolt Report on 'The Teaching of English in England' (Board of Education, 1921). George Sampson, a member of the Newbolt committee, writing in the same year (1921), had identified the following 'subjects' still being taught in elementary schools across the land: 'oral composition, written composition, dictation, grammar, reproduction, reading, recitation, literature, spelling, and handwriting.' (Shayer, 1972: 67) The Newbolt Report sought to change that and to bring together:

> under the title of English, 'taught as a fine art', four separate concepts: the universal need for literacy as the core of the curriculum, the developmental importance of children's self expression, a belief in the power of English literature for moral and social improvement, and a concern for 'the full development of mind and character'.
>
> (Protherough and Atkinson, 1994: 7)

This was how English became established as a subject in the secondary curriculum, and placed at the centre of the curriculum for all ages. Famously the

Newbolt Report suggested, of elementary teachers, that 'every teacher is a teacher of English because every teacher is a teacher in English' (Shayer, 1972: 70). The committee recommended that children's creative language skills be developed. They recommended the study of literature in the elementary schools. In addition they recommended the development of children's oral work, albeit in the form of 'speech training', which they saw as the basis for written work. Finally they challenged the nineteenth-century legacy of educational class division, placing English at the centre of an educational aim to develop the 'mind and character' of all children.

Change on the ground was slow to occur but it was happening. The old practice of reading aloud in chorus was disappearing, silent reading was being encouraged and, in the 1920s, textbooks were published that encouraged children's free expression and that questioned the necessity for formal grammar teaching. However, even though the Newbolt Report contained evidence of the uselessness of grammar teaching, the committee had the strong feeling that self-expression could go too far, and that the best way for children to learn to write was to study grammar and to copy good models.

The Hadow Reports

The years 1926, 1931 and 1933 saw the publication of the three Hadow Reports on secondary, primary and infant education respectively; the second (Board of Education, 1931) focused on the 7–11 age range. It had a number of specific recommendations about the curriculum in general and English in particular. Famously, it stated: 'We are of the opinion that the curriculum of the primary school is to be thought of in terms of activity and experience rather than of knowledge to be acquired and facts to be stored.' (Board of Education, 1931: 139)

In English, oral work was seen as important, with an emphasis on speaking 'correctly'. 'Oral composition' – getting the child to talk on a topic of their choice or one of the teacher's – was included. 'Reproduction' involved getting the child to recount the subject matter of the lesson they had just been taught. Class libraries were encouraged and silent reading recommended, although not in school time except in the most deprived areas. And the aim? 'In the upper stage of primary education the child should gain a sense of the printed page and begin to read for pleasure and information.' (ibid.: 158)

As for writing, children's written composition should build on oral composition and children should be given topics that interested them. Spelling should be related to the children's writing and reading: 'Any attempt to teach spelling otherwise than in connection with the actual practice of writing or reading is beset with obvious dangers' (ibid.: 160). The abstract study of formal grammar was rejected, though some grammar was to be taught. Bilingualism was addressed in the Welsh context, and teaching in the mother tongue was recommended. Welsh-speaking children were expected to learn English and, strikingly, English-speaking children were expected to learn Welsh.

The third Hadow Report (Board of Education, 1933) drew on ideas current at the time to suggest that formal instruction of the three Rs traditionally started too early in British schools, and recommended that for infant and nursery children: 'The child should begin to learn the 3 Rs when he [sic] wants to do so, whether he be three or six years old.' (ibid.: 133)

The report noted three methods of teaching reading that were used at the time: 'look and say', 'phonics' and more contextualised meaning-centred 'sentence' methods. It recommended that teachers use a mix of the three as appropriate to the child's needs. Writing should start at the same time as reading, and children's natural desire to write in imitation of the adult writing they saw around them at home or at school should be encouraged. The child should have control over the subject matter and his or her efforts should be valued by the teacher as real attempts to communicate meaning.

The report emphasised the importance of imaginative play, and noted, 'Words mean nothing to the young child unless they are definitively associated with active experience' (ibid.: 181), and 'Oral lessons should be short and closely related to the child's practical interests' (ibid.: 182). While 'speech training' was important, drama work was recommended for the development of children's language, and nursery rhymes and game songs were encouraged alongside traditional hymns. Stories should be told and read to the children.

The Hadow Reports read as remarkably progressive documents for their time, and the principles of child-centred education that are explicit in many of their recommendations continued to inform thinking in primary language teaching for the next 50 years.

Progressive education ☞, 1931–75

The central years of the twentieth century can perhaps be characterised as the years of progressive aspiration so far as primary language was concerned. The progressive views of the Hadow Reports began to be reflected in the Board of Education's regular guidelines, and teachers were on the whole free to follow them as they pleased. The 1944 Education Act itself offered no curriculum advice, except with regard to religious education, and central guidance on the curriculum ended in 1945. The primary curriculum in particular came to be regarded as something of a 'secret garden' to quote Lord Eccles, Tory Minister of Education in 1960 (Gordon et al., 1991: 287).

The 1944 Education Act finally established primary schools in place of elementary schools, though it would be another 20 years before the last school that included all ages of children closed. At secondary level a three-layered system of grammar, technical, and secondary modern schools was established, and a new exam, the 11+, was devised to decide which children should go where. Like the scholarship exam before it, the 11+ continued to restrain the primary language curriculum, particularly with the older children, despite the fact that more progressive child-centred measures were gaining ground with younger children. With the reorganisation of secondary schools along comprehensive lines in the 1960s (encapsulated in Circular 10/65), the 11+ was abolished and the primary curriculum was technically freed from all constraint.

In retrospect, the Plowden Report on primary education (DES, 1967) can be seen as centrally representative of the progressive aspiration of 'child-centred education'. Its purpose was to report on effective primary education of the time, and it was concerned to see to what extent the Hadow recommendations had been put into effect. It functioned as much to disseminate effective practice as it did to recommend future change. The child was central: 'At the heart of the educational process lies the child' (ibid.: para. 9); and language was crucial: 'Spoken language plays a central role in learning' (ibid.: para. 54) and 'The development of language is, therefore, central to the educational process' (ibid.: para. 55).

Like its predecessors, the report emphasised the importance of talk; like its predecessors, it emphasised the fact that effective teachers of reading used a mix of approaches. Drama work and story-telling were to be encouraged; the increased importance of fiction and poetry written for children and the development of school libraries were all emphasised. The report applauded wholeheartedly the development of personal 'creative' writing (→ Chapter 11) by the children, characterising it as a dramatic revolution (1967: para. 60.1). On spelling and punctuation the committee was more reticent, noting only that when inaccuracy impeded communication then steps should be taken to remedy the deficiencies (1967: para. 60.2). Knowledge about language was seen as an interesting new area but 'Formal study of grammar will have little place in the primary school' (1967: para. 61.2).

The Plowden Report was followed by the Bullock Report on English (DES, 1975). So far as primary age children were concerned, this spelled out in more detail much of what was already implicit in Plowden. Central to both the reports was an emphasis on the 'process' of language learning. From such a perspective, children's oral and written language would best develop in meaningful language use. A couple of quotes from the Bullock Report will illustrate the point. Of the development of oral language it suggested: 'Language should be learned in the course of using it in, and about, the daily experiences of the classroom and the home' (ibid.: 520). Where writing was concerned: 'Competence in language comes above all through its purposeful use, not through working of exercises divorced from context' (ibid.: 528).

So far as bilingual children and children from the ethnic minorities were concerned, the Plowden Report had already recognised the contribution that such children could make to the classroom, and the Bullock committee was concerned that such children should not find school an alien place:

No child should be expected to cast off the language and culture of the home as he [*sic*] crosses the school threshold, nor to live and act as though home and school represent two totally separate and different cultures which have to be kept firmly apart. The curriculum should reflect many elements of that part of his life which a child lives outside school.

(ibid.: para. 20.5)

Increasing political control, 1976 onwards

The ideas of progressive education remained important – despite increasingly frequent attacks – until the 1970s, when things started to change. Britain was declining in world economic importance and the oil crisis of the early 1970s was followed by an International Monetary Fund (IMF) loan which saw the Labour government of the time having to cut back on public spending. Effective child-centred education is teacher-intensive and requires small classes, and the previous decades had seen reductions in class size. That was no longer compatible with the financial constraints of the time and class sizes began to increase again. A more regulated curriculum is easier to cope with in such circumstances.

The National Curriculum itself was established by the 1988 Education Reform Act, which in the process gave the Secretary of State for Education considerable powers of direct intervention in curriculum matters. Following the Act, curriculum documents were drawn up for all the major subject areas. In line with the recommendations of the TGAT Report (DES, 1987: S227), attainment in each subject was to be measured against a ten-level scale and tested at ages 7, 11, 14 and 16. As the curriculum was introduced into schools, it became clear that each subject group had produced documents of considerable complexity. Discontent in the profession grew and a slimmed-down version was introduced in 1995. The original English document was prepared by a committee under the chairmanship of Brian Cox (DES, 1989, 1990; Cox, 1991). English was to be divided up into five 'attainment targets': Speaking and Listening, Reading, Writing, Spelling, and Handwriting. These were reorganised into three in Sir Ron Dearing's 1995 rewrite, as Spelling and Handwriting were incorporated into Writing (DfE, 1995).

During the mid to late 1980s, a number of large-scale projects were undertaken which aimed to improve the teaching and learning of English. The Schools Council, a body responsible for national curriculum development, had been replaced by the School Curriculum Development Committee (SCDC); the SCDC initiated the National Writing Project. This was in two phases: the development phase took place from 1985 to 1988 and the implementation phase from 1988 to 1989, although the Education Reform Act 1988 and the resulting National Curriculum and testing arrangements changed the focus of implementation.

One of the key problems of the time was that many children were being turned off by writing, something confirmed by some evidence from the Assessment of Performance Unit (APU). The APU found that as many as four in ten children did not find writing an enjoyable experience and 'not less than one in ten pupils [had] an active dislike of writing and endeavour[ed] to write as little as possible' (APU, 1988: 170). Somewhat later the National Writing Project gathered evidence that many children, particularly young children, tended to equate writing with transcription skills rather than composition.

The National Writing Project involved thousands of educators across the country. One of the main messages from the project was that writers needed to become involved in writing for a defined and recognisable audience, not just because the teacher said so. Connected to these ideas was the notion that writing should have a meaningful purpose. With these key concepts in place, teachers began to realise that writing tasks which were sequentially organised in school exercise books and consisting of one draft – or at best 'rough copy/ neat copy' drafts – were not helping to address the audiences and purposes for writing that needed to be generated.

The National Oracy Project was also initiated by SCDC and partly overlapped with the National Writing Project. During the period from 1987 to 1991, 35 local education authorities were involved in the oracy project. The recognition that oracy, or speaking and listening as it came to be called, needed a national initiative was in itself significant. Since the late 1960s, a number of enlightened educators had realised that talking and learning were very closely linked and that the curriculum should reflect that reality. But these people were in a minority and most educators continued to emphasise reading and, to a lesser extent, writing. The major achievement of the oracy project was to secure recognition that talk was important and that children could learn more if teachers understood the issues, and planned activities to support the development of oracy. As Wells pointed out: 'The centrality of talk in education is finally being recognised. Not simply in theory – in the exhortations of progressive-minded academics – but mandated at all levels and across all subjects in a national curriculum.' (Wells, 1992: 283)

The other large national project that we will touch on is the Language in the National Curriculum (LINC) project (→ Chapter 16). In 1987, a committee of inquiry was commissioned to make recommendations about the sort of knowledge about language that it would be appropriate to teach in school. The Kingman Report, as it was known (DES, 1988), disappointed right-wing politicians and sections of the press when it failed to advocate a return to traditional grammar teaching. The Cox Report (DES, 1989) ran into similar problems for the same reason, but both the 1990 and the 1995 orders for English in the National Curriculum (DES, 1990; DfE, 1995) contented themselves with general recommendations to use grammatical terms where and as the need arose. Between 1989 and 1992 most schools in England were involved with the LINC project. Its main aim was to acquaint teachers with the model of language presented in the Kingman Report. Kingman's work reaffirmed the idea that children and teachers should have sufficient 'knowledge about language' or 'KAL' if they were to become successful language users.

One of the strong features of the materials that were produced by the LINC project was that they were built on an explicit set of principles and theories:

Principles:

1   Teaching children should start positively from what they can already do.
2   The experience of using language should precede analysis.
3   Language should be explored in real purposeful situations rather than be analysed out of context.
4   An understanding of people's attitudes to language can help you understand more about values and beliefs.

Theories:

1   Humans use language for social reasons.
2   Language is constantly changing.
3   Language is a cultural phenomenon.
4   There are important connections between language and power.
5   Language is systematically organised.
6   The meanings of language depend on negotiation.

It may have been that some of these philosophies resulted in the politicians of the time refusing to publish the materials. In spite of this, the materials were photocopied and distributed widely and various publications independent of government were produced, e.g. Carter (1990).

The National Literacy Project ☞ was developed between 1996 and 1998. The project's main aim was to raise the standards of literacy in the participating schools so that they raised their achievements in line with national expectations. The project established for the first time a detailed scheme of work with term-by-term objectives that were organised into text-level, sentence-level and word-level goals. These were delivered through the use of a daily literacy hour with strict timings for the different sections. The project was supported by a national network of centres where literacy consultants were available to support project schools.

The National Literacy Project was important because it was claimed that its success was the reason that the National Literacy Strategy adopted the ideas of a Framework for Teaching and a prescribed literacy hour. However, it should be remembered that the schools which were involved in the project were schools which had identified weaknesses in their literacy teaching, and this has to be taken into account when any kind of evaluation is made about the success

of the project. The other important point to bear in mind is that it was originally conceived of as a five-year project; after that time, evaluations were to be
carried out. One of the features of these evaluations was that they were
supposed to measure the success of the three years of the programme when
schools were no longer *directly* involved in the project. In the event, the
approaches of the National Literacy Project were adopted as part of the
National Literacy Strategy in 1998. This occurred *before* any independent evaluation had been carried out and long before the planned five-year extent of the
National Literacy Project.

The only *independent* evaluation of the project carried out by the National
Foundation for Educational Research (INFER) found that:

> The analyses of the test outcomes have indicated that, in terms of the
> standardised scores on reading tests, the pupils involved in Cohort 1 of the
> National Literacy Project have made substantial gains. All three year
> groups showed significant and substantial increases in scores from the
> beginning to end of the project.
>
> (Sainsbury *et al.*, 1998: 21)

This outcome illustrates definite progress in the fairly restricted parameters of
standardised reading tests. It is not possible to conclude that the specific
approach of the National Literacy Project was more beneficial than other
approaches as this variable was not controlled. It is possible that the financial
investment, extra support and a new initiative were the dominant factors
in improved test scores rather than the particular characteristics of the recommended teaching methods. One area of concern about the findings from the
evaluation was that pupils eligible for free school meals, pupils with special
educational needs, pupils with English as an additional language (EAL) at the
'becoming familiar with English stage', and boys made less progress than other
groups.

It seems particularly regrettable, though not surprising, that no serious
attempts were made to evaluate what pupils thought of the project. Sainsbury
et al. admitted that:

> The reading enjoyment findings are less easy to interpret. The survey
> showed that children do, on the whole, enjoy their reading, with substan-
> tial majorities of both age groups expressing favourable attitudes both
> before and after involvement in the project. These measures, however, did
> not change very much, indicating that the systematic introduction of
> different text types that was a feature of the project did not have any clearly
> apparent effect on children's enjoyment of reading these varied text types.
> In the absence of a control group, however, it is difficult to draw any more
> definite conclusions.
>
> (ibid.: 27)

The National Literacy Strategy 1997–2006 and the Primary National Strategy Framework for Literacy, 2007–10

The Literacy Task Force was established on 31 May 1996 by David Blunkett, then Shadow Secretary of State for Education and Employment. It was charged with developing, in time for an incoming Labour government, a strategy to substantially raise standards of literacy in primary schools over a five- to ten-year period (Literacy Task Force, 1997: 4).

The Literary Task Force produced a final report that suggested how a National Literacy Strategy could be implemented. The recommendations heralded some of the most profound changes to English teaching. The single most important driving force behind the strategy was the introduction of target-setting: specifically that by 2002, 80 per cent of 11-year-olds should reach the standard expected for their age in English (i.e. Level 4) in the Key Stage 2 National Standard Assessment Tasks (SATs). Despite all the many changes to the curriculum since 1997, target-setting, and the associated publication of league tables, remain in place and now have an even more dominant effect on the curriculum and children's daily lives.

Earlier in this chapter we mentioned the important contribution of Brian Cox in relation to developing the guidance for the subject of English in the National Curriculum, a document that achieved a remarkable consensus in such a contentious area. Cox was extremely critical from the inception of the National Literacy Strategy: the policy on reading 'is too prescriptive, authoritarian and mechanistic', there should be 'more emphasis on motivation, on helping children to enjoy reading' (Cox, 1998: ix). Other contributors to the book were equally critical: Margaret Meek (1998: 116) criticised the 'repeated exercises in comprehension, grammar and spelling' and Bethan Marshall (1998: 109) suggested that 'the bleak spectre of utilitarianism ☞ hangs over our schools like a pall'. The words of an inspector in 1905 quoted by Marshall are another reminder of the history of the reading debates:

> A blackboard has been produced, and hieroglyphics are drawn upon it by the teacher. At a given signal every child in the class begins calling out mysterious sounds: 'Letter A, letter A' in a sing-song voice, or 'Letter A says Ah, letter A says Ah', as the case may be. To the uninitiated I may explain that No. 1 is the beginning of the spelling, and No. 2 is the beginning of word building. Hoary-headed men will spend hours discussing whether 'c-a-t' or 'ker-ar-te' are the best means of conveying the knowledge of how to read 'cat'. I must own an indifference to the point myself, and sympathise with teachers not allowed to settle it for themselves . . . 'Wake up, Johnny; it's not time to go to sleep yet. Be a good boy and watch teacher.'
>
> (Marshall, 1998: 115)

Most political education initiatives are introduced following claims that standards are falling, and the National Literacy Strategy was no exception. However, in spite of regular claims by the media, teachers, business people, politicians, etc., there was no evidence that standards of literacy had declined in England as Beard (1999) pointed out; something that Campbell (1997) also commented upon:

> On the current moral panic over the impact of the reforms on standards of attainment in literacy and numeracy, there are two things to say. First, no-one can be sure about standards in literacy and numeracy because of the failure – unquestioned failure – of the national agencies (NCC, SEAC and now SCAA) to establish an effective, credible and reliable mechanism for the national monitoring of standards over time since 1989.
>
> (Campbell, 1997: 22)

One of the first attempts to evaluate the strategies was commissioned by the New Labour government. Earl et al.'s (2003) evaluation of the NLS and NNS (National Numeracy Strategy) included collection of data from schools as follows: a) two postal surveys (in 2000 and 2002), each to two samples of 500 schools, one for literacy and the other for numeracy. Parallel questionnaires went to head teachers and teachers; b) a postal survey to all literacy and numeracy consultants in LEAs (Local Education Authority) across England in 2002; c) repeated visits to ten selected schools (with various sizes, locations, pupil populations, levels of attainment) and their LEAs: four to six days in each school. The research team interviewed head teachers and teachers, observed literacy and mathematics lessons, and analysed documents; d) interviews with literacy and numeracy managers and consultants from LEAs of the ten selected schools. The researchers also attended training sessions and staff meetings in some of those LEAs; and e) observations and interviews in 17 other schools (including special schools) and LEAs. Three of these were one-day visits to schools early in 2000, while the others were single visits as part of shadowing regional directors or HMI (Her Majesty's Inspectorate), or attending meetings locally.

Earl et al. (2003) found that the strategies had altered classroom practice: in particular greater use of whole class teaching, more structured lessons and more use of objectives to plan and guide teaching. Teachers' views about the strategies were more variable than head teachers', who were more likely to be in favour. Head teachers and teachers were more supportive of the NNS than they were of the NLS. For the most part, both teachers and head teachers believed that the NNS had been easier to implement and had had greater effects on pupil learning than the NLS. Overall, Earl et al. reported a wide range of variation in teachers' opinion of the NLS ranging from positive to negative.

Non-government-commissioned research explored a range of issues in relation to the strategies. For example, a series of research studies all reported that the recommended pedagogy of the NLS literacy hour was resulting in rather limited teacher–pupil interaction, which was tending towards short initiation-response sequences and a consequent lack of extended discussion. Observation schedules were used in studies such as those by Hardman *et al.* (2003), English *et al.* (2002) and Mroz *et al.* (2000). Mroz *et al.* (2000) noted the limited opportunities for pupils to question or explore ideas. English *et al.* (2002) found that there was a reduction in extended teacher–pupil interactions. Hardman *et al.* (2003) found that the NLS was encouraging teachers to use more directive forms of teaching, with few opportunities for pupils to explore and elaborate on their ideas. Skidmore *et al.* (2003) used audio recordings of teacher–pupil dialogue combined with video of non-verbal communication to support their finding that teachers were dominating interaction during the guided reading segment of the literacy hour. Parker and Hurry (2007) interviewed 51 Key Stage 2 teachers in 2001 and videotaped observations of the same teachers in class literacy sessions focusing on teacher and pupil questions and answers. They found that direct teacher questioning in the form of teacher-led recitation was the dominant strategy used for reading comprehension teaching and that children were not encouraged to generate their own questions about texts. Lefstein's (2008: 731) extended case study of one primary school found that open questions were suppressed as a result of 'teacher knowledge and policy support, conditions of teacher engagement with the curricular materials, and the durability of interactional genres'.

The answer to the question of whether the NLS Framework for Teaching and its pedagogy was effective is made difficult to answer because it was not subject to rigorous large-scale experimental trial. However there is now a significant amount of evidence in general about the effectiveness of the NLS: Wyse *et al.* (2010) summarised this in their research for the *Cambridge Primary Review* by analysing studies of primary classrooms and trends in national test outcomes. Although reading showed slightly better gains than writing according to some sources, the overall trend in national test scores can be explained as modest gains from a low base as teachers learned to prepare pupils for statutory tests followed by a plateau in scores as no further gains could be achieved by test coaching. Overall, the intense focus on testing and test results in the period of the NLS resulted in a narrowing of the curriculum driving teaching in the opposite direction to that which research indicates will improve learning and attainment.

In October 2006, the new *PNS* (Primary National Strategy) *Framework for Literacy* was released. The main elements that had been a feature of the NLS were still part of the PNS Framework. Teachers were offered a little more flexibility in some areas, such as in the teaching of writing, where longstanding criticisms finally and belatedly began to have an effect on policy makers. But overall the PNS Framework was little changed from the NLS. However, in 2010 a new period of radical reform began.

Control or freedom? 2010 onwards

The election of the Conservative–Liberal Democrat coalition government in 2010 in the UK brought with it radical, and in some cases immediate, change. A new National Curriculum for primary schools that the previous New Labour government had started to implement in 2010, published on an extensive fully functional website, was simply taken down and archived along with all the PNS resources and most other educational materials that had been developed during the New Labour terms. The ideological rationales for the rejection of previous materials were the dual promises of more freedom over the curriculum for teachers, and less bureaucracy. At the same time the new government announced yet another review of the National Curriculum (the third government-commissioned review of the primary curriculum in a period of less than ten years – for the first book-length analysis of this and other national curriculum developments in the countries of the UK, see *Creating the Curriculum*, Wyse et al., 2012).

Some new freedoms over the curriculum in England became available to an extent, but paradoxically at the same time even more control over key and influential elements of schooling were being placed in the hands of the Secretary of State for Education and the Minister for Schools (Wyse, 2008 and 2011 feature analysis of the implications for teaching of such control). In relation to the teaching of English, Language and Literacy a number of worrying developments took place. One was the decision to limit externally marked statutory assessment of writing for pupils aged 10–11 to the areas of spelling, grammar and punctuation; compositional aspects of writing were to be assessed by teachers. But even more troubling was the growing dominance of a single method of reading teaching called 'synthetic phonics'. As you will see in Chapter 9, phonics teaching has a long history of debate. One of the trends we have identified in successive editions of our book is the growing level of control over the teaching of reading. The influence of synthetic phonics has become so pervasive that it is part of teacher training, the vetting of publishers' teaching resources, selection of advisors to government and many other areas of policy. In opposition Nick Gibb MP was at the forefront of these trends and, as the Minister for Schools for the coalition government, intensified this work supported by Secretary of State for Education Michael Gove.

The most questionable development of all was the decision to implement a 'phonics screening check' for all six-year-old children in England. As you will see in Chapter 14, we are not against early identification of children who struggle with reading, and have clear ideas how they can best be supported. But we are very much against the likely distortion of the curriculum and the effects on children, parents, teachers, schools, and teacher trainers that such a national testing regime is likely to have.

The government response to a 'consultation' on whether the phonics screening check should be implemented was startling. The first problem with the consultation questionnaire design was that it did not include the question: do you think a phonics screening check should be implemented for all six-year-old children in England? The only question in the consultation that that came close to addressing the most important issue of whether the test was desirable overall or not was this one: 'do you agree that this screening check should be focused on phonic decoding?' (DfE, 2011: 12) The response rates were: Yes: 28%; No: 66%; Not Sure: 6%. This clearly showed a majority negative response to the main element of the phonics screening check. But in an extraordinary interpretation of the outcome of the survey the Minister concluded that '28% of respondents agreed the check should focus on decoding using phonics. 20% respondents argued that children learn to read using a variety of strategies, including using visual and context cues, and the check should take into account these alternative strategies' (op. cit.: 4). Therefore, 'Taking into account the consultation responses, findings from the pre-trialling and the academic evidence, we propose *to continue to develop the phonics screening check*' (op. cit.: 6, emphasis added). Surely this kind of interpretation and the resultant policy changes are undemocratic and unacceptable?

So the paradox of policy from 2012 was that some schools (particularly those that engaged with other government agendas such as becoming free schools or academies) were to have some freedom over the curriculum that was lacking during New Labour's time in government. But at the same time, the Department for Education and its Ministers were securing even greater control over early years and primary teaching.

Our predictions in relation to the impact of the policies on phonics are that:

- Schools will try to mitigate the worst effects.
- The curriculum will be narrowed (reading, and generally).
- League tables of schools' phonics screening test results will be compiled leading to high-stakes testing pressures.
- Gains in statutory test scores attributable to the increased emphasis on phonics are unlikely because there are other more important issues that will be squeezed, such as reading comprehension, an emphasis on which perhaps would have been much more likely to produce positive impacts.
- The overall outcomes for children as a result of such policy changes will be negative.

In spite of the potentially serious consequences of such policies we have not lost hope! In fact, such changes make us more determined than ever to fight for more appropriate curricula, pedagogy and assessment for the teaching of English, language and literacy that we hope we convey throughout this book. We are not the only people who are ready to challenge inappropriate policy. At the time of finishing this chapter, three of the members of the expert group on the National Curriculum in England had made clear their strong unhappiness with the government's response to their report, and the leaders of three of the teaching unions had written to the Minister to register their objections to the phonics screening check.

Practice points

- As a professional, you should evaluate all educational initiatives critically to ensure that they reflect the needs of the children that you teach.
- You need to develop a knowledge of historical developments as a vital tool for understanding educational change.
- Use the range of opportunities that are available to give your feedback about national developments in education, for example by responding to consultations, and contacting your local and national political representatives.

Glossary

Dialects – regional variations of language shown by different words and grammar.

Etymology – the origins of words.

Line justification – ensuring that the beginnings and ends of lines of print are all lined up.

Loanwords – words adopted from other languages.

National Literacy Project – a three-year professional development project that was carried out with authorities and schools who wanted to raise their standards of literacy.

National Literacy Strategy – a national strategy for raising standards in literacy over a five- to ten-year period.

Progressive education – teaching approaches that rejected old-fashioned rote-learning methods in favour of methods that put the child's interests and needs first.

Standard English – the formal language of written communication in particular. Many people call this 'correct' English.

Utilitarianism – the idea that education and learning can be reduced to crude skills and drills.

References

Andrews, R., Torgerson, C., Beverton, S., Locke, T., Low, G., Robinson, A., *et al.* (2004) 'The effect of grammar teaching (syntax) in English on 5 to 16 year olds' accuracy and quality in written composition', *Research Evidence in Education Library*. Retrieved 5 February 2007, from http://eppi.ioe.ac.uk/cms/.

APU (Assessment of Performance Unit) (1988) *Language Performance in Schools: Review of APU Language Monitoring 1979–1983*. London: HMSO.

Barber, C. (1993) *The English Language: A Historical Introduction*. Cambridge: Cambridge University Press.

Beard, R. (1999) *National Literacy Strategy Review of Research and Other Related Evidence*. London: DfEE.

Board of Education (1921) *The Teaching of English in England (The Newbolt Report)*. London: HMSO.

Board of Education (1931) *The Primary School (The Second Hadow Report)*. London: HMSO.

Board of Education (1933) *Infant and Nursery Schools (The Third Hadow Report)*. London: HMSO.

Boyle, B. and Bragg, J. (2006) 'A curriculum without foundation', *British Educational Research Journal*, 32(4): 569–582.

Bryson, B. (1990) *Mother Tongue: The English Language*. London: Penguin.

Campbell, J. (1997) 'Towards curricular subsidiarity?' Paper presented at the School Curriculum and Assessment Authority conference, 'Developing the Primary School Curriculum: the Next Steps', June.

Carter, R. (ed.) (1990) *Knowledge about Language and the Curriculum: The LINC Reader*. London: Hodder & Stoughton.

Cox, B. (1991) *Cox on Cox: An English Curriculum for the 1990s*. London: Hodder & Stoughton.

Cox, B. (1998) 'Foreword', in B. Cox (ed.) *Literacy Is Not Enough: Essays on the Importance of Reading*. Manchester: Manchester University Press and Book Trust.

Crystal, D. (1997) *The Cambridge Encyclopaedia of Language*, 2nd edn. Cambridge: Cambridge University Press.

Crystal, D. (2004) *The Stories of English*. London: Penguin/Allen Lane.

Department of Education and Science (DES) (1967) *Children and Their Primary Schools (The Plowden Report)*. London: HMSO.

Department of Education and Science (DES) (1975) *A Language for Life (The Bullock Report)*. London: HMSO.

Department of Education and Science (DES) (1988) *Report of the Committee of Inquiry into the Teaching of English Language (The Kingman Report)*. London: HMSO.

Department of Education and Science and The Welsh Office (DES) (1987) *National Curriculum Task Group on Assessment and Testing (The TGAT Report)*. London: DES.

Department of Education and Science and The Welsh Office (DES) (1989) *English for Ages 5–16 (The Cox Report)*. York: National Curriculum Council.

Department of Education and Science and The Welsh Office (DES) (1990) *English in the National Curriculum*. London: HMSO.

Department for Education (DfE) (1995) *English in the National Curriculum*. London: HMSO.

Department for Education and Employment (DfEE) (1998) *The National Literacy Strategy Framework for Teaching*. London: DfEE.

Department for Education and Employment (DfEE) and The Qualifications and Curriculum Authority (QCA) (1999) *The National Curriculum: Handbook for Primary Teachers in England. Key Stages 1 and 2*. Norwich: HMSO.

Earl, L., Fullan, M., Leithwood, K., Watson, N. *et al.* (2000) *Watching and Learning: OISE/UT Evaluation of the Implementation of the National Literacy and Numeracy Strategies.* Nottingham: DfES Publications.

Earl, L., Watson, N., Levin, B., Leithwood, K., Fullan, M., Torrance, N. *et al.* (2003) *Watching and Learning: OISE/UT Evaluation of the Implementation of the National Literacy and Numeracy Strategies.* Nottingham: DfES Publications.

English, E., Hargreaves, L. and Hislam, J. (2002) 'Pedagogical dilemmas in the national literacy strategy: primary teachers' perceptions, reflections and classroom behaviour', *Cambridge Journal of Education*, 32(1): 9–26.

Goody, J. and Watt, I. (1963) 'The consequences of literacy', *Comparative Studies in Society and History*, 5(3): 304–345.

Gordon, P., Aldrich, R. and Dean, D. (1991) *Education and Policy in England in the Twentieth Century.* London: Woburn.

Greenbaum, S. (1986) 'Spelling variants in British English', *Journal of English Linguistics*, 19: 258–268.

Hardman, F., Smith, F. and Wall, K. (2003) 'Interactive whole class teaching in the National Literacy Strategy', *Cambridge Journal of Education*, 33(2): 197–215.

Harris, R. (1986) *The Origin of Writing.* London: Duckworth.

Holmes, E. A. G. (1922) 'The confessions and hopes of an ex-Inspector of Schools', *Hibbert Journal*, vol. 20 (no further information in secondary source). Quoted in Gordon, P., Aldrich, R. and Dean, D. (1991) *Education and Policy in England in the Twentieth Century.* London: Woburn.

Lawson, J. and Silver, H. (1973) *A Social History of Education in England.* London: Methuen.

Lefstein, A. (2008) 'Changing classroom practice through the English national literacy strategy: A micro-interactional perspective', *American Educational Research Journal*, 45(3): 701–737. DOI: 10.3102/0002831208316256

LINC (Language in the National Curriculum) (1991) *Materials for Professional Development.* No publication details.

Literacy Task Force (1997) *The Implementation of the National Literacy Strategy.* London: DfEE.

Marshall, B. (1998) 'English teachers and the third way', in B. Cox (ed.) *Literacy Is Not Enough: Essays on the Importance of Reading.* Manchester: Manchester University Press and Book Trust.

Meek, M. (1998) 'Important reading lessons', in B. Cox (ed.) *Literacy Is Not Enough: Essays on the Importance of Reading.* Manchester: Manchester University Press and Book Trust.

Mroz, M., Smith, F. and Hardman, F. (2000) 'The discourse of the literacy hour', *Cambridge Journal of Education*, 30(3): 380–390.

Office for Standards in Education (OfSTED) (1998) *The National Literacy Project: An HMI Evaluation.* London: OfSTED.

Office for Standards in Education (OfSTED) (1999) *The National Literacy Strategy: An Interim Evaluation*, London: OfSTED.

Parker, M. and Hurry, J. (2007) Teachers' use of questioning and modelling comprehension skills in primary classrooms. *Educational Review*, 59(3): 299–314.

Protherough, R. and Atkinson, J. (1994) 'Shaping the image of an English teacher', in S. Brindley (ed.) *Teaching English*. London: Routledge.

Pyles, T. and Algeo, J. (1993) *The Origins and Development of the English Language*, 4th edn. London: Harcourt Brace Jovanovich.

Qualifications and Curriculum Authority (QCA) (2006a) Consultation: Implications of the Rose Review of early reading. Retrieved 1 June 2006, from http://www.qca.org.uk/232_16473.html

Qualifications and Curriculum Authority (QCA) (2006b) *Consultation on Proposed Changes to the Key Stage 1 English Programme for Reading and a Foundation Stage Early Learning Goal*. London: QCA.

Sainsbury, M., Schagen, I., Whetton, C. with Hagues, N. and Minnis, M. (1998) *Evaluation of the National Literacy Project Cohort 1, 1996–1998*. Slough: NFER.

Shayer, D. (1972) *The Teaching of English in Schools 1900–1970*. London: Routledge and Kegan Paul.

Skidmore, D., Perez-Parent, M. and Arnfield, D. (2003) 'Teacher-pupil dialogue in the guided reading session', *Reading Literacy and Language*, 37(2): 47–53.

Tymms, P. (2004) 'Are standards rising in English primary schools?', *British Educational Research Journal*, 30(4): 477–494.

Wells, G. (1992) 'The centrality of talk in education', in K. Norman (ed.) *Thinking Voices: The Work of the National Oracy Project*. London: Hodder & Stoughton.

Williamson, B. (1981) 'Contradictions of control: elementary education in a mining district 1870–1900', in L. Barton and S. Walker (eds) *Schools, Teachers and Teaching*. Lewes: Falmer Press.

Wyse, D. (2001) 'Grammar. For writing?: A critical review of empirical evidence', *British Journal of Educational Studies*, 49(4): 411–427.

Wyse, D. (2003) 'The National Literacy Strategy: A critical review of empirical evidence', *British Educational Research Journal*, 29(6): 903–916.

Wyse, D. (2008). 'Primary education: Who's in control?', *Education Review*, 21(1), 76–82.

Wyse, D. (2011) 'Control of language or the language of control? Primary teachers' knowledge in the context of policy', in S. Ellis and E. McCartney (eds) *Applied Linguistics and the Primary School*. Cambridge: Cambridge University Press.

Wyse, D., McCreery, E. and Torrance, H. (2010) 'The trajectory and impact of national reform: Curriculum and assessment in English primary schools', in R. Alexander, C. Doddington, J. Gray, L. Hargreaves and R. Kershner (eds) *The Cambridge Primary Review Research Surveys*. London: Routledge.

Wyse, D., Baumfield, V., Egan, D., Gallagher, C., Hayward, L., Hulme, M., Leitch, K., Livingston, K., Menter, I. and Lingard, B. (2012) *Creating the Curriculum*. London: Routledge.

Annotated bibliography

Cox, B. (ed.) (1998) *Literacy Is Not Enough: Essays on the Importance of Reading*. Manchester: Manchester University Press and Book Trust.

This was a powerful rejection of the concept of the Literacy Strategy. Many of its criticisms can be levelled at the PNS Framework.
L2 ★★

Crystal, D. (2004) *The Stories of English*. London: Penguin/Allen Lane.
A tremendous achievement. One of the central concerns of this book is the narrow way that English is often perceived, particularly notions of Standard English. Relevance to the National Curriculum here.
L2 ★★

Ellis, S. and McCartney, E. (eds) (2011) *Applied Linguistics and the Primary School*. Cambridge: Cambridge University Press.
Really useful account of the kinds of linguistic knowledge that can help primary teachers be more effective in the language and literacy teaching.
L3 ★★★

Goodwyn, A. and Fuller, C. (eds) (2011) *The Great Literacy Debate: A Critical Response to the Literacy Strategy and the Framework for English*. London: Routledge.
Dubbed 'the revenge of the professors' by the publisher! An excellent account of the NLS.
L2 ★★

Hall, K. and Harding, A. (2003) 'A systematic review of effective literacy teaching in the 4 to 14 age range of mainstream schooling', *Research Evidence in Education Library*. Retrieved 5 February 2007, from http://eppi.ioe.ac.uk/cms/.
Concluded that effective teachers of literacy balance direct skills teaching with more holistic approaches and 'avoid the partisan adherence to any *one* sure-fire approach or method' (p. 3).
L3 ★★★

National Literacy Trust http://www.literacytrust.org.uk/
A very useful site to find out about new initiatives and stories in the press about literacy and the teaching of English.
L1 ★

Shayer, D. (1972) *The Teaching of English in Schools 1900–1970*. London: Routledge and Kegan Paul.
A knowledge of history is vital if we are to make sense of the present. This book makes very interesting reading particularly by showing how the debates about English have progressed and in some cases recurred again and again.
L2 ★★

Wyse, D., Andrews, R. and Hoffman, J. (eds) (2010) *The Routledge International Handbook of English, Language and Literacy teaching*. London: Routledge.
A comprehensive overview of research and the implications for policy from leading international scholars. Has been used to inform some of the developments in this book.
L3 ★★★

Chapter 2

Learning and language

This book is based on our theories of the teaching of English, language and literacy (TELL). The chapter identifies some of the most important general theories and principles that underpin the other chapters in the book. Its interdisciplinary orientation draws on philosophical, cognitive, socio-cultural and linguistic perspectives.

Some people might question the need for theory ☞ at all. They could argue that becoming a teacher simply requires the learning of teaching techniques, that theory and research are not important, and all that needs to be learned can be learned through school practice. Of course it is not accurate to suggest that professional practice is simply that – practice. Teachers' theories reveal themselves all the time, sometimes in turns of phrase: 'They've got no language, these kids' (deficit models); 'She's a bright girl' (nature more than nurture); 'Boys are always naughty' (gender and stereotypes); etc. A particularly well-known phrase is to call children 'able' or not. If you think about this more deeply, the idea suggests an innate level of intelligence that is not going to change. This is another deficit theory which can lead to low expectations of children. For this reason we prefer to avoid altogether the general description of a child as being 'bright', 'clever' or 'able' and instead talk about the child's specific achievements. Theories and beliefs directly guide the practical decisions that you make all the time. They are particularly significant in guiding your decision-making in unfamiliar situations: you will encounter these throughout your career and without previous practical experience of a given situation, you will have to make decisions based on your theories.

This chapter explores the theoretical influences that inform the book as a whole, and our approach to the teaching of English, language and literacy (TELL – a longer version of this theory can be found in Wyse, 2011). The central focus of this book is an educational one: the teaching and learning of English, language and literacy in its pedagogical and societal context. But to understand this and any educational topic sufficiently requires interdisciplinary understanding, of a particular kind. The consideration of evidence from other disciplines must be fashioned by the most appropriate educational considerations. In a broad sense, interdisciplinarity has been used to refer to a range of practices, from borrowing and solving problems to increased consistency of subjects and methods, to the actual emergence of an interdiscipline. But central to the interdisciplinary methodology that informs TELL theory is integration, the blending or merging of concepts, methodology and/or theoretical perspectives from multiple disciplines or different fields of knowledge. True interdisciplinarity is difficult, not least because multidisciplinarity – where multiple perspectives on a problem or object are drawn upon using tools, theories and methods from different disciplines – is an easier, although still valuable, process. The process of integration that is key in interdisciplinarity entails a step in which the disciplinary perspectives are taken into a new configuration where something altogether new results from integration. In this introduction we portray TELL as a reconfiguration of philosophical, cognitive, socio-cultural and linguistic perspectives in order to articulate new theory.

Thinking about education

Matters of theory and the links with application and practice are part of all learning, not just education, and are rooted in a powerful historical tradition. Dunne's (1993) book showed the way that Aristotle established the concepts of *technē* and *phronésis* (or technical and practical reason). *Technē* is the kind of thinking required by the builder or the doctor when they make something or restore someone to good health. This is the thinking required for making things. *Phronesis* is a different kind of practical knowledge that emerges from conduct in a public space and is more personal and experiential. Practice, in a range of occupations, was seen by Aristotle 'as something nontechnical but not, however, nonrational' (ibid.: 10). In his book, Dunne argues for the modern relevance of the ideas of *technē* and *phronesis* by engaging in a written 'dialogue' with five modern philosophers.

In relating the book's complex philosophical exploration to practice, Dunne concludes overall that:

> In being initiated into the practice of teaching, student-teachers need not only experience in the classroom but also the right conditions for reflecting on this experience – so that reflectiveness (which we have all the time been clarifying under the name of 'phronesis') can become more and more an abiding attitude or disposition.
>
> (ibid.: 369)

Joseph Dunne's (1993) exploration of *technē* and *phronésis* was initially stimulated by a concern that behaviourism, most visibly applied as the objective-led teaching approach, was an inappropriate way to conceptualise and realise teaching and learning (for a critique of objective-led teaching, see Gallagher and Wyse, 2012). This kind of meaningful connection between modern educational problems and philosophy is seen at its most powerful through pragmatism. John Dewey's work is particularly illuminating, in particular his ideas about the curriculum. Although he did not address TELL directly in his work, Dewey's consideration of the curriculum is important because the work of the teacher necessarily involves locating TELL in a wider curriculum. Dewey regarded interaction between teachers and pupils as key to education:

> The fundamental factors in the educative process are an immature, undeveloped being; and certain social aims, meanings, values incarnate in the matured experience of the adult. The educative process is the due interaction of these forces. Such a conception of each in relation to the other as facilitates completest and freest interaction is the essence of educational theory.
>
> (Dewey, 1902: 4)

Dewey's main thesis was that good teaching is built on the educator's understanding that there should be an interaction between the child's experiences and ideas, and the school's aim to inculcate learning. Less effective learning takes place if, instead of interaction, an opposition is built between experience and learning. Over-emphasis on transmission of facts to be learned from a formal syllabus is one example of such opposition. Dewey was clear that the best knowledge available to society was the appropriate material for children's learning but only through teaching that made a connection with children's experiences and thoughts. He summed up the main role of the teacher by arguing that: 'Guidance [i.e. by the teacher] is not external imposition. *It is freeing the life-process for its own most adequate fulfilment.*' [Italics in original] (op. cit.: 17)

Language and thinking

Philosophy has long explored the nature of thinking and its relationship to language. But this relationship has also been explored from other perspectives including psychological ones. Much of Vygotsky's work is located in psychology, but one of the interesting aspects of his contribution was the fact that he viewed psychology as a tool or method rather than as a subject of investigation. Vygotsky's subjects of investigation were culture and consciousness, as the editor's introduction to one of his most well-known books explains:

> Vygotsky argued that psychology cannot limit itself to direct evidence, be it observable behaviour or accounts of introspection. Psychological inquiry is *investigation*, and like the criminal investigator, the psychologist must

take into account indirect evidence and circumstantial clues – which in practice means that works of art, philosophical arguments, and anthropological data are no less important for psychology than direct evidence.

(Vygotsky, 1986: xvi)

One of the reasons that Vygotsky's work has been so influential for educationists is the fact that he applied his theories directly to education. In the course of *Thought and Language*, Vygotsky develops some of the ideas of Jean Piaget, one of the best-known theorists on child development. In the revised edition of Vygotsky's book, the end notes include some of Piaget's responses to Vygotsky's reflections about Piaget's work. Part of their debate addresses the role of direct instruction and the learning of concepts. Piaget says:

All this raises at least two problems, which Vygotsky formulates, but in the solution of which we differ somewhat. The first concerns the 'interaction of spontaneous and nonspontaneous concepts.' This interaction is more complex than Vygotsky believes. In some cases, what is transmitted by instruction is well assimilated by the child because it represents in fact an extension of some spontaneous constructions of his own. In such cases, his development is accelerated. But in other cases, the gifts of instruction are presented too soon or too late, or in a manner that precludes assimilation because it does not fit in with the child's spontaneous constructions. Then the child's development is impeded, or even deflected into barrenness, as often happens in the teaching of the exact sciences. Therefore I do not believe, as Vygotsky seems to do, that new concepts, even at school level, are always acquired through adult didactic intervention. This may occur, but there is a much more productive form of instruction: the so-called 'active' schools endeavor to create situations that, while not 'spontaneous' in themselves, evoke spontaneous elaboration on the part of the child, if one manages both to spark his interest and to present the problem in such a way that it corresponds to the structures he had already formed himself.

(1986: 271)

Piaget and Vygotsky agreed that spontaneous learning is important. This is a side of their theories that needs to be re-evaluated in relation to modern educational practice, in particular by calling into question the over-emphasis on direct instruction and by reconsidering the role of spontaneous learning in the school curriculum.

Vygotsky's contribution includes his important concept of *mediated activity*, which he saw as central to the development of higher psychological processes in humans. It consists of an interplay between *sign* and *tool*. The tool's function is physical in character and leads to changes in objects externally. The sign is internally oriented and related to changes in behaviour. Vygotsky's theory suggests that physical resources and their links with learning are a vital consideration for teaching. For example a text – whether a book, a poster, a letter, etc. – is one of the most important tools, and is linked to a complex range of signs. The place of texts in mediation is vital for the learner but also for the teacher. Eun (2008) takes the idea of a link between pupil behaviour and teacher behaviour further forward in the suggestion that mediation can be linked with models of professional development of teachers, and characterised by: 'Continuous follow-up support that includes the three types of mediators: tools (material resources); signs (newsletters and journals); and other humans (professional networks).' (Eun, 2008: 144) While Eun's distinction between signs and tools may not fit comfortably with Vygotsky's original classification, the broadening of mediation to the professional collaborative context is helpful.

One of Vygotsky's best-known ideas was the 'zone of proximal development'. He recognised that most psychological experiments assessed the level of mental development of children by asking them to solve problems in standardised tests. He showed that a problem with this was that this testing measured only a summative aspect of development. In the course of his experiments, Vygotsky discovered that a child who had a mental age of eight as measured on a standardised test was able to solve a test for a 12-year-old child if they were given 'the first step in a solution, a leading question, or some other form of help' (Vygotsky, 1987: 187). He suggested that the difference between the child's level of problem-solving while working alone and the child's level with some assistance should be called the zone of proximal development (ZPD). He found that those children who had a greater zone of proximal development did better at school.

There are a number of practical consequences to ZPD. Vygotsky's ideas point to the importance of appropriate interaction, collaboration and cooperation. He suggested that, given minimal support, the children scored much higher on the tests. All teachers must make decisions about the kind of interventions that they make. Although the tests showed the influence of appropriate support, they also remind us that collaboration is an important way of learning and that in the right context, there is much that children can do *without* direct instruction.

If we accept the idea of ZPD, it leaves a number of questions about how teacher interaction can best support pupils' learning within the ZPD. The term 'scaffolding' has become common in discussions about literacy teaching. For example, it is often said that teachers should 'model' and 'scaffold' aspects of writing. Unfortunately the didactic context for these recommendations is not the same as the original concept of scaffolding. The term 'scaffolding' emerged as early as 1976 in the work of David Wood, Jerome Bruner and Gail Ross who argued that scaffolding requires the following functions of a 'tutor': recruitment (of the learner's interest); reduction in degrees of freedom (to simplify the task); direction maintenance; marking critical features; demonstration; and frustration control avoiding the 'major risk [of] creating too much dependency on the tutor' (Wood, Bruner and Ross, 1976: 98). Wood continued work on this in his research on the teaching techniques that mothers used with their 3–4-year-old children. The mothers, who were able to help their children complete a task that could normally only be completed by children older than seven, scaffolded their children's learning in specific ways:

- They simplified problems that the child encountered; they removed potential distractions from the central task.
- They pointed things out that the child had missed.
- The less successful parent tutors showed the child how to do the task without letting them have a go themselves, or they gave verbal instructions too frequently.

Overall, Wood (1998) identified two particularly important aspects. When a child was struggling, immediate help was offered. Then, when help had been given, the mothers gradually removed support and encouraged the child's independence. 'We termed this aspect of tutoring "contingent" instruction. Such contingent support helps to ensure that the child is never left alone when he is in difficulty, nor is he "held back" by teaching that is too directive and intrusive.' (ibid.: 100)

The vital point here is that scaffolding happens in the context of meaningful interaction that is not too didactic. This idea of scaffolding is not typically what is happening when a teacher is demonstrating some aspect of the writing process. Although demonstration has a useful purpose, it should not be referred to as scaffolding and given dubious theoretical authenticity by inaccurate reference to Vygotsky. Much more thought needs to be given to the encouragement of children's independence as part of the teaching of English.

Jerome Bruner built on Vygotsky's thinking in his articulation of the 'spiral curriculum' where 'an "intuitive" grasp of an idea precedes its more formal comprehension as part of a structured set of conceptual relationships' (Bruner, 1975: 25). The idea of a spiral curriculum is important in that it suggests that knowledge and concepts need to be revisited a number of times at increasingly higher levels of sophistication. It is also important because it calls into question the notion that learning is a simple sequence, where knowledge and concepts are addressed on only one occasion. In explaining older children's apparent abandonment of reliance on *signs*, Vygotsky uses the example of memorisation and concludes that the abandonment is illusory because: 'Development, as often happens, proceeds here not in a circle but in a spiral, passing through the same point at each new revolution while advancing to a higher level.' (Vygotsky, 1986: 56)

Bruner saw a close relationship between language and the spiral curriculum. He suggested that the spiral curriculum was supported by some essential elements in the learning process. Language learning occurs in the context of 'use and interaction – use implying an operation of the child upon objects' (ibid.: 25). In other words, it is important that children have first-hand experience of relevant 'objects' (including their local environment) to support their learning. In terms of English this suggests that the writing of texts should be supported by real purposes and that the reading of texts should first and foremost be about experiencing whole texts and, second, about analysis. There are many teaching strategies that encourage the direct use of objects and the environment to stimulate talking, reading and writing. Bruner argued that this kind of language learning was 'contextualised' and should be supported by people who were expert, like the teacher.

From language and linguistics to principles for teaching

One of the most important changes to the context for language and literacy in the curriculum of different countries has been the global growth in the use of English as a language. The growth of English is played out in the contexts of continent, country, state, district, city, town, school and classroom. This global phenomenon may seem a somewhat distant idea in relation to the daily lives of pupils and teachers in the UK. But if you pause to consider the language backgrounds and experiences of the pupils in any class you will find that *multi-vernacularism* is part of all children's lives so should be built on in schools (for research evidence on the related idea of *transcultural meanings* see Wyse *et al.*, 2011). Another reason why consideration of the broader aspects of language is important is that effective teaching is informed by appropriate knowledge. Part of this knowledge is as full an understanding of language as possible. This includes the international dimensions, coupled with appropriate linguistic principles to guide practice.

In all cities in the UK, and in many rural areas, there are populations of students who are multilingual. The range is broadest in London contrasting with the larger homogenous communities in other cities who have, for example, British Asian origins. If we look globally, in Africa every country has a different socio-political engagement with English. For example, the 13 languages enshrined in South African law contrast with the twin focus on Kiswahili and English in Tanzania. In primary schools in Tanzania, Kiswahili is the medium used for teaching; in secondary schools English is used. In other African countries, the influence of French and Dutch colonialists provides different contexts for English. In Scandinavian countries, the success of English language teaching supported by the use of European language frameworks is tempered by popular concerns that national languages may be endangered (Simensen, 2010). China and the Chinese language are also of particular interest, in their own right and in relation to the spread of English. Bolton (2003) reminds us that the early seventeenth century was the beginning of contact between speakers of English and speakers of Chinese.

Bolton (op. cit.) also raises the issues of total numbers of speakers of Chinese and English. Arriving at accurate figures is complex (Crystal, 2010). The first problem is the world population growth of about 1.2 per cent per annum, which means that figures for less-developed nations change rapidly. Even in more stable populations, acquiring information is difficult when most census questionnaires do not include questions about linguistic background. Even if you can ask people about their language(s) there are difficulties in relation to measuring proficiency of language use, the way that people name their languages versus other forms of language such as dialect, and political pressure to conform to particular ideas about the place of certain languages. Accepting these caveats, Crystal (op. cit.) estimated that the figures for numbers of speakers in 2010 were as follows:

- English, in countries where people are regularly exposed to English, including learning English in school, 2,902,853,000.
- English, second language speakers, 1,800,000,000.
- Chinese, mother tongue, all languages, 1,071,000,000.
- Mandarin Chinese, mother tongue, 726,000,000.
- English, mother tongue, 427,000,000.

A further problem for estimating the growing use of English is that there are no figures available for people who have learned English as a foreign language in countries where English does not have special status (including in China, where anecdotal accounts suggest that numbers of people learning English has grown dramatically). Halliday (2003) recognised English as a global language and made a distinction between this global spread and international variants of English that result from it. Crystal (2000) saw the possibility of an international Standard English with local and national variants. The spread of English, as is the case with any language, is an organic process that is impervious to attempts to divert it.

One of the most important implications of language change is how we should understand the multilingualism that all pupils will experience and/or encounter in their lives. As part of his *developmental interdependence* hypothesis and other work, Cummins (1979) proposed that the particular features of school discourse, such as the emphasis on particular forms of literacy learning, are part of what can make things difficult for bilingual pupils. Cummins' main conclusion was that support for bilingual pupils is necessary and there is a need to include assessments of pupils' language and literacy understanding in order to provide the most appropriate pedagogy. Reese *et al.*'s study (2000), conducted in the US with Spanish/English speaking pupils, provided support for some elements of Cummins' theories. Its most significant finding was that even if parents were not able to speak the first language (and therefore used a second language), their engagement with books and reading was beneficial for their children's learning to read in the first language and their education more generally. Research clearly shows that support for home languages benefits the learning of another language, and that impeding the use of home languages is damaging. This is supported by recent neuroscience work. For example,

Kovelman, Baker and Petitto's (2008) research showed that bilinguals have differentiated representations in the brain of their two languages. They also found no evidence to suggest that exposure to two languages might be a source of fundamental and persistent language confusion.

A linguistically informed view of TELL prompts further thinking about pedagogy. The New London Group (NLG, 1996) argued that traditional pedagogy represents 'page-bound, official, standard . . . formalized, monolingual, monocultural, and rule governed forms of language' (p. 61). Instead, the NLG promoted the idea of *multiple literacies* that involve: a) a necessary emphasis on cultural and linguistic diversity; b) the recognition of local diversity interacting with global connectedness; and c) the idea of *situated practice* that emphasised the important concept of a community of learners. The authors were critical of what they called 'mere literacy' that involves a limited focus on language only, and is based on rules and correct usage that leads to 'more or less authoritarian pedagogy' (p. 64).

Street proposed that *new literacy studies* recognised the idea of multiple literacies and that there was an important distinction to be made between *autonomous* and *ideological* models of literacy. Autonomous models assume that the improvement of literacy for example in economically disadvantaged groups of people will automatically lead to societal and material advancement. Ideological models require consideration of the social and economic conditions that led to disadvantage in the first place. A helpful distinction is made by Street (2003) between literacy *events* and literacy *practices*. A literacy event takes place when written language is integral to the participants' interactions. Street's literacy practices account for literacy events but add the social models of literacy that are brought to bear by participants. Street quite rightly argues that: 'The next stage of work in this area is to move beyond these theoretical critiques and to develop positive proposals for interventions in teaching, curriculum, measurement criteria, and teacher education in both the formal and informal sectors, based upon these principles.' (p. 82) An example from Queensland, Australia is given, but since Street's paper was written it appears that government policy has changed, moving away from the theory of new literacy studies as an influence on policy and practice (see Sawyer, 2010). One of the greatest threats to teaching approaches informed by multiple literacies and new literacy studies is the move internationally in the US, the UK, Australia and New Zealand, and others to more instrumental forms of literacy – perhaps what Street would call 'autonomous' forms.

I have addressed the English language in its global context and in relation to bilingualism and pedagogy, but further selection of linguistic theory relevant to a consideration of TELL requires principles that can delimit and focus the areas of most relevance to teaching. The following principles were derived from analysis of the linguistic and pedagogic aspects of three publications, one aimed at researchers and policy makers (Wyse et al., 2010), one aimed at researchers (Wyse, 2011) and the other aimed at teachers (the previous edition of this book: Wyse and Jones, 2008). The linguistic principles that underpin TELL are as follows:

- Communication of understandable meaning is the driving force of language.
- Analysis of language in use is the basis for appropriate knowledge for pupils and teachers.
- As a consequence of the natural processes of language change, descriptive accounts of language are more appropriate than prescriptive accounts.
- Experiencing and reflecting on the processes of reading and writing are an important resource to enhance teaching and learning.
- Language and social status (or power) are inextricably linked.

These principles underpin the book to varying degrees depending on the subject of the chapters. But for this introduction we will restrict ourselves to one or two illuminative examples of the implications for teachers' knowledge.

Since communication of understandable meaning is the driving force of language, the aims and objectives of teaching will ensure that meaning is a constant point of reference and a purpose for language activities and interaction. Exercises that narrowly focus on small components of language and literacy at the expense of whole 'texts' (in the very broadest sense) and understanding of meaning, are inappropriate. An example of a more appropriate approach that reflects the centrality of meaning can be seen in relation to the teaching of writing. The teaching of writing is most effective when the emphasis is on the process of writing, including the aim to communicate a range of meanings through chosen genres of writing, coupled with structured teaching such as strategy instruction (Wyse, Andrews and Hoffman, 2010).

An example of the second principle, the importance of the analysis of language in use, can be seen in relation to grammar. Teachers' knowledge of language is informed by the idea that accurate linguistic understanding draws on corpus data (e.g. Carter and McCarthy, 2006; Sealey, 2011). Data corpora are collections of real people's language in use that provide evidence for linguists. This approach to language can form the basis of enquiries in the classroom. For a simple example, take the teaching of punctuation. Custom and practice has often resulted in schools requiring pupils to use double speech marks to demarcate direct speech. But a cursory analysis of (for example) modern children's literature reveals that direct speech is often punctuated using single speech marks. Analysis of language in use enhances teacher knowledge and leads to more accurate teaching.

These examples also serve the next principle well as they remind us that although some conventions of language are relatively stable (spelling, for example), others are subject to much more change. Vocabulary is a particularly noticeable example of language change but new ways of combining words and phrases are also part of the evolving linguistic landscape. Perhaps one of the most dramatic features of this language change is the way that English progresses as a world language, and what the linguistic consequences of this are for teachers around the globe.

Teachers are experienced readers and writers relative to their pupils and have a personal linguistic expertise and resource to draw upon. Their experience needs to be enhanced by the opportunity to reflect upon their own processes of reading and writing, as a means to better understand the processes that their pupils might experience. Greater knowledge of the processes of writing can come from psychological accounts (e.g. Hayes, 2006), but knowledge of the craft of writing acquired by professional writers, which is increasingly accessible in published forms (e.g. Gourevitch, 2007), is also relevant, notwithstanding the differences between expert and novice writers.

The final principle reflects the idea that linguistic knowledge needs to include understandings about the language backgrounds of people in school communities that teachers are likely to encounter. To some degree, this is related to the idea of multiple literacies established by the NLG. But the central concern here is not only the way in which Standard English is established but also the implications that conceptions of Standard English, and its deployment, have for citizens. A particularly unfortunate example of (mis-)conception of Standard English is the way in which trainee teachers who use non-standard spoken varieties of English are sometimes criticised by tutors on the basis that their language does not represent a good model of the language – even though their meaning is entirely clear to their pupils. This brings us back to our first and most crucial principle: if communication of understandable meaning is the driving force of language, then the question is not whether a teacher uses Standard English or not, but rather whether they can be understood, and whether their communication helps their pupils learn.

Practice points

- Be receptive to theories of learning and consciously use the ones that you think are important to inform your teaching.
- Remember that to help children learn, you need to take account of social factors (such as motivation) as well as cognitive ones.
- Develop the confidence to explore different approaches to teaching on the basis of theories.

Glossary

Theory – a general idea, principle or set of principles that can form the basis for action.

References

Bolton, E. (2003) 'Chinese Englishes: from Canton jargon to global English', *World Englishes*, 21(2): 181–199.

Bruner, J. S. (1975) *Entry into Early Language: A Spiral Curriculum*. Swansea: University College of Swansea.

Carter, R. and McCarthy, M. (2006) *Cambridge Grammar of English*. Cambridge: Cambridge University Press.

Crystal, D. (2000) 'English: Which way now?', *Spotlight* (April 2000), 54–58.

Crystal, D. (2010) *The Cambridge Encyclopedia of Language*, 3rd edn. Cambridge: Cambridge University Press.

Cummins, J. (1979) 'Linguistic interdependence and the educational development of bilingual children', *Review of Educational Research*, 49(2): 222–251.

Dewey, J. (1902) *The Child and the Curriculum*. Chicago: The University of Chicago Press.

Dunne, J. (1993) *Back to the Rough Ground: Practical Judgement and the Lure of Technique*. Notre Dame, IN: University of Notre Dame Press.

Eun, B. (2010) 'From learning to development: a sociocultural approach to instruction', *Cambridge Journal of Education*, 40(4): 401–418.

Gallagher, C. and Wyse, D. (2012) 'Aims and objectives', in D. Wyse, V. Baumfield, D. Egan, C. Gallagher, L. Hayward, M. Hulme, K. Livingston, I. Menter and B. Lingard. *Creating the Curriculum*. London: Routledge.

Gourevitch, P. (ed.) (2007) *The Paris Review Interviews* (Vol. 2). Edinburgh: Canongate.

Halliday, M. (2003) 'Written language, standard language, global language', *World Englishes*, 22(4): 405–418.

Hayes, J. R. (2006) 'New directions in writing theory', in C. MacArthur, S. Graham and J. Fitzgerald (eds) *Handbook of Writing Research*. New York: The Guilford Press.

Kovelman, I., Baker, S. A. and Petitto, L. (2008) 'Bilingual and monolingual brains compared: a functional magnetic resonance imaging investigation of syntactic processing and a possible "neural signature" of bilingualism', *Journal of Cognitive Neuroscience*, 20(1): 153–169.

The New London Group (1996) 'A pedagogy of multiliteracies: designing social futures', *Harvard Educational Review*, 66(1), 60–93.

Reese, L., Garnier, H., Gallimore, R. and Goldenberg, C. (2000) 'Longitudinal analysis of the antecedents of emergent Spanish literacy and middle-school English reading achievement of Spanish-speaking students', *American Educational Research Journal*, 37(3): 622–633.

Sawyer, W. (2010) 'English teaching in Australia and New Zealand', in D. Wyse, R. Andrews and J. Hoffman (eds) *The Routledge International Handbook of English, Language and Literacy Teaching*. London: Routledge.

Sealey, A. (2011) 'The use of corpus-based approaches in children's knowledge about language', in S. Ellis and E. McCartney (eds) *Applied Linguistics and the Primary School* (pp. 93–106). Cambridge: Cambridge University Press.

Simensen, A. M. (2010) 'English in Scandinavia: a success story', in D. Wyse, R. Andrews and J. Hoffman (eds) *The Routledge International Handbook of English, Language and Literacy Teaching* (pp. 472–483). London: Routledge.

Street, B. (2003). 'What's "new" in new literacy studies? Critical approaches to literacy in theory and practice', *Current Issues in Comparative Education*, 5(2): 1–114.

Vygotsky, L. S. (1986) *Thought and Language*. Cambridge, MA: Harvard University Press.

Wood, D. (1998) *How Children Think and Learn*, 2nd edn. Oxford: Blackwell.

Wood, D., Bruner, J. and Ross, G. (1976) 'The Role of Tutoring in Problem Solving', *Journal of Child Psychology and Psychiatry*, 17: 89–100.

Wyse, D. (ed.) (2011) *Literacy Teaching and Education: SAGE Library of Educational Thought and Practice*. London: Sage.

Wyse, D. and Jones, R. (2008). *Teaching English, Language and Literacy*, 2nd edn. London: Routledge.

Wyse, D., Andrews, R. and Hoffman, J. (eds) (2010) *The Routledge International Handbook of English, Language, and Literacy Teaching*. London: Routledge.

Wyse, D., Nikolajeva, M., Charlton, E., Cliff Hodges, G., Pointon, P. and Taylor, L. (2011) 'Place-related identity, texts, and transcultural meanings', *British Educational Research Journal*. doi: 10.1080/01411926.2011.608251

Annotated bibliography

Siegel, H. (2009) 'Introduction', in H. Siegel (ed.), *The Oxford Handbook of Philosophy of Education*. Oxford: Oxford University Press.
An in-depth overview of the main philosophical issues and their relationship to education.
L3 ★★★

Vygotsky, L. S. (1986) *Thought and Language*. Cambridge, MA: Harvard University Press.
Probably Vygotsky's best-known book. Includes the description of the zone of proximal development.
L3 ★★★

Wood, D. (1998) *How Children Think and Learn*, 2nd edn. Oxford: Blackwell.
An excellent overview of the psychology of how children think and learn. Includes explanation of work on scaffolding learning.
L2 ★★★

Chapter 3

Children's literature

Children's literature is the lifeblood of the teaching of English, language and literacy. In this chapter, we consider its rich variety and the importance of teachers' knowledge of and enthusiasm for sharing texts with children. We explore picture books, poetry, fiction and non-fiction in a variety of forms as well as some of the issues related to their selection and use in the classroom and offer some practical suggestions for working with literature in the classroom. The chapter concludes with an examination of issues surrounding the use of published reading schemes.

Children's literature lies at the heart of teaching English. Meek (1988) argued powerfully that the specific texts that children experience are one of the most important aids to learning to read and that the challenges for young readers are to learn not merely how to decode, but to understand that there is meaning behind the words. Literature can help readers towards a better understanding of themselves, of others and of the world. It provokes readers to think about real and imagined worlds, and prompts reflection on what it is to be human. The *Cambridge Primary Review*, the most comprehensive review of primary education in the past 40 years, argued that children's imaginations need to be excited in order that children can:

> advance beyond present understanding, extend the boundaries of their lives, contemplate worlds possible as well as actual, understand cause and consequence, develop the capacity for empathy, and reflect on and regulate their behaviours . . . [W]e assert the need to emphasise the intrinsic value of exciting children's imagination. To experience the delights – and pains – of imagining, and of entering into the imaginative world of others, is to become a more rounded person.
>
> (Alexander, 2010: 199)

Children's literature is one of the prime sources to excite imagination.

Maynard, MacKay, Smyth and Reynolds (2007) investigated the reading habits of children aged 4–16 years. Data was collected from a total of 46 schools, 22 primary and 24 secondary. Questionnaires were used to ask participant children about what they like to read, which factors affected their choice of books and who they would recommend books to. Conclusions drawn demonstrated the clear importance of magazines for reading for pleasure, and that non-fiction was relatively important to boys and girls, both for support with schoolwork and also for pleasure. An overwhelming finding of the study was that children clearly do enjoy reading. First and foremost, therefore, is the need for teachers to find time to focus on reading for pleasure as a critical element of the early years and primary curriculum. Inspection reports from the Office for Standards in Education (OfSTED) confirm the link between children reading for pleasure and high attainment in reading (OfSTED, 2009, 2011).

It is helpful here to consider the perspective that reader–response theory ☞ brings to the act of reading. Rosenblatt (1938) emphasises the subjectivity of transactions between reader and text, formulating a continuum from 'aesthetic' (for pleasure) to 'efferent' (for meaning) styles of reading. Reader-response theory places the emphasis on reading as a creative act of meaning-making by the reader; meaning does not reside solely in the text but 'is made from the reader and the book' (Hunt, 1991: 66). Reading is, in effect, a performance in which the reader makes connections with existing knowledge and experience to make sense of the text. Reading and the choices of text to be read are therefore powerful tools for stimulating thinking in the classroom.

What is meant by the term 'children's literature'? Scholars in the field have contested the notion itself and for readers in the twenty-first century, the very concept of text includes representations of meanings in an expanding range of forms. For the purposes of this chapter, therefore, we will take Bearne and Styles' broad definition of the term, meaning 'texts written to entertain the young' (2010: 22).

More than 30 years ago, Hardy (1977) wrote that 'narrative is a primary act of mind' (1977: 13), arguing that story can play a key role in helping children structure and understand the world. From a socio-cultural perspective, reading and the texts that children read entails a shift of emphasis from the individual to the 'social and cultural context in which literacy occurs' (Hall, 2003: 134). In selecting texts to engage children in the classroom, teachers therefore need to be cognisant of the texts with which children engage outside the classroom and to support them in developing a critical approach to these.

A recent United Kingdom Literacy Association (UKLA) project, *Teachers as Readers: Building Communities of Readers* (Cremin, Mottram, Collins and Powell, 2008), collected data from 1,200 teachers about their personal reading habits, their knowledge of children's literature and the way they used literature in the classroom. When asked to list six 'good' children's writers, only 46 per cent of the teachers named six. In response to the same question about children's poets, 10 per cent listed six and 58 per cent of the respondents could only name one, two or no poets, 22 per cent named no poets at all. Well over half the sample (62 per cent) were only able to name one, two or no picture fiction creators, 24 per cent named no picture fiction authors/illustrators, while 10 per cent named six. In the Executive Summary of the report, its authors suggested that 'the question of teachers' knowledge of a diverse enough range of writers to enable them to make informed recommendations to young readers is a cause for concern' and that teachers' knowledge of children's poetry, picture fiction and global literature needed considerable development.

In the second phase of the project, teachers were supported to improve their subject knowledge of children's literature and to develop a more inclusive reading for pleasure pedagogy which included improving the classroom reading environment, read aloud programmes, opportunities for book talk, book recommendations and the provision of quality time for independent reading. The project was undertaken in five local authorities. The sample of 27 participating schools involved one primary-level pupil referral unit, five infant, two junior and 19 primaries. Forty-three teachers were involved, 80 per cent of whom were not responsible for literacy in their schools, and three 'focus' children were identified in each class. Findings showed that children who had been identified as reluctant and disaffected readers became drawn into reading; their perceptions of their abilities as readers and self-confidence subsequently improved. They demonstrated increased pleasure in reading and began to read both more regularly and more independently. Children's talk about reading and texts also became significantly more spontaneous, informed and extended. Finally, the majority of the children's attainment showed above average increases across the year. In the Executive Summary (2007–08), the report's authors concluded that 'reading for pleasure urgently requires a higher profile in primary education to raise both attainment and achievement and increase children's engagement as self-motivated and socially engaged readers'.

What are the implications then of national and international reports for beginning teachers? These studies of effective teachers of literacy show that knowledge of children's literature is important. They perhaps also reveal that anyone engaged in teaching children to read needs to be a reader themselves. As an interesting starting point, think about your memories of the texts you encountered as a child at home, in school and on the playground. To what extent were these shared or private experiences and how and by whom were you influenced in your choices? How might these early experiences influence the way you guide the less experienced readers in your class? Medwell, Wray, Poulson and Fox (1998) argued that successful teachers of literacy engage pupils in the pleasures of reading, ensuring that reading is not a chore but a shared, enjoyable experience.

How will you share your current reading of children's literature to enthuse the pupils with whom you work? Barrs and Cork (2001: 39) argue that when teachers and others read aloud, this enables children to 'attend more closely to the language of the text' without having to focus on decoding and allows teachers to model expression and intonation as well as reading strategies and behaviours.

Selecting literature for the classroom

For readers across the primary age range, we will consider picture books, poetry and fiction and non-fiction texts in a range of genres ☞. As Mallet (2010) points out, non-fiction has often been marginalised as a form of 'literature', as have more 'popular' types of texts such as comics and magazines. However, these are all part of the currency of children's reading and offer rich opportunities for developing critical reading skills in the classroom. Whilst many of the texts discussed in this chapter will include examples of multimodal ☞ and multimedia ☞ texts, these will also be considered in their own right in Chapter 25.

The quality of the best picture books is extremely high. There are a number of well-established classics ☞ that have been available for more than 40 years and the quality of the images and text in the best new books is breathtaking. Authors and illustrators now have available to them a sophisticated range of media and paper engineering to produce ever more inventive books. A wealth of research has shown that sharing picture books with children leads to highly satisfying and educationally rich experiences for children and adults alike (Arizpe and Styles, 2003; Sipe and Pantaleo, 2008). Picture books develop varied and complex skills and clearly stimulate children's pleasure in reading and writing in the classroom, inspiring confidence. In her study of young bilingual children responding to complex contemporary picture books, Coulthard (2003: 189) highlights 'the intellectual challenge and the capacity of these books both to stimulate and provide ways of demonstrating thinking . . . the power of these texts to inspire pupils to talk in a way that pushes their language to the outer limits'.

In simple terms, picture books use image as well as written text to convey meaning. Immediately, though, this statement requires clarification as there are many excellent examples of wordless picture books which provide opportunities for sophisticated reading and writing. Indeed Lewis (2001) testifies to the difficulty of providing a single definition, as many picture books are 'subtle, indeterminate and resistant to easy categorisation' (2001: 44). Generally, however, picture books' unique nature is based on the combination of verbal and visual modes of communication, of words and image. Anthony Browne (1997) talks about the gap that exists between the image and the words; the gap that has to be filled by the child's imagination. Often there is a disparity between word and image so children have to work hard to fill in the gaps and create meaning. It is the complexity of this relationship that offers endless possibilities for multilayered meanings and interpretation and makes picture books such a rich resource for use in both Key Stage 1 and 2 classrooms and indeed beyond.

Poetry too is a vital resource in early years and primary classrooms. Benton (1978) argued that poetry is the most condensed form of language we have and therefore has the potential to deepen a child's knowledge of what language is and does more subtly than any other form of literature. Whilst story is a significant influence in children's language development, poetry exists as an even earlier resource for children's steps towards language acquisition and learning, as well as being a rich introduction to literary heritages. As Rosen (1989) states, 'everything we remember, no matter how trivial: the mark on the wall, the joke at luncheon, word games, these like the dance of a stoat or the raven's gamble are equally the subject of poetry' (1989: 11). It is important to acknowledge that the majority of texts available to teachers come from a predominantly Western (and English/North American) tradition. However, there are a small number of publishers and booksellers who produce texts from a broader range of cultures and in dual language format. Some notable examples of these publishers are Letterbox, Tamarind, Mantrlingua and Milet. Recent work about identities and reading suggests that the choice of books, and teachers' mediation of them, has a profound effect on 'how [children] see themselves and who they want to be' (McCarthey and Moje, 2002: 237). In any classroom, it is essential that diversity is represented and celebrated through literature and that the imposition of any narrow social and cultural judgements is resisted.

In deciding which texts to use in the classroom, teachers are obviously constrained by budget considerations and the resources available to them. However, your selection might be influenced by:

- children's preferences and recommendations;
- guidance from English subject leaders and other colleagues;
- support from librarians;
- long and short lists from children's book awards;
- your own personal preferences, based on wide reading.

A good strategy for locating books is to use published guides. Hahn *et al.*'s (2008, 2009) *Ultimate Book Guides* covering books for children aged 0 to 12 are two such examples. The internet has a huge range of resources, not least from publishers who are finding increasingly imaginative ways to market their books, as well as information about numerous children's book awards, for example the Kate Greenaway, Carnegie and UKLA. Websites such as the Just Imagine Story Centre (www.justimaginestorycentre.co.uk) and Booktrust (www.booktrustchildrensbooks.org.uk) are valuable resources for teachers and will help them find out about new and established texts. These sites feature recommended books, reviews, regular interviews with authors and a range of practical resources to support teachers in selecting and working with texts in the classroom. Further recommendations for websites are included at the end of this chapter.

The issue of quality in relation to any text is clearly important, if contentious. How do we define quality? For teachers, one of the main criteria has to be about the learning that is likely to arise from the reading of the book. However, the genre of the text and the nature of the experience you are trying to provide will alter the type of learning. Another way to determine quality might be through children's preferences for and enjoyment of particular texts. But a dilemma exists here; if children have not had the opportunity to read a wide range of texts and actively discuss their quality, then their judgements may be incomplete. The same is true of teachers: if you have not read widely and analytically, it is difficult to have informed judgements about the quality of texts. One of the ongoing debates about decisions over the ways texts are selected, promoted and used in the classroom has centred on what are deemed to be the most 'suitable'.

Developing strategies for working with texts

Texts operate on a number of semantic levels. First and foremost, the texts should appeal directly and powerfully to children, but adults should also find aspects that engage their curiosity and analytic skills. High-quality texts, particularly fiction and poetry, are usually characterised by the different layers of meaning they contain, layers that reveal themselves only through rereading and analysis. The following list suggests things that you could be thinking about when selecting texts from the wide range of genres for your classroom/setting:

- How will the text support the children's learning?
- Is the subject of the text one that will interest the children?
- Does the text link with the children's experience in a meaningful way and/or offer new perspectives?
- Is the amount and level of print appropriate for the reading stamina of the children (this will include some texts which really stretch the children's capabilities)?
- What kind of prior knowledge might children need to access the text?
- What kind of knowledge will children acquire by reading the text?
- How effectively is language used?
- If present, how effectively are images used?

Your most important aim should be to inspire children to read for themselves. To do this, you will need to identify favourite books that you want to share with the children in your class. The first time you read a text aloud to the class is vital: it is a time to display your story-telling skills. How do you start? Sometimes it will be as simple as ensuring that the children are settled before launching into a dramatic telling.

One of the main principles of working with texts is that wherever possible, the children should experience whole texts, rather than extracts. This is because the meaning of an extract can be fully understood only in relation to the text in its entirety. Another principle is that these texts should be real texts with a genuine purpose and aimed at a genuine readership rather than poor imitations designed to address teaching objectives. Analysing the features of real texts leads to greater understanding and a more rewarding experience. Although there are some naturally short texts (such as some poems), working with complete novels necessitates longer periods of study in which the whole class can share the book and engage in activities that you devise.

A useful strategy for developing children's understanding of texts in the early years is the use of props to engage children's play. Story sacks contain items such as puppets for the characters, key objects from the story, non-fiction books related to the topic of the story, text or image extracts for matching, games to play, etc. Sometimes the story sacks remain in the setting, while at other times they are borrowed by families to enhance the reading experience with their child. A particularly worthwhile activity can be to involve children (and parents) in the making of story sacks which become a valuable resource. Additionally, making games related to books will help extend children's understanding by immersing them in play related to books.

In primary classrooms, puppets, objects and visual images relating to the texts are also useful ways of supporting children's understanding and enthusiasm, especially on initial readings. Having engaged the children's interest in the text, on subsequent readings, you will want to develop children's responses through discussion at various points during the reading. It is important to remember that the analysis of features of texts should not be at the expense of enjoyment, however, and that when talking about texts, discussion is promoted through open-ended questions. You do not always need to know the answer to the questions you ask but should provide space for children to develop personal responses. Chambers (1993) has identified many ways in which to initiate children's talk about texts and offers practical approaches about how to give ownership of book talk to children and generate discussion about books. The essential elements are four basic questions:

1   Was there anything you liked about this book?
2   Was there anything you disliked?
3   Was there anything that puzzled you?
4   Were there any patterns/connections – that you noticed?

Children's ownership of talk and learning can also be fostered by the use of literature circles (see Chapter 13) in which children meet and lead discussion of texts which they have taken the initiative in selecting. The main activities of the session will then develop the children's understanding of the text and their reading more generally. At this point, storyboxes and bags relating to the texts can be stimulating ways of developing talk and writing relating to the texts being shared. Drama is another very effective way into texts and specific strategies will be discussed in greater depth in Chapter 7. Threading rich opportunities for speaking and listening throughout interactions with texts is key.

For infant classrooms (ages five to seven), you may like to have a stock of very familiar texts, ones which have been recently introduced and texts that are completely new to your class to share on a daily basis. For junior classrooms it is often easy to feel that there simply is not time for you to read aloud to the class, but the benefits of having stories, poems and texts to share – again on a daily basis wherever possible – cannot be over-emphasised.

In the following sections, we will discuss the broad range of literature that children should encounter in the classroom, including picture books, poetry, and fiction and non-fiction in a variety of forms. We also select some favourite texts of our own which have successfully been used in classrooms, and include some text-inspired activities that might take place.

Picture books

A significant feature of picture books is the way that authors and illustrators use images and words to make links to other stories and texts (a feature called intertextuality ☞). A good example of this is Janet and Alan Ahlberg's *Each Peach Pear Plum* (1978), in which nursery rhymes are woven into the story through the device of the childhood game 'I Spy'. A whole range of nursery rhyme characters populate the story culminating in a picnic which includes plum pie:

> Three Bears still hunting
> THEY spy Baby Bunting
> Baby Bunting safe and dry
> I spy Plum Pie
> Plum Pie in the sun
> I spy . . .
> . . . EVERYONE!
>   (Ahlberg and Ahlberg, 1978: 24–31)

The text is structured in rhyming couplets with each double spread having one couplet and an accompanying illustration. The rhythm and rhyme is both appealing and also aids memory of the text, encouraging anticipation of words and phrases. In *The Jolly Postman or Other People's Letters* (1986), reference is made to a whole host of fairy-tale characters as the eponymous 'hero' delivers their letters and children can delight in taking out the various contents of the envelopes and detecting the many intertextual allusions and puns. There is a wealth of opportunities for children to adopt the format and create their own versions of the postman's journey.

The Ahlbergs' stories can rightfully be regarded as classics because of their longevity and continuing appeal. There are many more recent examples of postmodern picture books ☞ which play with intertextual links to traditional tales such as Child's *Who's Afraid of the Big Bad Book?* (2002), Browne's *Into the Forest* (2004) and Grey's *The Pea and the Princess* (2004). An important contribution of these authors and illustrators to children's literature is the manner in which they root their work in stories which increasingly are being narrated in a variety of formats, from oral tales and books to comics, television and films, that children may have encountered outside the classroom. Whilst being rooted in a Western tradition, they also enable children from a wide range of linguistic and cultural backgrounds to recognise stories and characters with which they may be familiar. Children delight in being 'detectives', spotting the clues to other texts and playing with the metafictive ☞ elements of the stories.

In selecting texts, and visual texts in particular, it is important to think about how images of race and culture are represented. Trish Cooke's book *So Much!* was a multiple prizewinner when it was published in 1994. Although prizes don't always identify the best books, on this occasion the awards of the Smarties Book Prize, the Kurt Maschler Award and the *She*/WH Smith awards were justified. Indeed, Anthony Browne is quoted on the back of the book: 'It is always a delight to see an established artist taking risks, breaking new ground and succeeding brilliantly.' *So Much!* explores an aspect of Black British children's culture and like many children's books has a naturally repetitive structure:

> They weren't doing anything
> Mum and the baby
> nothing really . . .
> Then,
> DING DONG!
> 'Oooooooh!'
> Mum looked at the door,
> the baby looked at Mum.
> It was . . .
> (Cooke, 1994: 7)

As can be seen from the extract, the text encourages children to predict what will happen next; this helps to develop an important reading strategy and recognises their enthusiasm for guessing and problem-solving. The illustrations show accurate and positive images of a British Afro-Caribbean extended family and as each character arrives at the house they first want to do something with the baby, such as squeeze him (Auntie Bibba), kiss him (Uncle Didi), eat him (Nanny and Gran-Gran), or fight him (Cousin Kay Kay and Big Cousin Ross):

And they wrestle
and they wrestle.
He push the baby first,
the baby hit him back.
He gave the baby pinch,
the baby gave him slap.
And then they laugh
and laugh and laugh.
'Huh huh huh!'

(ibid.: 28)

The language of the book brilliantly uses some of the rhythms and repetitions of African-English which links it with other writers such as the Guyanese poet John Agard. Once again, one of the core features of the book reflected in the title is based on a common childhood experience; the adult and child game: 'How big's baby?' or 'How much do we love you?'

Two books which continue this tradition of high-quality picture fiction and celebrate the power of children's imagination rooted in their everyday experience are *Billy's Bucket* (Gray and Parsons, 2003) and *Traction Man Is Here* (Grey, 2005). *Billy's Bucket* describes a boy who wants only one thing – a bucket – for his birthday. Once filled with water, he imagines all the amazing things that could be swimming around in it and, in a humorous twist at the end, confounds his parents' scepticism about his choice and the pleasure to be derived from a mundane household object. *Traction Man* is a wonderfully evocative depiction of a boy's imagination inspired by the Action Man figure that he receives for Christmas. Both text and illustration draw richly on many genres, including the comic, superhero and toy story. This is a wonderful book simply to share across the primary age range but can also be used as a stimulus for children's play, talk and writing. Some suggestions for starting points include:

- Discuss with the children stories/texts/films they know that feature superheroes. What qualities do superheroes have? What sorts of adventures do superheroes have?
- Before sharing the text, have a selection of objects displayed to represent the villains of the story (pillows, dishcloth, spade, sock, broom, scissors). Ask children to discuss what part the props might play in a story about a superhero.
- Act out the story for the children, using props and sound effects.

After reading the text:

- Ask children to act out a scene from the story, firstly with props and then without. They could try miming/freeze framing the scene and then invent their own dialogue and playscript.

- Have a role-play area with props, superhero outfits etc.
- Make a story box (with Action Man figure, spoons, scrubbing brush, etc.) for a book corner/role-play area.

Opportunities for writing:

- *The Further Adventures of Traction Man* – a sequel to the book in a form of your choice (adventure, mystery, sci-fi, fantasy, historical and contemporary fiction, dilemma stories, dialogue/play, myths, legends, fairy tales, fables, traditional tales).
- 'If I could be a Superhero' – a list poem, a haiku, adapt a nursery rhyme.
- 'The *Traction Man* Advertising Campaign' – a radio or TV script to perform, posters, packaging for Traction Man, letter to persuade head teacher to invite Mini Grey to World Book Day.
- 'My Christmas' – a diary entry, letter, newspaper report for Christmas Day.
- 'How to care for your Traction Man' – an instruction leaflet, a recipe for one of Granny's cakes, a map of one of the episodes in the story.
- A fact file, an alphabet book of superheroes, encyclopedia entries of the 'baddies' in the book, a catalogue of Christmas gifts.
- Other options – captions for role-play area, list of objects for Traction Man's survival kit, new endpapers ☞ for the book, packaging for Scrubbing Brush toy, thank you letter to Granny . . .

Fortunately for children, teachers and adults alike, there are now two further sequels to Traction Man's adventures!

Many picture books will appeal to children (and adults) of all ages. In considering the vast range available, it is worth stressing again that many can be used very effectively in Key Stage 2 classrooms as they offer ways of approaching complex issues. There are some excellent examples of wordless picture books which can engage children and lend themselves easily to cross-curricular work. Baker's *Window* (2002) and *Belonging* (2004) are concerned with issues of environmentalism and urban and human growth. The books are presented as a series of photographs of Baker's collages which deserve repeated scrutiny for the many messages and interpretations they offer. Tan's *The Arrival* (2006) is a haunting wordless graphic novel, depicting in a series of sepia-tinged images the journeys of migrants. Former Children's Laureate Anthony Browne's work is notable because of the way that his books often focus on important issues while maintaining genuinely interesting narratives. Examples of such issues include: sexism (*Piggybook*); self-esteem and bullying (*Willy the Champ*); one-parent families (*Gorilla*); freedom and captivity (*Zoo*); gender and sibling rivalry (*The Tunnel*). All of his books are accompanied by mesmeric illustrations and are excellent examples of picture books that can be used very successfully in Key Stage 2 classrooms.

Poetry

Poetry often has an uncertain place in national curricula, yet children have an innate response to rhythm and an instinct for musical language which may well start in the mother's womb and is a natural response in babies. Pleasures in patterned language are a marked, cross-cultural feature of childhood. Outside the classroom, young children are often exposed to the language, form and content of poetry through myriad advertisements, jingles and songs. These become supplemented with playground games and chants (often rude!) and songs learnt in school. It may be useful here to reflect on your own experiences of poetry from childhood, including the television and radio jingles, songs and patterned rhythmic texts you experienced at home and school. Which poems and poets do you recall? Can you remember any specific examples of lines, verses or classic poems and nursery rhymes?

Nursery rhymes and action rhymes are an early introduction to many features of the English language and these first experiences of poetry are often oral. They offer the child short snippets of language to remember, repeat and share. Rhyme can be invested with emphasis and physical action, for example 'Ring-A-Ring-Of-Roses' ends with the phrase 'all fall DOWN', which the child learns to accentuate by intonation and by literally falling down. Similarly, the rhyme:

> Round and round the garden
> like a teddy bear
> one step, two step
> and TICKLE HIM UNDER THERE

teaches the child anticipation, turn-taking, humour and the joy of another shared fragment of language. There are close links here with communal songs and stories, but poetry has the particularly important feature (at this stage) of brevity: it is manageable and memorable. The most successful poets for the young have always understood that poetry should be synonymous with play-fulness and daily pleasure in sharing rhymes in early years and infant classrooms is an essential part of a rich language curriculum.

Building on children's early oral experiences, how can poetry continue to be experienced and valued in the classroom? Regular opportunities to browse through a large range of poetry, both of individual poets' collections and also of anthologies to find favourites and returning to these should be a feature of the ongoing curriculum and not merely a function of English lessons. There are many high-quality classic and modern anthologies to have on your classroom bookshelf. *The Puffin Book of Utterly Brilliant Poetry* (1998) also includes interviews with the poets represented. Anthologies of classic poetry include *The Walker Book of Classic Poetry and Poets* (2001) and there are of course individual collections of older and 'classic' poets such as Stevenson's

(1885) *A Child's Garden of Verses*. An unusual anthology which brings together concrete (or shape) poetry ☞ is *A Poke in the I* (2005) and a favourite anthology of ours, which draws together poetry from a range of cultures, is *You'll Love This Stuff* (1986). Examples of single poet collections are also essential and the more you can acquaint yourself and children with, the better. Any list, even as a starting point, is of course incomplete, but some you might like to sample are: Carol Ann Duffy's *New and Collected Poems for Children*, Roger McGough's *All the Best*, Adrian Mitchell's *Daft as a Doughnut*, Tony Mitton's *Plum*, Grace Nichols' *Everybody Got a Gift* and Benjamin Zephaniah's *Wicked World*. CDs of nursery rhymes are also very useful in early years and infant classrooms, and nonsense verse and books of riddles are a rich of source of language play.

When reading poetry with children as part of a specific unit of work, there is a temptation to move into analysis and to ask 'what does the poet really mean?'. However, as reader-response theory shows, a more useful approach is to question 'what are the different ways that a poem can be read? What did this poem remind you of?'. This can offer illuminating insights into children's understandings and promote dialogue in the classroom. It should also be remembered that poetry is meant to be *heard*, and that children should be given opportunities to develop the specific skills required to listen to the sounds of words in poetry to interpret meaning. The Children's Poetry Archive is an invaluable resource here. Visitors can listen to aural clips of an ever-expanding range of contemporary English language poets and poets from the past as well as hear interviews with selected poets. All the poems and poets selected have been chosen with children in mind; they include work by well-known 'children's poets' such as Ahlberg, Berry, Bloom, Dahl, Nichols, Rosen and Wright and can be searched by poet, poem or theme. Many poets also have examples of readings on their own websites and the benefits of inviting a poet in to school, so that children can hear poetry read live and work with poets, cannot be over-emphasised.

Children's everyday contact with spoken language is a useful starting point for their poetry writing. Simply asking children to collect together the language they come across builds naturally on early oral experiences of rhyme, rhythm and language and leads into experimentation with form and content based on personal experience. Children are capable of extraordinary observations and often make startling conceptual links between what they see, hear, feel, know and imagine and how they compare those understandings. Working on the Northumbrian coastline, a group of children studied one village's fading relationship with the sea. One child looked at the slight film of oil on the surface of the water and wrote:

> Anchored kittiwakes bob calmly
> on the vinegar water
> A bitter scent lingers in the air.
> Sweet shards of crystal nuzzle

into the knotted rocks.
A lilted tongue tilts to its side
whispering
tish
tish

The child's perception of the water's surface is something that would have
been difficult to predict, and responses such as these become crucial starting
points for creative poetry writing as they allow metaphors to be played with,
expanded and explored linguistically. At another (stormier) part of the coast,
other children variously described the sea as a cobra, a lion, a porpoise and a
wolf, developing animal metaphors and similes which were often insightful
and occasionally surprising. Waves were variously described as 'carelessly
turquoise', 'hypnotising', 'pearl diamonds' and 'silk sheets'. The noise of the
water became a lullaby, a quarrel, a whisper, a growl, a lisp and a roar.
Observations such as these offer powerful starting points for discussion and for
further investigations into poetry and children's instinctive use of metaphor
and simile.

As primary teachers typically spend longer periods of time with the same
children, it is possible for them to develop methods of writing which build on
shared previous experiences. After a period of working on the development of
new images to describe observations, one of the authors (Russell) arrived at
school one morning after a particularly heavy frost. He took his Year 3 class
into some woodland adjacent to the playground. A girl wrote:

Sour frost swirls through the air,
mist killing the sun.
A solid surface
protecting the undergrowth.
The ice crumbles on frozen puddles, spikes on branches
frozen
like fingers trying to crack the air.
Sun beaming through a line
of gleaming frost,
lost
in a crystal clear desert of ice.
Cracked and empty.

Using the constructs of particular poetic forms such as the haiku or the cinquain
can be interesting starting points for writing poetry. Giving children specific
numbers of lines (three in the case of haiku and five for cinquains) and then
moving on to the classic syllabic patterns in each line can provide a supportive
framework (in a haiku, the syllabic pattern is 5, 7, 5 and in a cinquain, 2, 4, 6,
8, 2). Regular rhythmic patterns such as the limerick also provide similar

opportunities for children to work within specific poetic structures that are light-hearted and offer reasonably quick returns for their linguistic investment, although like many classic forms this takes time to master. Teachers can also use poems as a model to act as a framework for children to write their own. Examples that are often used are Kit Wright's *The Magic Box* and Miroslav Holub's *Go and Open the Door*. However, while having a framework can be a helpful tool, it should of course be remembered that these are wonderful poems in their own right and that using models for imitation can detract from children's ability to experiment with form and content in order to create new meaning.

If any of the genres of literature were likely to offer the opportunity for children to find their 'voice' and draw on their language resources to express their own ideas and feelings, it would be hoped that poetry could do this. Poetry-rich classrooms offer children the chance to exercise real choice over the content and form of their poetry. Finding a balance between form and freedom, however, is a challenge. Whilst models and structures may be helpful to an extent, children should be encouraged to experiment both with form and, importantly, with the development of voice; children need both to know about how working within poetic form requires the poet to adjust and adapt language, thought and feeling. This can come about only through extensive experience of reading poetry.

Writing poetry can be a liberating and challenging experience both for children and teachers. At its best, it can be vigorous, committed, honest and fascinating and is probably the most personal writing we ask children to do. As such, we also need to respond to their writing with care. Poetry writing should above all be about searching for things that genuinely matter to the writer. As Ted Hughes said: 'Almost everybody, at some time in their lives, can produce poetry. Perhaps not very great poetry, but still, poetry they are glad to have written.' (Hughes, 1967: 33)

Ideas for working with poetry

- Read poetry all the time and expose children to an eclectic range of it.
- Listen to poets reading their own work as well as actors reading poems.
- Play games with language.
- Put together displays of children's and poets' work with poems of the week/month.
- Ask children to review and then collate their own anthologies.
- Provide opportunities for children to write their own collections of poetry.
- Provide opportunities for children to learn poems by heart and for choral speech and poetry performances.
- Organise school poetry assemblies and festivals.
- Encourage children to take part in poetry competitions.
- Invite poets into the classroom.

It is also worthwhile to be mindful of Mitchell's exhortation at the beginning of his collection *Daft as a Doughnut*:

> GOOD LUCK, TEACHERS!
> Please don't use these poems or any
> Of my other work in exams or tests.
> But I'm happy if people choose to read
> Them aloud, learn them sing, dance
> Or act them in or out of school.
> (Mitchell, 2004)

Fiction

National curricula often require the teaching of a range of fiction and poetry (including modern, classic and texts drawn from a variety of cultures), play-scripts, myths, legends and traditional folk and fairy stories. Traditional stories are a key feature of the infant curriculum and folk tales. They have a particularly important role to play in children's narrative experience because of their origin in oral traditions and speech patterning (Fox, 1993). Fairy tales also lend themselves easily to oral retelling and role play. Modern retellings and parodies are available in poetic, short story, film and picture book versions offering many opportunities for younger and older children to engage and play with traditional versions in dramatic and written formats. Little Red Riding Hood, for example, has been recast in the Roberts' *Little Red* picture book (2005) as a boy; in *Beware of the Bears*, MacDonald and Williams (2001) give the bears their opportunity to wreak their revenge on Goldilocks.

As children move through the primary years, it is to be hoped that they will develop their reading stamina and engage with an increasing variety and length of texts, being willing to tolerate the uncertainty when starting the process of getting into a new book. This is not to say that children should not also be allowed to revel in the pleasures of rereading favourite texts and authors, but this may be where the 'class reader' and your personal knowledge of literature comes again into its own; in sharing texts with the whole class and making individual recommendations, you can introduce your pupils to imaginative and exciting writing that they may not otherwise choose to encounter. It is worth persevering here and also seeking out the recommendations of others, including the children, which may mean that you have to challenge your own prejudices. Short stories, shorter fiction and longer novels should all be part of this varied reading diet.

A rewarding and challenging read for upper Key Stage 2 children, both as part of a unit of work or as a class novel, is David Almond's *Skellig* (1998) which has been a Carnegie Medal and Whitbread Children's Book Award winner. The plot focuses on something that the protagonist, Michael, finds at the back of the dilapidated garage that is part of the house he has just moved into. The other plot line concerns the health of Michael's baby sister who has a heart problem. Throughout the book, Almond portrays Michael's uncertainties and worries about his sister in an authentic and touching way. Towards the end of the book, his sister recovers from an operation, and mum and the baby return home:

> Welcome home, Mum,' I whispered, using the words I'd practised.
>
> She smiled at how nervous I was. She took my hand and led me back into the house, into the kitchen. She sat me on a chair and put the baby in my arms.
>
> 'Look how beautiful your sister is,' she said. 'Look how strong she is.'
>
> I lifted the baby higher. She arched her back as if she was about to dance or fly. She reached out, and scratched with her tiny nails at the skin on my face. She tugged at my lips and touched my tongue. She tasted of milk and salt and of something mysterious, sweet and sour all at once. She whimpered and gurgled. I held her closer and her dark eyes looked right into me, right into the place where all my dreams were, and she smiled.
>
> 'She'll have to keep going for check-ups,' Mum said. 'But they're sure the danger's gone, Michael. Your sister is really going to be all right.'
>
> We laid the baby on the table and sat around her. We didn't know what to say. Mum drank her tea. Dad let me have swigs of his beer. We just sat there looking at each other and touching each other and we laughed and laughed and we cried and cried. (p. 168)

The use of language in this passage is exquisite. The human senses of sight, touch, smell and taste overwhelm us. The image of the view through the eyes to 'the place where all my dreams were' is striking. The profound relief about the baby's recovery is made more poignant by the seemingly mundane language of 'swigs' of beer. An initial way to encourage discussion might be to ask children if anything in the passage resonates with their own lives: for example, being worried about a brother or sister.

By demonstrating that you do not have all the answers, you will be showing that literature can have different meanings depending on personal experience. You might start further questions with some some straightforward literal ones to check understanding and then proceed to much more searching questions that require inference ☞:

- What happens in the passage?
- Which sentences describe the use of the senses?
- What does 'swigs' mean? Why does Almond use this word here?
- Why did they laugh *and* cry?
- Where is the place, 'where all my dreams were'? How do you think this works as a metaphor?

Skellig is a gripping story. But like all the best children's literature, it also encourages a greater depth of thought in its readers through its recurring themes; celebration of life is contrasted with exploration about what happens to things when they die. Another theme concerns learning and education. Michael meets a new friend called Mina. One of their discussions is about owls and Almond uses the opportunity to present factual information about owls in the guise of the children's curiosity. During another of their conversations, we hear Mina's description of her learning:

> 'My mother educates me,' she said. 'We believe that schools inhibit the natural curiosity, creativity and intelligence of children. The mind needs to be opened out into the world, not shuttered down inside a gloomy classroom' (p. 47).

Since *Skellig's* publication in 1998, Almond has revisited Mina in a thought-provoking prequel, *My Name Is Mina* (Almond, 2011).

Ideas for working with fiction

Reader-response perspectives have demonstrated convincingly that children bring their own experiences to make sense of texts but this of course does not mean that teachers do not have a role to play; the texts you bring to the class-room and the activities you plan will enable readers to reflect on their reading and enhance meanings already made. Some suggestions for general strategies that you might use are:

- Reading aloud.
- Asking open-ended questions.
- Encouraging oral response.
- Role play, improvisation and drama.
- Focus on the author/author studies.
- Analysing story features: genres, plots, structures, characters, settings, styles and themes.
- Comparing versions and adaptations of texts.
- Cross-curricular activities, including art and DT.
- Written response/writing in role, scripts, book-making.
- Reading journals and reviews.

Non-Fiction

Non-fiction texts written for children have shown dramatic improvements – notably in terms of organisation and layout – over the last 30 years and now differ widely in mode and media. Some of the major publishers of non-fiction for children – Dorling Kindersley, Usborne, Kingfisher, Heinemann, Franklin

Watts, Oxford University Press, Evans Brothers, A&C Black and Collins have made available a wide range of non-fiction content in print and (increasingly) in multimedia formats. Many recent editions of non-fiction texts have CD-Roms and links to websites which can add an extra dimension to children's engagement. Multimedia texts involve a different approach to reading print text and can offer a motivating experience for some young readers into accessing information. This will be discussed more fully in Chapter 25.

It is important, therefore, not to have a narrow view of particular text types and technical details about their structures and language feature; 'real' non-fiction texts shift boundaries and often contain a mixture of types, forms and structures. A leaflet for a local attraction, for example, will contain elements of persuasion, report and instruction. If you consider the writing styles of Jamie Oliver, Delia Smith and Nigel Slater, it is clear that recipes can be written in a variety of instructional formats! Walker's *Read and Wonder* was a breakthrough series that provides text with a poetic narrative voice accompanied by informative captions. 'Stories' such as *Think of an Eel* (Wallace, 2008) are told in lyrical style and use features of characterisation, pace, tension, drama which are more commonly associated with fiction texts and make the books very readable. The latest edition also has a CD-Rom. The text in the book is accompanied with beautiful illustrations. As with picture book fiction, exploring the contribution of illustrators and their different styles to these texts is a very worthwhile activity with children.

For older children, the recent books of the award-winning Manning and Granström partnership, are examples of non-fiction texts organised narratively. In the *Fly on the Wall* series published by Frances Lincoln, information about Greek, Egyptian, Roman and Viking life is provided through a cast of characters, animated with direct speech in a sketchbook format. The authors' *What Mr Darwin Saw* (2009) combines diary entries, text boxes and illustrations to provide information about Darwin's life and the reception of his ideas offering lots of opportunities for cross-curricular work. Marcia Williams is another author who incorporates an extensive range of text types, notably in *Archie's War* (2007) which, in scrapbook format, recounts a child's experience of the First World War. Another favourite is Gravett's *Little Mouse's Big Book of Fears* (2007). This is an ingenious book, impossible to categorise because it combines so many different layers and text types and, in true postmodern fashion, invites readers to contribute to the book through drawing, writing or collage. As a final recommendation, Part II of Mallet's *Choosing and Using Fiction and Non-fiction, 3–11* is an invaluable and comprehensive guide.

Ideas for working with non-fiction

Many of the strategies already outlined apply to non-fiction texts. Reading aloud, sharing your own and children's enthusiasm and discussing responses to a variety of texts beyond those that have been created as teaching tools will help to engage and motivate children with a sense of purpose and pleasure. Wray and Lewis (1997) advocate a model for teaching non-fiction which moves from teacher modelling through joint and scaffolded activity into independent activity. They recommend the use of oral discussion, writing frames and writing located in meaningful experiences. Mallet (2010) summarises her response to this model, adding greater emphasis to the active, social and oral experiences which need to accompany these stages and also stresses that the process may not be linear. She asserts that:

> children need to be at the controls when it comes to using reference and indeed all information texts. We encourage this by making critical reading important from the earliest stages so that children can develop their own viewpoints and their own 'voice' when they speak and when they write
>
> (Mallet, 2010: 374)

Finally, she states that the teacher's role is central. These are statements which apply to all the forms of texts that have been addressed in this chapter.

Published reading schemes

Historically there has been much debate about the merits of reading scheme books versus 'real' books. (In the US, reading schemes are known as 'basals'.) There are many commercial reading schemes designed to help teach reading across the primary age range. Many schools buy into reading schemes which organise texts according to levels of difficulty and, increasingly, include texts from a wide range of genres. Many people have commented on the disjointed flow in older reading scheme books due to their controlled vocabulary, stilted text and limited punctuation. There are some shocking (and sometimes amusing!) examples of these texts and the stereotypical social messages they convey. However, the old criticism of uninspiring language and pictures applies much less now and books in reading schemes are often written by respected authors (although recent moves towards government-promoted synthetic phonics schemes have reintroduced some books of dubious quality for children). Frequently, schools will use a core scheme (or schemes) of the school's choice alongside selections of 'real' books and organise their own packs according to levels of difficulty using a system called 'book banding' to support individual and guided reading (→ Chapter 13 for an overview of guided reading). However, it is worth remembering that some schools successfully teach reading using only 'real' books.

Each time significant modifications are made to guidance for the teaching of literacy, publishers have responded by producing new schemes and resources for teachers. This has been particularly evident recently with the focus on the *simple view of reading* and the teaching of systematic synthetic phonics since 2006. Publishers have also responded to the genre-based approach to literacy teaching which has been recommended since 1997 and have produced programmes organised in levelled sets designed for use in guided reading sessions of 20 minutes. For example, Oxford University Press and the Heinemann, Rigby and Ginn publishing group have produced guided reading programmes and packs of fiction, non-fiction, poetry and playscripts which often make explicit cross-curricular links.

However, this is not to say that there are still many issues surrounding the use of published schemes. The impact of the use of reading schemes with very young children in particular has been highlighted by Levy (2011) in her research with children aged three to five. In her analysis of children's views about reading, she found worrying evidence that children perceived that 'real' reading could happen only with reading scheme books and that these perceptions had a profound influence on children's confidence and motivations for reading. Whereas in the nursery, children believed that a reader was someone who could read print, for reception children, a reader was someone who had completed all the stages in a reading scheme. We discuss these findings further in relation to young children's wider reading skills and strategies, for example in relation to digital texts, in Chapter 25.

Another issue is the choice of texts in these schemes. In the period between 1997 and 2005, frequently short extracts were used. As you will have gathered, one of the guiding principles for our approach to teaching English is that complete, real texts should be used whenever possible in order to inspire children and as the basis for developing understanding and critical analysis. Furthermore, these schemes are not flexible enough to reflect the changing needs of your particular class as the objectives are set by the scheme, not by the teacher, and this can result in lack of clear learning focus in your classroom. We argue that the textual and teaching content of these materials need to be approached with a critical stance.

Witnessing a class of children engrossed in the novel being read to them, a group sprawling on cushions in the library avidly arguing about the non-fiction text they have chosen or coming across an individual buried in a book of poetry are moments that teachers are privileged to share. To return to Meek once more, the most important single lesson that children learn from texts is the nature and variety of written discourse, the different ways that language lets a writer tell, and the many and different ways a reader reads (1988: 21). Teachers have the exciting challenge of introducing less experienced readers and writers to the vast array of texts available and to help equip children to see the potential literature has to open doors to new understandings and possibilities. Deep subject knowledge of children's literature will provide you with a foundation for effective teaching and learning in English and beyond.

Practice points

- Start a reading journal to document texts you have read across a range of narrative and non-narrative examples and include notes about possible ways to use these in the classroom.
- Provide frequent opportunities for literature of all types to be shared, and also moments of quiet reflective pleasure.
- Consider the interests and attitudes of the children in your class to build reading stamina for children at different stages of development.

Glossary

Classics – books that remain of interest to significant numbers of people long after their initial publication date. They are also regarded to be of special significance.

Concrete poem – a poem which forms a shape that complements the meaning of the poem.

Endpapers – pages at the beginning and end of a picture book on which there may be illustrations or images relating to the theme of the book.

Genre – a kind or type of text bound by rules and conventions.

Inference – the understanding of textual meanings that goes beyond the literal to what is implied rather than made fully explicit.

Intertextuality – where allusions to other texts are made within a text.

Metafictive – a term applied to a text which, in creating the story, comments on the process of its creation.

Multimedia – a communication combining different sorts of media.

Multimodal – a combination of any of the four modes of communication (print, image [moving and still], sound, gesture).

Postmodern picture books – picture books which expand the conventional boundaries of picture book format, often containing non-linear structures, multiple perspectives and elements of playfulness, ambiguity and irony.

Reader-response theory – a theory which explores how readers respond to, and make sense of, texts.

Books for children

Ahlberg, A. and Ahlberg, J. (1978) *Each Peach Pear Plum*. London: Penguin.

Almond, D. (1998) *Skellig*. London: Hodder Children's Books.

Almond, D. (2011) *My Name Is Mina*. London: Hodder Children's Books.

Baker, J. (2002) *Window*. London: Walker Books.

Baker, J. (2004) *Belonging*. London: Walker Books.

Browne, A. (1983) *Gorilla*. London: Random Century.

Browne, A. (1985) *Willy the Champ*. London: Little Mammoth.

Browne, A. (1989) *Piggybook*. London: Reed Consumer Books.

Browne, A. (1992) *The Tunnel*. London: Walker Books.

Browne, A. (1992) *Zoo*. London: Random House.

Browne, A. (2004) *Into the Forest*. London: Walker Books.

Child, L. (2002) *Who's Afraid of the Big Bad Book?* London: Hodder Children's Books.

Cooke, T. (1994) *So Much!* London: Walker Books.

Cremin, T., Mottram, M., Collins, F. and Powell, S. (2008) *Building Communities of Readers*. Leicester: UKLA.

Duffy, C.A. (2010) *New and Collected Poems for Children*. London: Faber and Faber.

Gravett, E. (2007) *Little Mouse's Big Book of Fears*. London: Macmillan.

Gray, K., and Parsons, G. (2003) *Billy's Bucket*. London: Red Fox.

Grey, M. (2004) *The Pea and the Princess*. London: Red Fox.

Grey, M. (2005) *Traction Man Is Here*. London: Jonathan Cape.

Janeczko, P. and Raschka, C. (illus) (2005) *A Poke in the I*. London: Walker Books.

MacDonald, A. and Williams, G. (illus) (2001) *Beware of the Bears*. London: Tiger Press.

McGough, R. and Monks L. (illus) (2004) *All the Best. The Selected Poems of Roger McGough*. London: Puffin.

Mallet, M. (2010) *Choosing and Using Fiction and Non-fiction 3–11*. London: Routledge.

Manning, M. and Granström, B. (illus) (2009) *What Mr Darwin Saw*. London: Frances Lincoln.

Maynard, S., Mackay, S., Smyth, F. and Reynolds, K. (2007) *Young People's Reading in 2005: The Second Study of Young People's Reading Habits*. London: National Centre for Research in Children's Literature.

Mitchell, A. and Ross, T. (2004) *Daft as a Doughnut*. London: Orchard.

Mitton, T. (2010) *Plum*. London: Barn Owl Books.

Nichols, G. (2005) *Everybody Got a Gift: New and Selected Poems*. London: A & C Black Publishers.

Patten, B. (ed.) (1999) *The Puffin Book of Utterly Brilliant Poetry*. London: Puffin.

Roberts, L. and Roberts, D. (illus) (2005) *Little Red: A Fizzingly Good Yarn*. New York: Abrams.

Rosen, M. and Howard, P. (illus) (2001) *The Walker Book of Classic Poetry and Poets*. London: Walker Books.

Styles, M. (1986) *You'll Love This Stuff*. Cambridge: Cambridge University Press.

Tan, S. (2007) *The Arrival*. London: Hodder Children's Books.

Wallace, K. and Bostock, M. (illus) (2008) *Think of an Eel*. London: Walker Books.

Williams, M. (2007) *Archie's War*. London: Walker Books.

Zephaniah, B. (2000) *Wicked World*. London: Puffin.

References

Alexander, R. (ed.) (2010) *Children, Their World, Their Education: Final Report and Recommendations of the* Cambridge Primary Review. London: Routledge.

Arizpe, E. and Styles, M. (2003) *Children Reading Pictures: Interpreting Visual Texts*. London: RoutledgeFalmer.

Barrs, M. and Cork, V. (2001) *The Reader in the Writer: The Links Between the Study of Literature and Writing Development at Key Stage 2*. London. CLPE.

Bearne, E. and Styles, M. (2010) 'Children's literature', in D. Wyse, R. Andrew and J. Hoffman (eds) *The Routledge International Handbook of English, Language and Literacy Teaching*. London: Routledge.

Benton, M. (1978) 'Poetry for children: a neglected art', *Children's Literature in Education*, 9(3): 111–126.

Bromley, H. (2004) 'Storyboxes', *The Primary English Magazine*, 9: 5, June.

Bromley, H. and McEwan, K. (illus.) (2000) *Book-based Reading Games*. London: CLPE.

Browne, A. (1997) 'Never too old for picture books', *Times Educational Supplement*, 15th December 1997.

Brownjohn, S. (1994) *To Rhyme or Not to Rhyme?: Teaching Children to Write Poetry*. London: Hodder Education.

Chambers, A. (1993) 'The difference of literature: Writing now for the future of young readers', *CLE*, 24(1): 1–18.

Chambers, A. (1993) *Tell Me: Children, Reading and Talk*. The Thimble Press.

Coulthard, K. (2003) ' "The words to say it": young bilingual learners responding to visual texts', in E. Aripe and M. Styles (eds) *Children Reading Pictures: Interpreting Visual Texts*. London: RoutledgeFalmer.

Cremin, T., Mottram, M., Collins, F. and Powell, S. (2008) *Building Communities of Readers*. Leicester: UKLA.

Fox, C. (1993) *At the Very Edge of the Forest: The Influence of Literature on Storytelling by Children*. London: Cassell.

Hahn, D., Flynn, L. and Reuben, S. (eds) (2008) *The Ultimate First Book Guide: Over 500 Good Books for 0–7s*. London: A & C Black.

Hahn, D., Flynn, L. and Reuben, S. (eds) (2009) *The Ultimate Book Guide: Over 700 Great Books for 8–12s*, 2nd edn. London: A & C Black.

Hall, K. (2003) *Listening to Stephen Read: Multiple Perspectives on Literacy*. Buckingham: Open University Press.

Hardy, B. (1977) 'Towards a poetics of fiction: an approach through narrative', in M. Meek, A. Warlow & G. Barton (eds) *The Cool Web: The Pattern of Children's Reading*. London: The Bodley Head.

Hughes, T. (1967) *Poetry in the Making*. London: Faber and Faber.

King, C. and Briggs, J. (2005) *Literature circles: Better Talking, More Ideas*. Leicester: UKLA.

Levy, R. (2011) *Young Children Reading*. London: Sage.

Lewis, D. (2001) *Reading Contemporary Picturebooks: Picturing the Text*. London: Routledge.

McCarthey, S. J. and Moje, E. B. (2002) 'Identity matters', *Reading Research Quarterly*, 37(2): 228–238.

Martin, J. R., Christie, F. and Rothery, J. (1987) 'Social processes in education: A reply to Sawyer and Watson (and others)', in I. Reid (ed.) *The Place of Genre in Learning*. Melbourne, Victoria: Deakin University.

Medwell, J., Wray, D., Poulson, L. and Fox, R. (1998) *Effective teachers of literacy: Final report to the Teacher Training Agency*. University of Exeter.

Merchant, G. and Thomas, H. (eds) (1999) *Picture Books for the Literacy Hour*. London: David Fulton.

Rosen, M. (1989) *Did I Hear You Write?* London: Andre Deutsch.

Sipe, L. and Pantaleo, S. (2008) *Postmodern Picture Books: Play, Parody, and Self-referentiality*. London: Routledge.

Wray, D. and Lewis, M. (1997) *Extending Literacy*. London: Routledge.

Wray, D. and Medwell, J. (1997) *QTS English for Primary Teachers*. London: Letts.

Annotated bibliography

Arizpe, E. and Styles, M. (2003) *Children Reading Pictures: Interpreting Visual Texts*. London: RoutledgeFalmer.
    A wonderful exploration of children's responses to contemporary picture books, highlighting the significance of visual literacy to children's engagement with literature.
    L2 ★★★

Gamble, N. and Yates, S. (2008) *Exploring Children's Literature*, 2nd edn. London: Sage.
    An extremely comprehensive and readable exploration of the range of children's fiction with excellent suggestions for further reading.
    L2 ★★

Goodwin, P. (ed.) (2008) *Understanding Children's Books: A Guide for Education Professionals*. London: Sage.
    A high-quality collection demonstrating the importance of sharing the rich and varied experience of children's books.
    L2 ★★

Hunt, P. (ed.) (2004) *International Companion Encyclopedia of Children's Literature*, 2nd edn. Vol. 1. London: Routledge.
    A comprehensive, scholarly account of recent work in the field of children's literature.
    L3 ★★★

Mallet, M. (2010) *Choosing and Using Fiction and Non-fiction 3–11: A Comprehensive Guide for Teachers and Student Teachers*. London: Routledge.
    An invaluable guide, packed full of useful advice and recommendations illustrated with insightful case studies.
    L2 ★★

Meek, M. (1988) *How Texts Teach What Readers Learn*. Stroud: The Thimble Press.
A seminal text in the field of children's literature. Meek argues strongly for the importance of specific high-quality texts as one of the main things that will help children learn to read.
L2 ★★

Useful websites

www.achuka.co.uk/books.php
www.booksforkeeps.co.uk
www.booktrustchildrensbooks.org.uk
www.carnegiegreenaway.org.uk
www.justimaginestorycentre.co.uk
www.literacytrust.org.uk
www.poetryarchive.org/childrensarchive/home.do
www.readingzone.com/home.php

Part II

Language

Chapter 4

The development of language

Theories and stages of language acquisition are addressed at the beginning of this chapter. We then explore how to maximise children's capacity to learn, achieve and participate through dialogic approaches to teaching. A brief account of educational policy for language in national, statutory government curricula is presented. The chapter reveals how understanding of the centrality of language to a child's development has grown over the last 30 years.

There are two important elements of language: communication and representation. Communication is the transmission of meanings, and we know that babies engage with communication from birth. But language is also a representational system that emerges with children's cognitive skills, enabling them to understand and organise the world. Language comprises different elements that are important for effective understanding and communication: phonology, vocabulary, grammar, and pragmatics are the four basic strands which mutually support and influence each other's development. To communicate effectively, children need to develop receptive language skills in order to become increasingly able to understand the language they hear. They also need to develop expressive language skills to convey their own thoughts, feelings and desires. Thus from a very early age children are learning through language, learning to use language and learning about language.

Nature versus nurture arguments are still a potent force in discussions about how child language develops. One of the most famous advocates of the idea that language development is innate was Noam Chomsky. In his early work, he hypothesised that children made use of a Language Acquisition Device (LAD). This device, he argued, is a special capacity of the brain that enables children to use the rules systems of their native language. Jerome Bruner countered that Chomsky's theory correctly identified this aspect of the child's capacity but that this was only part of the process of language acquisition:

> The infant's Language Acquisition Device could not function without the aid given by an adult who enters with him into a transactional format. That format, initially under the control of the adult, provides a Language Acquisition Support System (LASS). It frames or structures the input of language and interaction to the child's Language Acquisition Device in a manner to 'make the system function'. In a word, it is the interaction between the LAD and the LASS that makes it possible for the infant to enter the linguistic community – and, at the same time, the culture to which the language gives access.
>
> (Bruner, 1983: 19)

Messer (2006) shows the ways that such debates have continued to be an important part of thinking about children's language acquisition, while at the same time showing how theory has progressed. Messer cautions that there has been a welcome resurgence of interest in how adults speak to children and scepticism about all-encompassing grand theories such as Chomsky's LAD.

Chomsky's later work involved theories of minimalism. One of the important features of minimalist theory is the idea that many aspects of grammar are contained in the vocabulary of a language and its semantic information. Previous theories proposed that grammatical representations were independent of vocabulary. Minimalist ideas and other developments in the field have resulted in language-development theorists focusing on the way that the human brain operates more generally. Neuro-scientists have defined the brain's activity in terms of connectionist networks, neural networks or parallel distributed processes, which are different terms describing the same general phenomena. Connectionist networks have been explored by encouraging computers to learn grammatical features such as past tense. Computers have had success with both regular and irregular past tense forms. The point of such work is to research the extent to which language features are innate, hence not learnable by computers, or can be learned. Kuhl (2004) argues that infants use computational strategies to detect the statistical and prosodic patterns in language input which leads to the discovery of phonemes and words (see also the chapters on the development of reading and reading difficulties).

Language acquisition

Infants learn language with remarkable speed: by the age of five, provided they do not have language difficulties, all children have acquired the grammar for the main constructions of their native language (Peccei, 2006). This is true across all cultures and in all languages (Kuhl, 2004). The term 'acquired' in this context is important because linguists make a distinction between emergent language constructions and ones which are acquired fully.

The main stages of children's syntactic development begin with single words and then move on to two-word phrases. After this, children's syntax develops rapidly and on many fronts. Negative sentences such as 'I am not walking' and the use of complex sentence types will be areas that develop during the nursery stage. The ability to ask questions is another aspect of syntax that develops at this time.

The word morphological comes from morpheme. A morpheme is the smallest unit of language that can change meaning. For example, if we take the singular 'apple' and turn it into the plural 'apples', then the letter 's' is a morpheme because it changes the meaning from singular to plural. Morphemes that can stand alone, such as 'apple', are called 'free' morphemes, and those which cannot, such as -s in apples, are called 'bound' morphemes. Children's development of morphological understanding can be seen in their capacity to invent words, such as 'carsiz' (cars).

Lexical ☞ development is concerned with the development of vocabulary and so is not something that has a particular end point because we continue to add vocabulary throughout our lives. One of the features of children's lexical development is over-extension. An example of this is where children call all meats 'chicken' because they are familiar with that word but not others, such as 'beef', 'pork', etc. Another feature of lexical development is learning about the way that the meanings of words relate to each other, something called 'sense relations'. Synonyms such as 'happy/joyful' and antonyms such as 'happy/sad' are part of this. This means that children can learn about vocabulary from words that they know without having to directly experience the concept of the word in question.

Phonological development ☞ has been much studied, partly because of its link with learning to read. As far as talk is concerned, there are some understandings and skills that have to be acquired before those which are beneficial for literacy. For example, the young child learns to control their vocal chords. The sound/airflow which passes from the vocal chords is obstructed in various ways in order to form sounds which eventually become words. The place of articulation involves use of the teeth, lips, tongue, mouth and glottis. The manner of articulation involves obstructing the airflow to varying degrees such as completely stopping it or allowing some to pass through the nose.

Table 4.1 is a summary of Peccei's (2006) introductory chapters on children's language development. It shows the typical ages when significant developmental milestones in the areas described above occur.

Adults model (in an unplanned way) the conventions of language, providing feedback on the effectiveness of a child's ability to communicate by responding to them. They scaffold the child's language learning and enable the child to test their current hypotheses about how language works. The ability of adults to take into account the limited abilities of the child and adjust their language accordingly (so that the child can make sense of them) is intuitive for most. To this end, one of the important ideas in relation to children's language acquisition was the concept of 'motherese', the impact, appropriateness and helpfulness of language interactions particularly between mothers and their children

Table 4.1 Summary of stages of children's language acquisition based on information from Peccei (2006)

Age	Phonological development	Sense relations	Vocabulary	Morphological development	Syntactic development	Discourse development
Birth to two months	Vowel-like sounds such as crying and grunting					
Two to four months	Cooing					
Four to six months	Vocal play including rudimentary syllables such as /da/or/goo/					
Six months	Babbling such as/ba/ba/ba/ or /ga/ba/da/do					
One year	First meaningful words					
Nine months to one year three months						Prelinguistic directive such as speech sounds and pointing
One year and six months to one year and eight months			First 50 words acquired			
One year three months to two years						Telegraphic directives: e.g. 'that mine', 'gimme'

Age		
Two years	Average vocabulary = 200–300 words	Begin to put words together in sentences. Noun phrases with premodification of the noun: e.g. more biscuit. Pronouns appear: e.g. 'me want that'
Two years and three months	Past tense inflection appears	Limited routines: 'Where's my X?', 'What's that?'
Two years to two years four months		
Two years and six months	Starting to acquire rules for inflecting nouns and verbs: e.g. 'breaked it' or 'mouses'	Multiple premodification of nouns: e.g. that red ball
Two years eight months		Compound sentences: e.g. 'The dog bit the cat and then he ran away'

(Continued overleaf)

Table 4.1 (Continued)

Age	Phonological development	Sense relations	Vocabulary	Morphological development	Syntactic development	Discourse development
Two to three years		Refer to all members of category as the same: e.g. all flowers as flower				
Two years nine months						Greater precision of articulation in self-repairs, increased volume and use of contrastive stress: e.g. 'It was on the chair!' (not under it)
Three years					Post-modified phrases: e.g. 'the picture of Lego town'. Complex sentences	Can cope with non-situated discourse
Two years four months to three years eight months						Embedded requests: 'Can I have big boy shoes?'

Age		
Three years eight months to four years		Conversation consists largely of initiation/response (I/R) exchanges
Four years		Elaborate oblique strategies: 'We haven't had any sweets for a long time'
Four years to four years seven months		Acquisition of auxilliary verbs (might, may, could) and negation. Child's response itself increasingly becomes R/I
Four years seven months to four years ten months		Greater ability to encode justifications and causal relationships allows for longer exchanges
Four to five	Spontaneously use category names: e.g. rose or daisy	

(Continued overleaf)

Table 4.1 (Continued)

Age	Phonological development	Sense relations	Vocabulary	Morphological development	Syntactic development	Discourse development
Four years six months					Coordination with ellipsis: e.g. 'The dog bit the cat and ran away'	
Three years eight months to five years seven months						Advanced embedding: 'Don't forget to buy sweets'
Six years old			Average vocabulary understood = 14,000 words. Average spoken vocabulary = 6,000 words			

(see Tizard and Hughes, 1984). This is now called Child-directed Speech (CDS) in recognition of the fact that it is not just mothers who modify their speech when talking to young children. The notion of CDS has helped our understanding of the degree to which a rich language environment assists language development, which has been well documented within research. Two examples of relevant studies here are those of Tizard and Hughes (1984) and Wells (1986). Both demonstrate the influence of language experiences on a child's ability to use language and communicate effectively. Wells' study, for example, found a correlation between the amount of conversation experienced with parents and other members of their family circle and children's rates of progress in language learning. Peccei (2006) points out that there is no clear evidence that CDS should be seen particularly as a teaching tool. She accurately observes that CDS is probably just a natural response to the fact that young children use talk which is semantically and syntactically simple; therefore if adults are to communicate effectively with them, they need to use a similar kind of language. This perhaps suggests that natural forms of communication between adults and children, commensurate with the child's language at different stages, are beneficial.

Language and the bilingual child

Kuhl (2004) argues that young children usually learn their mother tongue rapidly and effortlessly, following the same developmental path regardless of culture. Bilingual children are hearing two languages – or two distinct systems – which they have to internalise and respond to. At an early age, neither language is likely to interfere with the other so young children can learn two languages easily. Reese et al.'s (2000) research showed that bilingual pupils' success in learning to read in English does not rest exclusively on primary language input and development. The most significant finding was that parents' engagement with reading using the second language is beneficial both for their children's reading in the first language and their education more generally. Time spent on literacy activity in a child's native language – whether at home or at school – is therefore not time lost with respect to English reading acquisition.

The social and cultural aspects of language development are important as children learn, through talk, to place themselves within a specific social context; in this way, the development of language and identity are closely linked. The quality of social experience and interaction will vary greatly between children, and, during the early years, teachers need to be aware that some children will arrive at school appearing to be confident, articulate users of the English language, whereas others seem less comfortable language users. However, teachers should beware deficit models and remember that it is too easy to label a child's spoken language as 'poor', or even to say that they have 'no language', without sufficient thought. To illustrate some of the issues with labelling, Bearne analysed a transcription of a discussion including Sonnyboy, a six-year-old boy from a Traveller community, demonstrating his ability to 'translate' language for other children:

Emily: I loves them little things.

Sonnyboy: Yeah . . . I loves the little sand things – that tiny wee spade . . . And this little bucket . . .

Teacher: Do you think it would be a good idea to ask Cathy to get some? *(Cathy runs a playgroup for the Traveller children on their site).*

Emily: What for?

Teacher: So that you'd have some at home.

Sonnyboy: And who'd pay for them? Would Cathy pay?

Teacher: No, it would be part of the kit.

Emily: I don't know what you mean. Kit – who's Kit? Me Da's called Kit – would me Da have to pay?

Sonnyboy: Not your Da – it's not that sort of kit, Emily. It's the sort a box with thing in it that you play with . . . like toys and things for the little ones.

(Bearne, 1998: 154)

It is important then that teachers understand about language diversity and the ways in which judgements are made about speakers in the classroom. From this perspective, it is equally important that teachers recognise their own histories and status as language users, and resist the temptation to impose their own social criteria on the child's ongoing language development. As Bearne goes on to point out:

> Language diversity is . . . deeply involved with social and cultural judgements about what is valuable or worthy . . . Judgements are often made about intelligence, social status, trustworthiness and potential for future employment on the basis of how people speak – not the content of what they say, but their pronunciation, choice of vocabulary and tone of voice. Such attitudes can have an impact on later learning.

(ibid.: 155)

The following ideas can help to support bilingual children in the mainstream classroom:

- Encourage pupils' use of their first language in the classroom. If your knowledge of the language is poor, learn simple key phrases such as 'hello' and 'goodbye', 'please' and 'thank you'.
- Create a focus for speaking and listening activities.
- Include the child in activities and lessons right from the start; build bilingual learners' needs into the overall language and literacy objectives for the whole class.

- Integrate language learning within the lesson content of subjects other than literacy.
- Model speaking the English language. It is worth noting that some monolingual learners may also benefit from this strategy.
- Consider the use of visual aids such as pictures, photographs and real objects to support language learning.
- Involve parents in their children's learning if you can.

Chapter 26 talks in greater detail about supporting the language development of bilingual children.

Dialogic teaching

Classroom dialogue contributes to children's intellectual development and their educational attainment (Mercer and Littleton, 2007). Research has further shown that both interaction with adults and collaboration with peers can provide opportunities for children's learning and for their cognitive development (Alexander, 2000, 2004). Barnes (1971) found that language is a major means of learning and that pupils' uses of language for learning are strongly influenced by the teacher's language, which prescribes them their roles as learners. Barnes suggested that pupils have the potential to learn not only by listening passively to the teacher, but by verbalising, by talking, by discussing and arguing. Mercer and Hodgkinson (2008) built on the work of Douglas Barnes to further explore the centrality of dialogue in the learning process.

Alexander (2004: 48) argues that 'talk in learning is not a one-way linear communication but a reciprocal process in which ideas are bounced back and forth and on that basis take children's learning forward'. During dialogue, participant children (and their teachers) are equal partners striving to reach an agreed outcome and trying out and developing what Mercer (2000) has described as the joint construction of knowledge or 'interthinking'. Interthinking can be achieved through dialogue with pupils, but pupils can interthink with each other in a process of joint enquiry. Dialogic approaches to teaching are therefore based on two main premises: 1) children as active participants in learning; 2) children using language to learn.

Whole-class interactive teaching has been shown to increase pupil achievement (Alexander, 2000). The key word here is 'interactive', where pupils are allowed time for talk within a framework of effective direct teaching approaches. In order to be effective at direct teaching, teachers need to understand the complexities. Direct teaching does not mean simply one-way lecturing or 'traditional' teaching: it is interactive, it can occur between pupils and the teacher and/or between pupils and pupils, and it can involve several elements:

- clear, sequenced, structured presentations;
- effective pacing and timing;

- effective demonstrations and modelling of a particular skill or procedure;
- effective interactive structured questioning and discussion;
- relaying information that pupils do not know;
- introducing and modelling technical language/key vocabulary;
- relating to and building upon existing knowledge or understanding (for example refreshing pupils' memories of previous work);
- clarifying a sequence of cognitive or practical steps appropriate to learners;
- paired discussion work between pupils;
- pupil response and feedback;
- effective summarising;
- effective consolidation.

Whole-class interactive teaching also requires skilful questioning, and the kinds of questions that are asked to check understanding. The teacher might ask for examples, pursue an issue in greater depth with a particular pupil or check understanding of a process as well as the product or the single right answer. Underlying whole-class interactive teaching enables the teacher to have more communicative contact with pupils, which is itself a critical factor in effective learning.

Questioning is a powerful tool for teaching because it allows for supporting, enhancing, and extending children's learning. There are essentially two types of questions that teachers can use to elicit children's understanding: lower-order and higher-order questions. Lower-order questions are sometimes called 'closed' or 'literal' questions. They do not go beyond simple recall and children's answers are either 'right' or 'wrong'. Higher-order questions require children to apply, reorganise, extend, evaluate and analyse information in some way. Both types of question have their place within an effective pedagogy; the type of question asked and the form in which it is posed will vary in relation to its purpose.

In addition, questions need to be formulated to match children's learning needs. It is possible to differentiate questions for different abilities and different children. Different questioning *techniques* can be used in order to support children's learning more thoroughly, such as prompting, probing and redirecting. Prompting may be necessary to elicit an initial answer to support a child in correcting his or her response, for example simplifying the framing of the question, taking them back to known material, giving hints or clues, accepting what is right and prompting for a more complete answer. Probing questions are designed to help children give fuller answers, to clarify their thinking, to take their thinking further, or to direct problem-solving activities, for example, 'Could you give us an example?'. Questions can also be redirected to other children, for example, 'Can anyone else help?'.

In dialogic talk, the questions asked by children are as important as the questions asked by the teacher, as are the answers given. The teacher is not using questions solely for the purpose of testing pupils' knowledge, but also to enable them to reflect, develop and extend their thinking. Wragg and Brown (2001) suggest several types of response that can be made to pupils' answers and comments. Teachers can:

- ignore the response, moving on to another pupil, topic or question;
- acknowledge the response, building it into the subsequent discussion;
- repeat the response verbatim to reinforce the point or to bring it to the attention of those that might not have heard it;
- repeat part of the response, to emphasise a particular element of it;
- paraphrase the response for clarity and emphasis, and so that it can be built into the ongoing and subsequent discussion;
- praise the response (either directly or by implication in extending and building on it for the subsequent part of the discussion);
- correct the response;
- prompt the pupils for further information or clarification;
- probe the pupils to develop relevant points.

These features indicate the type of response that can be made to pupils' utterances. It is easy for the teacher to miss important clues to children's understanding when they are too concerned with leading children towards a predetermined answer, so it is important to give children time to respond and, wherever possible, build further questions from their contributions. There are other matters to consider, for example allowing thinking time (particularly for complex responses); affording pupils the opportunity to correct, clarify and crystallise their responses once uttered, i.e. not 'jumping onto' a response before a pupil has had time to finish it; building a pupil's contribution into the teacher's own plans for the sequence of the discussion; and using a pupil's contribution to introduce another question to be put to another pupil. Galton and Hargreaves (2002) found that on average a classroom teacher waits only two seconds before either repeating a question, rephrasing, it, directing it to another child or extending it themselves. Their research showed that increasing wait time from just three to seven seconds results in an increase in the following:

1   the length of pupil responses;
2   the number of unsolicited responses;
3   the frequency of pupil questions;
4   the number of responses from less capable children;
5   pupil-to-pupil interactions;
6   the incidence of speculative responses.

Additionally, it is important to think about pace in relation to purpose – a series of closed questions may be appropriate, but at other times we want pupils to give more thoughtful and considered responses. To summarise: discovering what pupils know and what their misconceptions are requires good communication skills, language skills and empathy. Unlike questions from teachers which elicit only brief responses from pupils, we can see that dialogic talk is a type of interaction where teachers and pupils make substantial and significant contributions.

Exploratory talk

Barnes (1976) and Mercer (2000) argue that exploratory talk is the kind of talk that teachers should aim to develop. When children engage in exploratory talk, they are almost certain to be working in a small group with their peers. They will be sharing a problem and constructing meaning together; exchanging ideas and opinions, considering and evaluating each other's ideas, building up shared knowledge and understanding. In other words, children are thinking together and we can hear them thinking aloud, hypothesising and speculating. Children might use words and phrases such as 'perhaps', 'if', 'might' and 'probably'; they give reasons to support their ideas using words such as 'because', and seek support from the group. In this kind of scenario, children are listening to each other and considering their response. When children are working in this way, their reasoning becomes apparent through their talk. However, this kind of talk does not come naturally to them: they need to be guided by their teachers to understand the value of collaborative talk.

Collaborative learning in group work occurs when knowledge and under-standing is developed through pupils talking and working together relatively autonomously (Blatchford et al., 2003, Mercer and Littleton, 2007). Mercer and Littleton (2007) define children as being engaged in collaborative learning 'when they are engaged in a coordinated, continuing attempt to solve a problem or in some way construct common knowledge'. The role of talk and knowledge and understanding of speaking and listening skills is therefore crucial to this process.

For successful classroom interaction to occur, a collaborative climate must be established where children feel part of a learning community in which problems are solved and understandings are developed through collective cognitive action; simply grouping children and asking them to talk together will not necessarily help them to develop talking skills. Children need to understand what is meant by 'discussion', and have the skills to engage one another in speaking and listening in order to gain value from the talk activity. Children need to be taught how to talk to one another; they have to understand and share the aims for their talk. They need to recognise that if all the group can agree on a set of rules, 'ground rules for talk', then talk can proceed in a way which will make the whole group more likely to achieve success and develop new ways of thinking. These are some of the ground rules for exploratory talk:

- Everyone in the group must be encouraged to contribute.
- Contributions must be treated with respect.

- Reasons are asked for.
- Everyone must be prepared to accept challenges and justify responses.
- All relevant information should be shared and alternative outcomes need to be discussed before a group decision is taken.

The teacher should encourage the children to talk about and develop their own list of 'ground rules for talk', written in their own words. This can be placed on the wall or printed out as a reminder for small groups when they are working on their own. In order to assess the quality of group interaction, the teacher must be clear about the objectives for the task.

Speaking and listening in policy and practice

Prior to the 1960s, the idea that talk should be an important part of the English curriculum would have been greeted with some scepticism. However, educational researchers became increasingly interested in the idea that learning could be enhanced by careful consideration of the role of talk. Andrew Wilkinson's work resulted in him coining the new word 'oracy' as a measure of how important he thought talk was, a fact confirmed by the *Oxford English Dictionary* which lists Wilkinson's text historically as the first time the word was used in print:

> **1965** A. WILKINSON *Spoken Eng.* 14 The term we suggest for general ability in the oral skills is *oracy*; one who has those skills is *orate*, one without them *inorate*.

The coining of a new word is perhaps the most fitting sign of Wilkinson's legacy. The work of Wilkinson and other educationists resulted in speaking and listening becoming part of the National Curriculum programmes of study for the subject English and since the 1980s, the recognition of oracy as part of the early years and primary curriculum has been growing. Recent reviews of curricula in England further support a central emphasis on oracy. The *Cambridge Primary Review* concluded that oracy must have its proper place in the language curriculum. Indeed, spoken language is central to learning, culture and life, and is much more prominent in the curricula of other countries (Alexander, 2010). In addition, an increased understanding and focus on the importance of supporting children to develop early language skills has emerged (Sylva *et al.*, 2010). This recent work suggests, amongst other key findings, the importance of what happens in relation to a child's language experiences (both at home and in early years settings) during their formative years in relation to later educational outcomes.

Whilst few would now argue that speaking and listening is not an important feature of early years and primary teaching and learning, there are still a number of questions that need to be asked. One of the key questions concerns the balance between speaking and listening, reading, and writing. To answer this question, there is a need to separate the curriculum content to be covered from considerations of teaching style. It seems to us that most of the debates about oracy and the recent considerations of talk in teaching and learning may have more to do with teaching style than a careful consideration of programmes of study. If national curricula are present, as they are in many countries, then it is appropriate that they should specify the content of the curriculum. This can apply to communication and language/speaking and listening just as it can apply to reading and writing and other subjects in the curriculum. However, there is a need for clear thinking about what this content should be. We would argue that if teachers' practice more routinely encouraged elements such as exploratory talk and dialogic teaching (Mercer, 2000; Alexander, 2006; Mercer and Hodgkinson, 2008), then it may be appropriate to reduce the overall content of the programmes of study for speaking and listening. This would require renewed thinking about what the content should be and might lead to more of a focus on some of the kinds of language exploration quite rightly advocated by the Language in the National Curriculum (LINC) project of the 1980s. Following this line of thinking, an increased understanding of how language is acquired and the importance of developing a speaking and listening pedagogy would give teachers a set of tools with which to support children's language skills and the confidence to interpret curriculum content creatively.

The National Curriculum in England divided the subject of English into Speaking and listening, Reading, and Writing. Four main areas of speaking and listening were addressed: children should learn how to speak fluently and confidently; listen carefully and with due respect for others; become effective members of a collaborative group; and participate in a range of drama activities. There was further emphasis on the importance of using spoken Standard English (→ Chapter 5) and some thought given to language variation. However, the emphasis of language variation lay more on the functional linguistic emphasis of language in different contexts than learning centred on topics such as accent and dialect, language and identity, language and culture, etc.

In 2003, the Qualifications and Curriculum Authority (QCA) published a resource called *Speaking, Listening, Learning: Working with Children in Key Stages 1 and 2*. The pack was designed to support the teaching of speaking and listening in primary schools and consisted of a set of materials reflecting National Curriculum requirements in English. There were several premises supported by research cited in this chapter upon which these materials were built, the first of which emphasised the fact that children need to be taught speaking and listening skills, and acknowledged that those skills develop over time and as children mature. It put forward an argument as to why speaking and listening is so important, linking it with children's personal and social development. The materials described the value of talk in helping children to organise their thoughts and ideas, pointing out that speaking and listening should not be seen as part of English as a subject alone, but as extending to all curriculum areas, acknowledging that different types of talk will be appropriate in different subject areas. The interdependency of speaking and listening, reading and writing was discussed and finally, approaches to assessment. Assessment of talk is looked at in detail in Chapter 8.

Language in the early years

England's Early Years Foundation Stage (EYFS) put the development and use of communication and language at the heart of young children's learning. It targeted the importance of supporting children to become skilful communicators from an early age, arguing that learning to speak and listen begins from birth, emerging out of non-verbal language. The premise behind this approach is the recognition of the importance of the development of speaking and listening skills which, as they become more refined, provide children with key skills with which they can build the foundations for reading and writing. This is an ongoing process which moves through several stages, beginning with early reading skills and mark-making and ending with the ability to read and write conventionally. The ability to communicate verbally is therefore seen as a very important element in a child's overall progress.

Practitioners who understand the ongoing development of communication and language are better placed to create a language-rich environment in which talk has high status. In the early years setting, children do the following:

- Develop their knowledge and understanding about how language works.
- Develop an increasingly broader range and variety of vocabulary to use.
- Develop awareness of their audience – the people they are speaking to (there is some evidence to suggest that by the age of four, children have learned to adjust their speech according to different audiences).
- Think about the appropriate language to use according to the circumstances of the situation.
- Learn to speak coherently and with clarity to make themselves understood.
- Learn to speak with confidence.

As children develop their language, they build the foundations for literacy, for making sense of visual and verbal signs and ultimately for reading and writing. Children need varied opportunities to interact with others and to use a wide variety of resources for expressing their understanding, including mark-making, drawing, modelling, reading and writing.

Purposeful situations must be planned in order for children to practise their language skills and become aware of what is appropriate or suitable for a specific context. Children need to learn to take turns, negotiate, share resources, listen to and appreciate another person's point of view and function in a small group situation. Opportunities for purposeful language situations are many: in role-play areas, for example, or round a talk table. Collaborative interaction can be encouraged round the water and sand trays. If there are two chairs by the computer, one child can discuss with another the applications they are using and children can also learn to wait for their turn (the use of an egg timer to make the waiting time fair can help). The practitioner can skilfully draw children into various activities and discussions in the setting, both indoors and outdoors.

Children need to know that the setting is a place where emotions can be expressed but that there may be undesirable consequences for expressing emotions in particular ways. Being able to manage some of these emotions through talk is the challenge both for the individual child and the practitioner. For example, young children experience an intense sense of injustice if they feel they have been wronged. Consider the scenario where one child hits another who immediately responds by hitting back. The practitioner should aim to support the child to use language as a tool for thinking by, for example, prompting the child who was hit to think about these kinds of questions: Why did they hit me? Did I do anything to provoke or upset them? Why am I upset? How should I respond to being hit? What should I do if this happens again? A strong early years setting will provide guidelines for children to follow or appropriate support systems if they find themselves in this kind of situation.

Non-verbal language such as facial expressions, effective eye contact, posture, gesture and interpersonal distance or space is usually interpreted by others as a reliable reflection of how we are feeling (Nowicki and Duke, 2000). Mehrabian (1971) devised a series of experiments dealing with the communication of feelings and attitudes, such as like–dislike. The experiments were designed to compare the influence of verbal and non-verbal cues in face-to-face interactions, leading Mehrabian to conclude that there are three elements in any face-to-face communication: visual clues, tone of voice and actual words. Through Mehrabian's experiments it was found that 55 per cent of the emotional meaning of a message is expressed through visual clues, 38 per cent through tone of voice and only 7 per cent from actual words. For communication to be effective and meaningful, these three parts of the message must support each other in meaning; ambiguity occurs when the words spoken are inconsistent with, say, the tone of voice or body language of the speaker.

Young children are naturally physically expressive, such as when they are tired, upset or happy, yet they do not always understand straightaway the full meaning another child is conveying. In a situation of conflict, for example, it can be useful when practitioners point out the expression on a 'wronged' child's face to highlight the consequences of someone else's actions. Conversely, if a child is kind to another child and that child stops crying or starts to smile, then this too can be highlighted.

Similarly, the practitioner needs to be aware of the messages they are sending out to a child via their use of non-verbal language. It is important to remember that whenever we are around others, we are communicating non-verbally, intentionally or not, and children need to feel comfortable in the presence of the adults around them. According to Chaplain (2003: 69), 'children are able to interpret the meaningfulness of posture from an early age'. Even locations and positions when talking can be important. For example, it is beneficial when speaking with a young child to converse at their physical level, sitting, kneeling or dropping down on one's haunches alongside them. This creates a respectful and friendly demeanour and communicates genuine interest in the child and what they are doing.

Practice points

- Talk with children so that they feel that you respect them, are interested in them and value their ideas.
- Give children your full attention as you talk with them; use direct eye contact to show that you are really listening.
- Find ways of encouraging children to talk in a range of contexts.
- Using specific positive praise such as 'I really liked the way that you waited patiently for your turn on the computer'.
- Smile!

Glossary

Lexical – relates to the words or vocabulary of a language, i.e. the lexicon.
Phonological development – development of understanding of sounds (phonemes) and ability to use phonemes as part of speech or recognise them when reading.

References

Alexander, R. (2000) *Culture and Pedagogy: International Comparisons in Primary Education.* Oxford: Blackwell.

Alexander, R. (2004) *Towards Dialogic Teaching: Rethinking Classroom Talk.* Cambridge: Dialogos UK.

Alexander, R. (2006) *Towards Dialogic Teaching*, 3rd edn. Dialogos.

Alexander, R. (2010) *Children, Their World, Their Education. Final report and recommendations of the* Cambridge Primary Review. London: Routledge.

Baines, E., Blatchford, P. and Kutnick, P. (2003) 'Changes in grouping practices over primary and secondary school', *International Journal of Educational Research*, 39: 9–34.

Barnes, D. (1971) 'Language and learning in the classroom', *Journal of Curriculum Studies,* 3(1): 27–38.

Barnes, D. (1976) *From Communication to Curriculum.* Harmondsworth: Penguin.

Bearne, E. (1998) *Making Progress in English.* London: Routledge.

Bearne, E. (1998) *Use of Language across the Primary Curriculum*. London: Psychology Press.

Blatchford, P., Kutnick, P., Baines, E. and Galton, M. (2003) 'Toward a social pedagogy of classroom group work', *International Journal of Educational Research*, 39: 153–172.

Bruner, J. S. (1983) *Child's Talk: Learning to use Language*. Oxford: Oxford University Press.

Chaplain, R. (2003) *Teaching Without Disruption in the Primary School*. London: RoutledgeFalmer.

Department for Education (DfE) (2012) *Statutory Framework for the Early Years Foundation Stage*. London: DfE.

Department for Education and Employment (DfEE) (1998) *The National Literacy Strategy Framework for Teaching*. London: HMSO.

Department for Education and Employment/Qualifications and Curriculum Authority (DfEE/QCA) (1999) *The National Curriculum: Handbook for Primary Teachers in England: Key Stages 1 and 2*. London: DfEE/QCA.

Galton, M. and Hargreaves, L. (2002) *Transfer from the Primary School: 20 Years On*. London: Routledge.

Galton, M., Simon, B. and Croll, P. (1980) *Inside the Primary Classroom (the ORACLE project)*. London: Routledge.

Kuhl, P. K. (2004) 'Early language acquisition: cracking the speech code', *Nature Reviews Neuroscience*, 5(11): 831–843.

Littleton, K., Mercer, N., Dawes, L., Wegerif, R., Rowe, D. and Sams, C. (2005) 'Talking and thinking together at Key Stage 1', *Early Years*, 25(2): 165–180.

Mehrabian, A. (1971) *Silent Messages*. Belmont, CA: Wadsworth.

Mercer, N. (2000) *Words and Minds: How We Use Language to Think Together*. London: Routledge.

Mercer, N. and Hodgkinson, S. (2008) *Exploring talk in school*. London: Sage.

Mercer, N. and Littleton, K. (2007) Dialogue and the Development of Thinking: A Sociocultural Approach. New York: Routledge.

Messer, D. (2006) 'Current perspectives on language acquisition', in J. S. Peccei (ed.) *Child Language: A Resource Book for Students*. London: Routledge.

Nowicki, S. and Duke, M. (2000) *Helping the Child who Doesn't Fit In*. Atlanta, GA: Peachtree.

Peccei, J. S. (ed.) (2006) *Child Language: A Resource Book for Students*. London: Routledge.

Qualification and Curriculum Authority (QCA) and Department for Education and Skills (DfES) (2003) *Speaking, Listening, Learning: Working with Children in Key Stages 1 and 2*. London: DfES.

Reese, L., Garnier, H., Gallimore, K. and Goldenburg, C. (2000) 'Longitudinal analysis of the antecedents of emergent Spanish literacy and middle-school English reading achievement of Spanish-speaking students', *American Educational Research Journal*, 37(3): 633–662.

Siraj-Blatchford, I. and Clarke, P. (2000) *Supporting Identity, Diversity and Language in the Early Years*. Buckingham: Open University Press.

Sylva, K., Melhuish, E., Sammons, P., Siraj-Blatchford, I. and Taggart, B. (2010) *Early Childhood Matters: Evidence from the Effective Pre-school and Primary Education Project*. Oxford: Routledge.

Tizard, B. and Hughes, M. (1984) *Young Children Learning*. London: Fontana.

Wells, G. (1986) *The Meaning Makers: Children Learning Language and Using Language to Learn*. London: Hodder & Stoughton.

Wragg, E. C. and Brown, G. (2001) *Questioning in the Primary School*. London: RoutledgeFalmer.

Wray, D., Bloom, W. and Hall, N. (1989) *Literacy in Action*. Barcombe: Falmer.

Annotated bibliography

Bearne, E. (1998) *Making Progress in English*. London: Routledge.
While this is not a book purely about speaking and listening, it contains wonderful examples of children's talk (often with teachers) and provides keen insight into the way in which this talk is related to reading and writing development.
L2 ★★

Mercer, N., and Hodgkinson, S. (2008) *Exploring talk in school*. London: Sage.
In addition to the valuable advice in this book, a website developed from Neil Mercer's research can be found at: http://thinkingtogether.educ.cam.ac.uk/. The website looks at research in the area of talk and provides some downloadable materials for teachers, with links to book, research projects and other websites.
L1 ★★

Norman, K. (ed.) (1992) *Thinking Voices: The Work of the National Oracy Project*. London: Hodder & Stoughton.
A collection of voices which includes children, teachers, project coordinators, LEA advisers, academics and researchers, combining to present a readable and comprehensive introduction to speaking and listening issues.
L2 ★★

Qualification and Curriculum Authority (QCA) (2003) *New Perspectives on Spoken English in the Classroom*. London: QCA Publications.
There is a series of excellent contributions to this publication which summarise various kinds of work on speaking and listening.
L3 ★★

Chapter 5

Accent, dialect and Standard English

The emphasis in this chapter is on accent and dialect ☞ as rich resources of the English language. A discussion on Standard English ☞ flags up the political factors that are at work. We conclude with some thoughts on language and identity.

The Jay makes answer as the Magpie chatters;
And all the air is filled with pleasant noise of waters.
(Wordsworth, 1807: 270)

William Wordsworth's regional accent meant that water would have been pronounced 'watter' in the extract above; chatter' and 'water' represent a natural rhyme. Many poets have embraced the wonderful variation and authenticity that come from accent and dialect. The study of accent and dialect is an important part of knowledge about language (→ Chapter 16).

One of the reasons why the English language is considered to be so rich is because of the many intriguing and fascinating variations it has to offer. These variations reveal themselves in many ways, including through accent and dialect. While there are many people in society who regard accents and dialects as a rich source of language, there is sometimes a tendency to treat them differently in schools. Some teachers feel that they are obliged to correct children's 'mispronunciations' because of the National Curriculum's insistence on the use of Standard English. It is not difficult to become confused about the differences between accent, dialect, Standard English, the Queen's English, etc. The whole business of the child's language can seem like a linguistic minefield. A strong understanding of some of the terms can help you to know when it is appropriate to correct a child and when it may be inappropriate.

Accent is the more straightforward term because it refers only to differences in pronunciation. Accents are associated with regional and social characteristics. Issues of language and power are inseparable from consideration of accent. For example, consider the small number of speakers of accents other than *received pronunciation* ☞ that you hear in news broadcasts, or the attitudes that people have to accents from the UK cities of Liverpool, Birmingham or Glasgow. One of the engaging things about accents is trying to guess a speaker's geographical origins from their speech. However, you cannot guess this about speakers who use *received pronunciation*.

Received pronunciation (RP) is sometimes referred to as 'the Queen's English' or 'BBC English'. It is the 'posh' accent which we have come to associate with public schools, 'high society' and radio broadcasters from 50 years ago. It is different to other accents because it denies the listener any indication of the speaker's geographical origin. It is primarily a socially influenced accent rather than a geographically influenced one, and it locates the speaker in a particular social group.

All speakers of English use a dialect. Dialect refers to a specific vocabulary and grammar which is often influenced by geographical factors. It does not refer to the ways in which words are pronounced. Regional dialect includes particular words that are special to the locality. For example, a flat, circular slice of potato cooked in a fish and chip shop has a large range of names across the country: in Warrington it is a *scallop*, in South Wales it is a *patty*, in Liverpool it is a *fritter*, in West Bromwich it is a *klandike* and in Crewe it is a *smack*. Dialect also contains grammatical differences: for example, in Stoke the phrase 'Her's gone up Hanley, duck' (she's gone into Hanley) is an example of the ways in which regional dialect alters the grammatical structure of the sentence while maintaining meaning (the joke in Stoke is that this is all one word: gonnerpanley!).

It is possible to distinguish between *traditional dialects* and *mainstream dialects*. An example of a traditional dialect would be the following (see if you can work out where the speaker might come from – answer at end of chapter):

> *Ah telt thee to seh thoo hazn't to gan yem the neet*
> I told you to say you mustn't go home tonight
> (Kerswill, 2007: 41)

Mainstream dialects include non-standard dialects spoken now, such as this:

> *She come up Reading yesterday.*
> She came to Reading yesterday.
> (op. cit.)

More controversially, to the lay person, it is also more accurate to describe Standard English as a dialect. Standard English is a distinct form of the language that differs from other forms in some of its vocabulary and grammar, hence it is a dialect even though it does not have particular pronunciation associated with it.

A more recent phenomenon is the idea of *dialect levelling*. This is where the features of local accents and dialects are reduced in favour of new features that are adopted by speakers that cover a wider area. So-called *Estuary English* can be seen as relatively homogenised accents or dialects spoken in the South East of England (op. cit.).

In order to see the direct interaction between children's language and teaching consider the example of Neil's writing (Figure 5.1).

Can you guess where the writer, Neil, lived? No? The writing was the first page of a book that Neil had been creating as part of the writing workshop approach that Dominic adopted in his first teaching post in Somers Town in London – a pretty dramatic opening to a story, ambush, death, mourning, burial, Roman history and an imaginary race called the Hojibs all in the first page! Now try reading the writing out loud with a London Cockney accent! You can see how Neil's accent shows in his spelling because he attempts to convert the spoken versions of words to the written versions. Dialect also features, for example in 'two Romans *was going* to another land; the people *was the* Hojibs; and the Romans *was very* sad'. He was grappling with the conventions of Standard English writing using the linguistic experience that formed part of his identity.

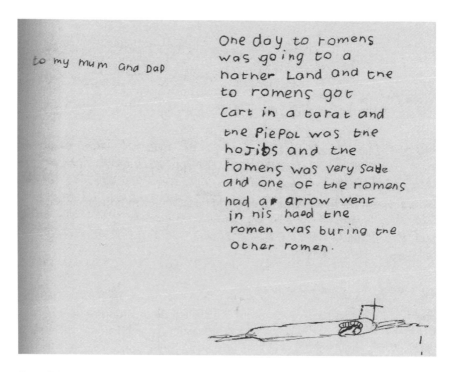

Figure 5.1   An example of Neil's handwriting.

Standard English

The question of spoken 'Standard English' is one that has also been particularly influenced by political factors. It is a complex issue that is centrally about the social context of language use, and it is bedevilled by prejudice and misunderstanding. The Cox Report contained a sensible discussion of the issue (DES, 1989) and the 1990 National Curriculum orders required only that older primary pupils should have opportunity to use spoken Standard English 'in appropriate contexts' (DES, 1990: 25) and that knowledge should rise out of the pupil's 'own linguistic competence' (DES, 1989: 6.11). The 1995 National Curriculum highlighted the issue of Standard English in a separate section which included the misleading requirement that 'To develop effective speaking and listening pupils should be taught to use the vocabulary and grammar of Standard English' (DfE, 1995: 2, 3) but otherwise left the Cox approach intact. The statement is misleading because effective speaking and listening develops in all dialects, not just Standard English. In 2012, the draft proposals for new programmes of study in England's new National Curriculum largely ignored talk as an area of the English curriculum, a retrograde step.

Language and identity

Trudgill (1975) offers a pyramid of social variation, at the peak of which are those who use Standard English and speak with RP, resulting in high social status. The base of the pyramid is made up of a wide range of regional accents and dialects which are afforded low social status. Given that accents and dialects are closely linked to perceptions of social status, then there are issues for teachers to consider if one form of dialect is accepted as superior in the classroom:

> There is a particular danger that, if Standard English is held up as a superior dialect which ought to replace the child's own, the child will come to resent and reject anything that has to do with Standard English – especially reading . . . there is evidence to suggest that some children at least may not learn to read because they do not want to: and that they do not want to for reasons which have to do with group identity and cultural conflict, in both of which dialect certainly plays a role.
>
> (Trudgill, 1975: 67)

As an example of identity and conflict we offer the following anecdote. When one of the authors of this chapter was completing his initial teacher training, he was told by a supervising tutor that he could not be a teacher until he had lost his 'working-class accent'. Over ten years later, while completing classroom-based research, the author watched a lesson given by a student teacher in a classroom where she, the teacher and the children all shared the same strong

Potteries accent and dialect. Despite the fact that the lesson had progressed perfectly well, and the children had achieved the aims of the lesson, the student was failed outright by the university tutor who 'could not understand a word that was said'. The student reported that 'I was told I can't speak. I'm common'.

These examples illustrate the close connection between accent, dialect and personal identity. The insensitive correction of regional dialects runs the risk of upsetting people, whether they are children or adults. It is for this reason that activities which encourage reflection on language in different contexts (such as role play for different degrees of formality and looking at the differences between speech and writing) are preferable to continual correction. There have been arguments to suggest that non-standard dialects should be purged from the classroom and teachers have resorted to all kinds of tactics to attempt to ensure this takes place:

> Generations of teachers have employed persuasion, exhortation, punishment, scorn and ridicule in attempts to prevent children from using nonstandard dialects – and all of them without success. And there is no reason to suppose that they will be any more successful in the future.
>
> (Trudgill, 1975: 66)

The issue for the teacher therefore is how to achieve the balance between using the child's own language as a motivational and cultural tool for development while at the same time illustrating that certain language forms are deemed more appropriate than others at certain times and in certain social situations. Much of this is achievable by establishing particular audiences and contexts for talk activities. However, although children have to be aware that Standard English is the norm in formal situations, they also need to be aware that there is considerable prejudice against regional accents and dialects.

Practice points

- Regional dialects should be respected, enjoyed and seen as a rich language resource.
- Standard English is often best discussed in the context of writing or role play.
- Helping students to understand standard conventions of writing is essential but this always needs to be done sensitively.

Glossary

Dialect – regional variations of grammar and vocabulary in language.
Received pronunciation – a particular accent often called 'BBC English' or 'The Queen's English'.

Standard English – the formal language of written communication in particular. Many people call this 'correct' English.

References

Department of Education and Science and The Welsh Office (DES) (1989) *English for Ages 5–16* (*The Cox Report*). York: National Curriculum Council.

Department of Education and Science and The Welsh Office (DES) (1990) *English in the National Curriculum*. London: HMSO.

Department for Education (DfE) (1995) *English in the National Curriculum*. London: HMSO.

Kerswill, P. (2007) 'Standard and non-standard English', in D. Britain (ed.) *Language in the British Isles*. Cambridge: Cambridge University Press.

Trudgill, P. (1975) *Accent, Dialect and the School*. London: Open University Press.

Wordsworth, W. (1807) 'Resolution and independence', in *Oxford Library of English Poetry*, Vol. 2. Bungay: Book Club Associates.

Annotated bibliography

The British National Corpus: http://www.phon.ox.ac.uk/SpokenBNC
A wealth of spoken and written examples of the English language.
L1 ★

Crystal, D. (2004) *The Stories of English*. London: Penguin/Allen Lane.
A tremendous achievement. David Crystal shows how language and the English language in particular continue to change, driven by the need to communicate meaning. The social status of different kinds of English is clearly shown.
L2 ★★

Milroy, J. and Milroy, L. (1985) *Authority in Language*. London: Routledge.
A mainly theoretical, but lively, examination of attitudes towards 'correct' and 'incorrect' uses of English. The third (1999) edition of this book addresses the increasing debate about Standard English in schools.
L3 ★★★

Trudgill, P. (1975) *Accent, Dialect and the School*. London: Open University Press.
Trudgill's work is seminal text in its field. This is short, readable and very informative about a complicated area of language development.
L2 ★★

Answer to dialect question: The speaker would be from Durham in the North East of England.

Chapter 6

Planning for talk

The reasons for systematic planning for talk are followed by examples of children talking and interacting. The chapter concludes with some examples of strategies which can promote effective talk in classrooms.

As you saw in Chapter 4, 'The development of language', language is a vital part of teaching and learning. Mercer and Littleton (2007), for example, have shown that focusing on the quality of spoken dialogue in primary classrooms can significantly improve children's educational attainment. Speaking and listening has been a programme of study in England's National Curriculum since 1988. There has been an expectation that opportunities for talk should be planned systematically, not only within English or literacy sessions, but across the curriculum so that the development of children's ability to use talk for thinking and learning is given the same level of attention as key literacy skills. Planning opportunities for talk can broaden and enhance children's command of language by providing them with a range of different contexts in which to use their speaking and listening skills. It is also important for teachers to understand language development and that speaking and listening skills must be taught from an early age. Whilst for nearly all children the development of language occurs naturally, *how* to use language effectively is a facet that benefits from teaching.

Planning for talk therefore begins with the conviction that talk is valuable and has the potential to focus children's attention on learning and understanding in unique ways. Talking allows children to question, elaborate and reflect on a range of ideas. By planning lessons that offer overt opportunities for different types of talk children are, for example, given the experience of discussing tasks with their peers, exploring their thinking, presenting their ideas and working collaboratively to reach an agreement.

Examples of children talking

Mercer and Hodgkinson (2008) argue that *exploratory talk* is the optimum type of talk that teachers should aim to develop amongst pupils in their classrooms. Exploratory talk is a way of interacting which emphasises reasoning, the sharing of relevant knowledge and a commitment to collaborative endeavour. This contrasts with Mercer's definitions of *disputational talk* in which speakers are competitive rather than cooperative, each sticking to their own point of view, and *cumulative talk* in which speakers share ideas and agree with each other but there is no critical evaluation of ideas.

In the two contrasting examples of talk that follow, a group of three children aged six and seven years old discuss what they see in a snailery. In the first extract, the teacher attempts to focus their discussion; in the second extract, the children are working alone:

Teacher:	Can you tell me how you think they move?
Emma:	Very slowly.
Teacher:	Jason, you tell me, how are they moving?
Jason:	They're pushing themselves along.
Teacher:	How many feet can you see?
Susan:	Don't think they have got any feet really.
Teacher:	None at all?
Susan:	No.
Emma:	I should say they've got . . . can't see 'em. No.
Susan:	Haven't exactly got any feet.
Emma:	Slide . . . the bottom . . . so it slides . . . they can go along.
Teacher:	Doesn't it look like one big foot?
All:	Yes . . . yes (murmur hesitantly).
Teacher:	Where do you think its eyes are?
Emma:	On those little bits.
Susan:	I can see . . . little.
Teacher:	Which little bits?
Susan:	You see those little bits at the bottom.
Teacher:	Yes? You think the top bits? Which ones do you think, Susan?
Susan:	I think the bottom one.
Teacher:	You think the bottom . . . well, have a close look at the bottom horns. What is the snail doing with the bottom horns?
Susan:	He is feeling along the ground.
Teacher:	He's feeling along, so what would you call the bottom horns, Jason?
Susan:	Arms? No . . . sort of . . .
Emma:	Legs?

Teacher: You think they're legs, you think they're arms. What do you think they are Jason, if he's feeling with them?

Jason: Feelers?

(Grugeon *et al.*, 1998: 2)

Although within this extract the teacher has the best of intentions and is keen to draw in all members of the group, there are a number of ways in which the talk is not productive:

- Typically, the teacher asks closed questions which necessitate single word, 'correct' answers.
- The teacher asks short questions which are followed by short answers and which lead to further short questions.
- Exploratory talk is non-existent as a response to the teacher's questioning.

Contrast the same children's experience of talking about the snailery before the teacher arrived:

Susan: Yes, look at this one, it's come ever so far. This one's stopped for a little rest . . .

Jason: It's going again!

Susan: Mmmm . . . good!

Emma: This one's smoothing . . . slowly.

Jason: Look, they've bumped into each other (laughter).

Emma: It's sort of got four antlers.

Susan: Where?

Emma: Look! I can see their eyes.

Susan: Well, they're not exactly eyes . . . they're a second load of feelers really, aren't they? They grow bigger, you know, and at first you couldn't hardly see the feelers and then they start to grow bigger, look.

Emma: Look, look at this one. He's really come . . . out . . . now.

Jason: It's got water on it when they move.

Susan: Yes, they make a trail, no . . . let him move and we see the trail afterwards.

Emma: I think it's oil from the skin . . .

Jason: Mmm . . . it's probably . . . moisture. See, he's making a little trail where he's been. They . . . walk . . . very . . . slowly.

Susan: Yes, Jason, this one's doing the same, that's why they say 'slow as a snail'.

Emma: Ooh look, see if it can move the pot.

Jason: Doesn't seem to . . .

Susan: Doesn't like it in the p . . . when it moves in the pot . . . look, get him out.

Jason: Don't you dare pull its . . . shell off.
Emma: You'll pull its thing off . . . shell off . . . ooh it's horrible!
Jason: Oh look . . . all this water.

(ibid.: 2)

From this transcript, several learning points are clear:

- The children are unafraid to hypothesise ('I think it's moisture', for example).
- The children generate more creative, descriptive and insightful observations *without* their teacher.
- The children operate as a group, they share their ideas, they listen to one another and they respond positively to new suggestions.
- They look for opportunities to draw one another into the task, typically using 'tag' questions ☞.

These extracts serve as a reminder that direct instruction and intervention can only achieve so much. It is important to remember that the teacher's ability to plan exciting learning opportunities and to sometimes *leave* children to talk is an important skill in itself. Guidance often stresses the need for teachers to model features of speaking and listening, but it is important to remember that there are times when good teaching also consists of planning which allows children to explore and interact independently. This type of talk, however, also benefits from sensitive teaching. In the following extract, the teacher rehearses collaborative strategies with the children:

Teacher: What do we need to remember in our groups?
Student A: That everybody gets a turn to talk.
Teacher: That everybody gets a turn to talk.
Student B: Everybody needs to share their opinions.
Teacher: Yeah – and are we all the same?
Students: No.
Teacher: Will there be someone in your group that perhaps wants to talk all the time?
Students: Yes.
Teacher: Will there be someone in your group who doesn't want to talk at all?
Students: Yes.
Teacher: How are you going to get that person who doesn't want to talk at all to say something? Shane? What do you think? How are you going to get that person who sits there and doesn't say anything to say something in your group? Help him out, Tyber.
Student C: Ask them.

Teacher:	Ask them – brilliant. What about that person who talks *all* the time?
Student D:	Tell them to shut up.
Teacher:	Ooh! Are you? I hope not, because that's not positive language is it? What can you do to help them out?
Student A:	Ask them and then ask somebody else and then ask the other person.
Teacher:	Brilliant. Making sure that you ask everybody in the group. Excellent.

(Mercer and Littleton, 2007: 118)

Here, the teacher has explicitly reminded children of teaching points in relation to group talk and has supported the development of ground rules for discussion (→ Chapter 4).

Creating a learning environment which promotes talk

As can be seen from the previous example, conditions need to be established for effective talk to happen in classrooms. This includes the physical environment; from this perspective, the following should be considered:

- furniture organised to facilitate collaborative work in pairs and small groups;
- interactive displays;
- a collection of props and artefacts to stimulate and promote discussion and story telling;
- a listening area which might include a CD player and headphones/ computer and cushions;
- a role-play area;
- posters displaying ground rules for discussion.

Strategies to promote effective talk in classrooms

When planning for talk, the teacher can draw on a repertoire of strategies to support the planning process. Strategies which can be deployed during paired work, group work and whole class teaching are outlined below.

Talk partners

Children are put into pairs and allocated time for each to talk to the other at specific points during a teaching sequence. They might, for example, share experiences, generate ideas or reflect on what they have just learned. *Talk partners* is a strategy which means that all children are given the opportunity to think and discuss and express themselves orally. Some children may feel more confident when expressing their ideas in a paired situation rather than to the whole class. Talk partners also allows children to organise their thoughts, giving them time to think ahead of speaking out loud to a larger group.

Group work

Group work can help children to develop the language and social skills needed for cooperation and collaboration; to use exploratory language to try out ideas; to extend their ideas as they share these with others; to support and build on each other's contributions; and to take their turns in discussion. All of these enable children to 'interthink' (Mercer and Littleton, 2007). Some examples of strategies to consider when planning for group work include the following:

Twos to fours

The teacher sets a particular problem for a pair to discuss. After discussion, the pair meets with another pair who have been given *exactly the same task* in order to compare and elaborate on their findings.

Envoying

When working in groups, one member of each group is allocated the role of 'envoy'. The envoy has the responsibility of gathering further information and resources as required, reporting progress to the teacher and seeking further clarification for the group. This is a particularly effective way of managing practical group activities as the teacher can focus attention on a much smaller number of children in order to maintain progress.

Jigsawing

Children are organised into 'home' groups (of four to six children) to begin to solve a particular problem or to work on a collaborative activity. Each child in the group then has the responsibility of finding out more about one particular aspect of the problem. These children gather together in 'expert' groups in order to gather as much information as possible to then take back and share with their 'home' group. Once each child in the group has given their expert opinion to their home group, the problem-solving continues until an end point is reached.

Assigning roles

There may be occasions when assigning roles to individuals within group work can further enhance talk. Such roles include:

- Leader/chair – the leader organises the group, encouraging all group members to participate and to complete the task.
- Scribe – the scribe notes main points of discussion and any decisions, and checks accuracy of notes with group members.
- Reporter – the reporter works with the scribe to organise the report on findings, and by summing up and presenting ideas.
- Mentor – the mentor helps group members to carry out the task, supporting them and explaining what is needed.
- Observer – the observer makes notes on how the group works and on different contributions, then shares the observations with the group.

Whole class talk

Studies show that children learn more in classrooms where teachers use a mixture of different types of question. 'Closed' questions require relatively brief, factual answers while 'open-ended' questions are broader, inviting a range of possible answers. In order to get the most out of whole class talk, include open-ended questions to elicit children's understanding and ideas; you may want to target individual children and specific groups in this way. Exploratory questions to promote exploratory talk might include:

- What do you think? Why?
- What makes you think . . .?
- How do you feel about . . .?
- Do you like the bit where . . .? Why?
- Can you explain why . . .?
- I wonder why the writer has decided to . . .?
- Do you agree with . . .'s opinion?
- Is there anything that puzzles you?
- What would happen if . . .?

Children as researchers

Children could either be given the opportunity to research an area of their choice or to research a given topic. They could begin their research on their own, before taking their findings to a group forum. Some of the group work techniques outlined above can be used to disseminate their expertise. This can be a good way to motivate children and promote peer-to-peer learning. The benefits of this way of working are that:

- The children feel some ownership over their area of study and are consequently better motivated.
- The teacher has the potential to focus in more closely on particular groups of children because they are working independently.
- The work demands a high level of negotiation and cooperation.

Practice points

- Talk-based activities require specific planning, just as reading and writing activities do.
- Talk should be promoted within an environment that values children's contributions.
- A range of strategies should be used to promote paired, group and whole class talk.

Glossary

Tag questions – questions that are added onto the end of a statement, e.g. '... isn't it?' or '... aren't they?'

References

Alexander, R. (ed.) (2010) *Children, Their World, Their education: Final Report and Recommendations of the* Cambridge Primary Review. London: Routledge.

Grugeon, E., Dawes, L., Smith, C. and Hubbard, L. (1998) *Teaching Speaking and Listening in the Primary School*. London: David Fulton.

Mercer, N. and Hodgkinson, S. (2008) *Exploring Talk in School*. London: Sage.

Mercer, N. and Littleton, K. (2007) *Dialogue and the Development of Children's Thinking*. London: Routledge.

Annotated bibliography

Barnes, D. (1976) *From Communication to Curriculum*. Harmondsworth: Penguin. (2nd edn, 1992, Portsmouth, NH: Boynton/Cool-Heinemann). A classic text and an early advocacy of the importance of language in the curriculum.
L2 ★★

Blatchford, P., Kutnick, P., Baines, E. and Galton, M. (2003) 'Toward a social pedagogy of classroom group work', *International Journal of Educational Research*, 39: 153–172. An important contribution to the research on group work in classrooms, including the difference between effective and ineffective group work.
L3 ★★★

Thinking Together. For more information and resources on the possibilities of talk in the primary classroom, visit http://thinkingtogether.educ.cam. ac.uk/.
L1 ★

Chapter 7

Drama

Reasons for teaching drama are outlined. Drama is linked to play, particularly role play, in the early years and to story telling and writing creatively across the primary curriculum. A theoretical model of the 'building blocks of drama' is provided and some practical ideas are presented as starting points. Drama is perceived as concerning the making of meaning rather than necessarily the making of plays.

The importance of drama in its own right and as a tool for learning has been formally recognised since its inclusion in 1999 as a separate section in the speaking and listening requirements of the National Curriculum. From 2006, drama was also recognised as essential in the development of literacy with its own strand of learning objectives as part of the literacy framework for teaching. Drama incorporates the use of talk and self-expression and has been shown to be a potentially powerful stimulus for writing. Drama can enable children to experience and explore a situation with their teacher and peers and to organise their thoughts ahead of committing them to paper.

Some teachers might feel a lack of confidence about drama, claiming that it is like teaching without a 'safety net', while others will find it one of the most liberating and invigorating aspects of their job. Drama sessions can provide some of the most memorable, challenging, enjoyable and rigorous moments of the child's time at school. Good drama teaching builds on positive relationships and trusting interaction between teachers and learners.

Why teach drama?

- Drama helps children to understand their world more deeply and allows them an opportunity to find ways to explore and share that understanding.
- Drama promotes an awareness of the self.

- Drama encourages self-expression and focuses the child on the art of communication.
- Although not exclusive to speaking and listening, drama includes a large oral element which allows children to use, practise and develop their language skills, sometimes broadening their vocabulary.
- Drama offers the early years and primary teacher a route into language study that is not covered by any other form of teaching.
- Drama helps children to cooperate and collaborate with their peers. It encourages them also to see themselves in a wider social context and should help them become more sensitive to others.
- Drama allows children to explore and experience familiar and not so familiar situations.
- Drama can help bring a story and its characters alive.
- Drama can invigorate children's writing (Cremin et al., 2006).
- Drama can raise the self-esteem of even the most disaffected of pupils (Woolland, 2010).
- Relationships between the teacher and the child through their shared language are different in drama sessions. Expectations change, negotiated progress is a more prominent feature and there is a greater sense of active participation for the child.
- Drama creates direct links across the curriculum into other areas of study.
- Drama can be highly motivating for children and highly productive for teachers as learning becomes a more dynamic process.
- Drama offers an element of negotiation and unpredictability within the curriculum.
- Drama is an art form which has played a central part in our cultural heritage.

The growing interest in language as a vital part of learning has included an increased emphasis on drama. Drama can be used across the curriculum, opening up a form of language-based study which is beneficial for the child not just educationally, but also spiritually, morally and socially. Teachers should plan accordingly, encouraging children to use the richness of the experience in a multitude of ways.

The early years

When children first arrive at their early years settings, they are not bound by the formal conventions of learning; for them, play is an intrinsic part of the process by which they come to know about the world and come to refine and communicate their knowledge. Early years teachers recognise the importance of play and provide a wealth of opportunities for the child to explore a variety of roles and social situations. This should never be perceived as 'mere' play. Wood and Attfield (2005), for example, describe the significance of dramatic and socio-dramatic play as a means for learning within the early years which involves 'complex cognitive, social and emotional processes' (p. 42). Dramatic play is about pretending to be someone else, role taking, imitating a person's speech and actions, using real and imagined props, first-hand and second-hand experience and the child's developing knowledge of characters and situations. Socio-dramatic play involves cooperation between two or more children where play develops on the basis of interactions between players acting out their roles, both verbally and in terms of the acts performed (p. 41). Children might act out a well-known story or a trip to the shops, for example. Socio-dramatic play may involve an element of thematic-fantasy play (Hendy, 2008) where children create stories from their imagination. Role-play areas can be situated both within the indoor and outdoor learning environment, providing opportunities for dressing-up, and other 'real life' and fantasy scenarios (for example, playing 'shop' or a castle for knights and princesses). Role-play areas offer children crucial opportunities to enact, to imitate, to imagine, to confront, to review and to understand the social world they inhabit. Strong early years practice builds on this understanding, acknowledging that dramatic and socio-dramatic play is part of the way in which children come to make sense of their world.

Early drama teaching builds on the child's natural inclination for play and usually develops into two areas. Firstly, there are a variety of drama games which often involve walking and clapping or mime and movement activities, often though the use of songs and music. These activities introduce some structure to drama times and establish the position of the teacher within a specific exploratory context. Secondly, and more importantly, there is a movement towards the provision of structured imaginative play, allowing the teacher to plan more carefully and encouraging the child to use their intrinsic sense of participation to explore some issues in greater detail. An example of this might be exploring characterisation within a text.

Story regularly provides a natural and productive initiation for more detailed drama sessions. Story is a familiar and important feature of early years class-rooms, and there are clear links between the thematic features of children's stories (finding/losing, friends/enemies, deception, hiding, escaping, etc.) and early explorations into movement and drama. Stories also serve as a perfect medium through which the teacher can begin to introduce the speculative ideas associated with drama: What would happen if . . .?; Let's suppose that . . .; Perhaps there might be . . .? By using familiar characters and story settings, a new discourse opens through which children can explore possibilities. These can be discussed, debated and transformed into a turn-taking game with the teacher controlling the narrative and children providing dialogue, or re-enacted using classroom resources, either already available or created with the children. Airs and Ball (1997), for example, used established children's stories such as *Goldilocks* and Janet and Allan Ahlberg's *Burglar Bill*, to investigate a range of dilemmas through drama; dilemmas such as: should Goldilocks have entered the Three Bears' house? Why/why not? Was Burglar Bill a good man? Why/

why not? How could both characters have acted differently? Hendy (2008) suggests children becoming a group of servants worried about the disappearance of Snow White. What could they do to help? Can they come up with a plan of action together?

Understanding drama

The movement towards more formally planned drama work with older children needs to be capable of being both spontaneous and well structured. Woolland (2010) suggests that the building blocks for music are *pitch, melody, harmony, tempo, rhythm* and *texture*. What then are the building blocks of drama? Woolland offers one such possible set which begins to indicate a conceptual route for intending teachers of drama:

- **Role or character**
  Acting as if you were someone else or placing yourself as someone else in another situation.
- **Narrative**
  Ordering a sequence of events or images in such a way that their order creates meaning. Narrative involves the way in which the drama is moved forward – withholding information; sudden turn of events; surprise ending or beginning, etc.
- **Language**
  Verbal (this may include: naturalistic dialogue; a formal, heightened style of language such as a proclamation, or the beginning of a ritual; a direct address to an audience; characters talking to themselves; choral speech); or non-verbal (this may include symbols; body language; facial expression; the use of space; ritual).

Finally, Role or character, Narrative and Language all operate within a particular

- **Context**
  Where does the action of the drama occur?
  Is it set in a particular historical period?
  What are the relevant social / political conditions?

(Woolland, 2010)

Teachers need to know how to use these 'building blocks' to construct meaningful and valuable drama. One method which is cited by almost all drama books is that of 'Teacher-in-Role'. At its most basic, this involves the teacher adopting the role of another person (typically historical, fictional or imagined) for the purposes of questioning and answering. An example might be based on *The Rainbow Fish* (Pfister, 1992), who has lost all his friends. Teacher-in-Role is a technique which can also be used to explore the motivation of historical figures or to generate debate about current (perhaps local) social issues. More importantly, as Bolton (1992: 32) argues, 'the main purpose of Teacher-in-Role is to do with ownership of knowledge'. While the teacher (in this simplified version) is potentially in control at all times, the nature and origin of knowledge begins to shift, so that children become instrumental not only in generating new understandings, but also (and most importantly) in understanding the process of social interaction. As children learn how to interact within this context they, of course, become capable of reversing roles and assuming the 'mantle of the expert'. This is a term originally devised by Heathcote and Bolton (1995) with its origins firmly in drama and which has experienced something of a renaissance as part of early years and primary practice.

Drama and texts

When drama work is linked with a text, in addition to its intrinsic merits it can deepen pupils' understanding and interpretation of that text. Here are two examples: *Little Red Riding Hood*, which is a text suitable to use with early years (children in the EYFS and Key Stage 1), and *Goodnight Mr Tom*, suitable for children in upper Key Stage 2.

Early years and early primary: drama techniques using *Little Red Riding Hood*

Choose a version of the traditional tale that you and your class or group of children are familiar with.

Talking partners

Half of the class (in pairs) discuss why Little Red Riding Hood should go into the woods. Half of the class discuss why she should not. Take this to whole class discussion. Consider drawing up a 'For' and 'Against' list as part of a shared write.

Mime

This can take place either with the whole class or in small groups. It can involve making and eating cakes; walking through the wood; entering the house; Little Red Riding Hood encountering the wolf in bed and realising he is a wolf! Depending on the age of the children, a script could be developed.

Hot seating

Select volunteers to play Little Red Riding Hood, Little Red Riding Hood's mother and the wolf. The other children in the class need to ask each character questions.

Provide opportunities for socio-dramatic play through providing a role-play area linked to the text such as Grandma's Cottage. Use props such as a wolf mask and a red cape for children to play in role. You might also consider taking the children for a walk in role as Little Red Riding Hood through the woods to find Grandma's Cottage in the outdoor area of your setting. What or who might the children find along the way?!

Upper primary: drama techniques using Chapter I of Goodnight Mr Tom

Mime

After reading the opening extract from the book *Goodnight Mr Tom*, ask children to identify a character, their likely location/stance in the scene and their body language. They should back up their ideas by reading between and beyond the lines. Ask them to give a rationale for their choices.

Freeze frame

Children work in small groups to create the opening scene then 'freeze' the position.

Speaking thoughts

Select children from the freeze frame and ask them to voice the thoughts of their character.

'Conscience alley'

Divide the class into two large groups. One half of the class should think about reasons why Mr Tom *should* take the child, the other half argue why he shouldn't. After the preparation time, 'Mr Tom' walks down the 'alley' formed by the two groups facing each other. He approaches and/or indicates children to 'voice their conscience' about the issue when Mr Tom passes them.

Acting in pairs

Tom and Willie – the tour of Tom's house or the first meal.

Storying

Three large groups represent the billeting officer(s), the evacuees and the hosts. Each of the sets discusses experiences with others in a similar position. Individuals from the groups are encouraged to share their experiences, in role.

Hot seating

Three children play Tom, Willie and the billeting officer. Others in the class come up with questions for each character.

Moving to film

Draw a picture to show what the first three scenes of a film will look like. Make a list of sounds/music that will be heard in the first scene.

Compare with the film

Show opening and analyse differences between children's interpretations, the text and the film.

(Dominic is grateful to Ainé Sharkey for the origins of some of these ideas.)

Drama and writing

There is evidence that drama can be a useful precursor to children's writing (e.g. Cremin *et al.*, 2006). To end the chapter, the following example shows some of the power of drama for writing. The example is taken from research carried out by Helen and Dominic that evaluated the work of museum–school partnerships to enhance writing.

Four children from a class of Year 5/6 children had been focusing on biography as a writing genre and had each written a biography of the writer Michael Morpurgo in school. In preparation for a visit to Ely Stained Glass Museum (located inside Ely Cathedral), they then started to look at the life of John the Baptist using books and internet information to stimulate class discussion.

During the museum visit, they re-enacted the Dance of Salome. The class teacher chose children to play the main characters, and the rest of the children became guests at the feast. To support the children getting into role, there were costumes to dress up in, real food to eat (grapes, dates, Turkish delight, pineapple and apricots), authentic music for Salome to dance to, and John the Baptist's head (made from papier mâché), authentically gruesome, carried in on a silver platter!

In an interview before the museum visit, the class teacher felt the drama experience that was planned as part of the trip would have a particular impact on the children's motivation to write. This was in line with the recent changes to the whole school policy that had moved towards using speaking and listening as a stimulus for writing. The school's reading levels had traditionally surpassed writing levels, so the new approach was designed as part of a whole school initiative to support raising writing levels to match those of reading. On a practical level for the school, this had meant planning a lot more role play and drama work as part of literacy lessons, which the children enjoyed and were responding to well. These experiences were generally felt to be having a positive impact on writing outcomes. In the interview with the education officer at Ely Stained Glass Museum, she highlighted the importance of absorption and engagement leading to vivid memories during visits by school parties in order to impact on children's motivation to write.

Following the visit, the children wrote up their biography of John the Baptist, organising their work into four clear paragraphs with headings. The drama experience clearly had an impact on the children's ability to organise their material for writing. For example, the children found that they didn't need their notes as a scaffold for their writing because they had vivid memories to rely on:

Reasearcher: Did you make any notes before you did this?
Annie: Well, we made a few.
Researcher: Did that help at all?
Annie: I didn't really use them at all.
Sarah: I used my notes and the pages from the other sheets about John the Baptist because they told me all the names of the people and where all these things happened.

Charlie was able to compare his experience of writing in the same genre pre- and post-museum experience:

Researcher: You said earlier that it was better than doing the biography on Michael Morpurgo, why is that do you think?
Charlie: We've had a lot more time to learn about him because we've also been to the church and learned a lot about him and how he died. He had his head chopped off and put on a silver plate and taken to Salome who gave it to her mum, who was married to Herod.

For his Michael Morpurgo biography, Charlie wrote 175 words in total. However, at 300 words, his John the Baptist biography was nearly twice the length, an impact that was common to other children in the class.

Practice points

- You do not have to be a good actor in order to teach or use drama as part of your practice.
- Drama does not always have to take place in the school hall; good drama can take place in five or ten minutes in the classroom without necessarily moving any of the furniture, as well as outside the school environment.

- Use children's natural creativity by giving them the chance to invent their own collaborative drama at times.
- Use the observation of drama experiences as an opportunity to plan for new skills/subject matter.

References

Airs, J. and Ball, C. (1997) *Key Ideas: Drama*. Dunstable: Folens.

Bolton, G. (1992) *New Perspectives on Classroom Drama*. Hemel Hempstead: Simon & Schuster.

Cremin, T., Goouch, K., Blakemore, L., Goff, E. and Macdonald, R. (2006) 'Connecting drama and writing: Seizing the moment to write', *Research in Drama Education*, 11(3): 273–291.

Heathcote, D. and Bolton, G. (1995) *Drama for Learning: Dorothy Heathcote's Mantle of the Expert Approach to Education*. Portsmouth, NH: Heinemann.

Hendy, L. (2008) ' "It is only a story, isn't it?" Interactive story-making in the early years classroom', in D.Whitebread and P.Coltman (eds) *Teaching and Learning in the Early Years*, 3rd edn. London: Routledge.

O'Sullivan, C. and Williams, G. (1998) *Building Bridges: Laying the Foundations for a Child-Centred Curriculum in Drama and Education*. Birmingham: National Association for the Teaching of Drama (NATD).

Pfister, M. (1992) *The Rainbow Fish*. New York: North-South Books.

Wood, E. and Attfield, J. (2005) *Play, Learning and the Early Childhood Curriculum*, 2nd edn. London: Sage.

Woolland, B. (2010) *Teaching Primary Drama*. Harlow: Pearson Education Ltd.

Annotated bibliography

Cremin, T. and Macdonald, R. (forthcoming) 'Developing creativity through drama', in R. Jones and D. Wyse (eds) *Creativity in the Primary Curriculum*, 2nd edn. London: David Fulton.
Shows how teachers can employ drama, as an art form of social encounters, both to teach creatively and to teach for creativity.
L2 ★★

Cremin, T., Goouch, K., Blakemore, L., Goff, E. and Macdonald, R. (2006) 'Connecting drama and writing: Seizing the moment to write', *Research in Drama Education*, 11(3): 273–291.
A detailed analysis of the possibilities for enhancing children's writing through drama. It is particularly persuasive about the advantages of spontaneous writing emerging from drama work.
L3 ★★

Heathcote, D. and Bolton, G. (1995) *Drama for Learning: Dorothy Heathcote's Mantle of the Expert Approach to Education* Portsmouth, NH: Heinemann.

This book concerns itself primarily with the study and promotion of drama. It provides an excellent link between theories of drama education and their application in primary education.
L3 ★★★

Winston, J. and Tandy, M. (2001) *Beginning Drama 4–11*, 2nd edn. London: David Fulton.
Usefully structured for the non-specialist, this book offers advice for developing drama across the curriculum.
L2 ★★

Chapter 8

Assessing talk

Until relatively recently, speaking and listening has not been given such prominence within the curriculum (→ Chapter 4). However, given the centrality of talk in children's learning, we would argue that assessment of talk is crucial. This chapter offers guidance on principles for the assessment of talk, and includes way in which these principles may be put into practice with the help of a transcribed conversation between a teacher and pupil. This chapter should be read in conjunction with Chapter 15, 'Assessing reading', and Chapter 22, 'Assessing writing', as some tools for assessment – such as Assessing Pupil Progress (APP) – are applicable to all three modes, whereas other strategies are specific to one mode.

The underlying premise of this chapter is that talk is central to learning. If teachers are to help children develop their skills in speaking and listening, they will have to assess the ways that children talk. There are practical problems when attempting to assess talk in the primary classroom mainly because it is more difficult to *record* than other curriculum areas. In order to assess talk, a number questions need to be thought about: What criteria am I going to apply? What contexts for talk will I include? How will I record the talk? How will I ensure that my assessments are fair?

Assessment of talk serves two primary functions. First, it allows the teacher to make judgements about the development of talk itself. Second, it affords the teacher an opportunity to assess other forms of understanding which are communicated through that talk:

> A child who feels confident with her or his knowledge in a particular area is more likely to be fluent, at ease, capable of communicating information, making explanations or being persuasive, than a child who has no partic-ular expertise in that area. On the other hand, a child might know a great

deal yet not wish to voice that knowledge publicly, or show the ability to use particular talk strategies on any given occasion.

(Bearne, 1998: 174)

Helping any child improve their current competence therefore requires some sort of assessment. Different forms of assessment are needed at different stages of development and in order to record different features of talk. According to Grugeon *et al.* (2005: 137), in the early years, the assessment of talk usually takes the form of observable features such as:

- Does the child initiate and carry on conversations?
- Does the child listen carefully?
- Can the child's talk be easily understood?
- Does the child describe experiences?
- Does the child give instructions?
- Does the child follow verbal instructions?
- Does the child ask questions?
- Can the child contribute to a working group?
- Does the child 'think aloud'?
- Does the child modify talk for different audiences?

The Early Years Foundation Stage in England recommends that children are likely to develop more complex language when they talk about what they are most interested in. This has implications for planning opportunities for talk and highlights the importance of the teacher knowing what children's interests are. At later stages, other features of talk will take on greater significance in the assessment process. Teachers will find that they begin to look for evidence where the child is seen to be hypothesising, imagining, directing, exploring, practising, recalling, developing critical responses, explaining and sustaining talk. It is important to understand that a good listener is essential for developing good talkers, so the teacher's role as a sensitive partner in sustained shared thinking about children's activities, ideas, approaches to problem-solving and questions is key.

Talk is very much dependent on the context of its occurrence. For example, when early years teachers observe children in play contexts, they often see a very different language user. Some children, freed of the pressures of performance in front of the teacher, begin to demonstrate skills as language users and a preparedness to explore and experiment which teachers would otherwise never witness. These kinds of contexts are equally applicable among older children who perceive themselves as poor language users in the classroom, yet seem to be perfectly articulate and imaginative when outside at play. The point here is that teachers who are concerned about a child's development in this area should look at that same child at play for further evidence of language use.

The National Oracy Project (NOP) established six aspects of assessment that were applicable to speaking and listening:

- *Planning* – the groupings, the activities, the learning environment.
- *Observing and gathering information* – through notes, children's talk-diaries, file-cards, hand-held tape recording, etc.
- *Recording* – on observation sheets, audio and video tape, to build evidence of talk cumulatively for each child.
- *Summarising* – by reviewing the collected evidence and considering the main areas of achievement and needs.
- *Making judgements* – about the progress of each child, linked closely to your summaries.
- *Reporting* to parents, to children, to the school.

(Baddeley, 1992: 65)

A short case study

The example below is an extract from a fully transcribed conversation between a teacher and a Year 4 child called Stephen. Stephen was a boy who wrote very little and, over the previous three months, had offered the teacher little evidence of his ability. The task set by the teacher was to investigate 'What is a poem?', and a number of questions had been established to focus ideas along the lines of 'what colour is a poem?', 'what season is a poem?', etc. Stephen arrived late for the lesson after a visit to the dentist and missed the focused introduction. He discussed the task with some of his peers, worked for some 20 minutes and then arrived at the teacher's desk with an indecipherable piece of writing. The teacher was taping a conversation with another child as Stephen arrived (as part of an Oracy Project investigation) and the tape was left running as Stephen began to explain his ideas.

The extract below begins to indicate that the teacher's initial assessment of the child's reasoning and language skills were inadequate. Yet it also indicates the ways in which Stephen began to sharpen and consolidate his ideas in response to the teacher's inexperienced questioning. It is clear that Stephen had not been intimidated by the challenging nature of the task, nor by his lack of ability in writing. The extract shows that he had clear ideas and wanted to be able to clarify and communicate them effectively:

Teacher: Let's find out what you've got. What colour is a poem?
Stephen: I put 'white and innocent' because it's ready for your thoughts to . . . (inaudible) the paper.
Teacher: I'm sorry, Stephen, it's for your thoughts to what the paper?
Stephen: Sweep. Or dazzle.
Teacher: That's a nice picture in my mind. Why did you use the word 'sweep'?

Stephen: Well, I just thought it sounded right. It does sweep across the paper really. As you write it. It just goes across the paper. That's what I think.

Teacher: How did you answer 'What does a poem taste like?'?

Stephen: I put 'It tastes like a lemon because when you bite into it, it stings.'
Like when you get into the actual poem it tingles in your head. Sometimes it stings. Sometimes it makes you go all excited.

Teacher: So how is that like a lemon?

Stephen: Well the lemon stings and the poem kind of stings.

At this point, there is already clear evidence that Stephen has responded thoughtfully to the task, that he is still clarifying his responses (he is unsure whether to use 'sweep' or 'dazzle'), but that he is engaged in a challenging process of sifting through his own ideas, searching for the most appropriate responses. It is interesting that sometimes he thinks about the physical comparisons he is drawing, and at other times he is thinking carefully about the *sounds* that the words make; in both cases providing evidence of poetic thought at a high level. However, he went on to develop a larger idea he had been developing:

Teacher: What was the next question?

Stephen: 'What season is a poem?'
I put 'winter' because it's hibernating in your head until you write it down. Then it becomes spring.

Teacher: Oh! After it's written down it becomes spring. Why do you think that is?

Stephen: Because in spring everything comes out new, and with a poem it's brand new to everybody else.

Teacher: That's a really nice way of thinking about it.

Stephen: The next question was 'What sound is a poem?' and that is to do with winter as well, because in winter it's muffled.

Teacher: Why does it sound muffled?

Stephen: Because it's in a deep sleep.

Teacher: The poem is?

Stephen: Yes, until it comes out you don't hear it that well in your mind. Then it's been unblocked. Or unmuffled.

Teacher: 'Unmuffled'! What a lovely word. What's the next question?

Stephen: 'Where is a poem?' Again it's in the mind of the author until it's written down, and then it starts to grow up.

Teacher: Say that again slowly.

Stephen: A poem is in the mind of the author until you get it written down, and then it starts to grow up.

Teacher: Why does a poem start to grow up once it's written down?

Stephen: Well, it's like a human, because when a human leaves home it's kind of like a sign of growing up and finding its own way around in the world by itself. Stuff like that.

Stephen went on to develop his ideas throughout the conversation and was extremely pleased with his results.

If you compare this case study with the NOP assessment framework above, you will see that this description addressed four of the categories:

- Planning – the poetry activity.
- Observing and gathering information – noting that Stephen arrived late and that he asked his peers about the activity.
- Recording – literally, on a tape-recorder.
- Summarising – revealed by our analysis in this section.

There is sufficient evidence in these short extracts to indicate that had Stephen's talk not been part of an ongoing assessment process, the teacher would not have been able to establish valid statements about Stephen's language abilities. Space restricts further extracts, but an examination of the full transcription ☞ would indicate that Stephen *does* think aloud, he *does* ask questions, he continually modifies his idea using talk as a vehicle, he tests the ways that words sound out loud, he thinks about his audience, he is confident in his own ability and he is prepared to take chances with words he has invented to communicate his ideas. It is worth repeating that this is a child whose previous language assessments had been meagre to say the least.

Assessing Pupil Progress (APP) and the Assessment Focuses (AFs) for Speaking and Listening

Assessing Pupils' Progress (APP) is the national approach to periodic assessment in England. APP materials are available for speaking and listening, reading and writing. It is a tool used to refine judgements made using assessment for learning and combines a range of outcomes to inform a level judgement. Evidence for speaking and listening can be recorded in a variety of ways, including using post-its (notes of observations), noting activities and achievements on an APP guidelines sheet, annotating plans and using pupils' own log books.

The APP process involves teachers selecting a sample of pupils (usually six, with two from each ability group). Each term, they review the full range of evidence for each Assessment Focus (AF), across a range of speaking and listening experiences throughout the curriculum. They then refer to the APP assessment criteria and arrive at judgements using the assessment guidelines sheet. You may find further information created during the development of APP at http://webarchive.nationalarchives.gov.uk.

One of the intentions of APP is to be able to identify which AFs children are struggling with and to modify planning accordingly. It also enables teachers to establish where there is insufficient evidence to make a judgement and therefore to again modify planning accordingly.

The Assessment Focuses (AFs) for Speaking and Listening are:

- **AF1: Talking to others.** Talk in purposeful and imaginative ways to explore ideas and feelings, adapting and varying structure and vocabulary according to purpose, listeners and content.
- **AF2: Talking with others.** Listen and respond to others, including in pairs and groups, shaping meanings through suggestions, comments and questions.
- **AF3: Talking within role-play and drama.** Create and sustain different roles and scenarios, adapting techniques in a range of dramatic activities to explore texts, ideas and issues.
- **AF4: Talking about talk.** Understand the range and uses of spoken language, commenting on meaning and impact and draw on this when talking to others.

Since 1999, materials in the QCA document *A Language in Common* have been used to assess progress in speaking and listening (as well as for reading and writing) for English as an Additional Language (EAL) learners. The AFs for speaking and listening can also be used as an effective means of monitoring EAL pupils' achievements, providing specific feedback on their progress in different aspects of spoken language development.

Unlike the areas of reading and writing, assessment of speaking and listening in classrooms has not been given such attention, perhaps because of the difficulty in recording evidence and because assessment opportunities are evident in such a wide range of contexts.

Planning strategies for assessment

Here are some strategies to use for building the assessment of speaking and listening into curriculum planning. These suggestions come from a useful pack of materials called *Speaking, Listening, Learning: working with children in Key Stages 1 and 2* (DfES, 2003).

- *Focusing on two or three children each week* (to ensure systematic coverage of the whole class).
- *Using objectives for whole class monitoring* (developing whole class lists of which children meet specific teaching objectives).
- *Integrating speaking and listening assessment with other records* (possibly building a page-per-pupil record which incorporates talk).

- *Termly checks* (looking for patterns, omissions, etc.).
- *Annual review* (to provide feedback for children and to enable target-setting and future planning).

(Department for Education and Skills (DfES) and Qualifications and Curriculum Authority (QCA), 2003: 31)

A main concern for assessment is to consider how well the talk suits the kind of event in which children are participating, for example retelling a story or participating in a debate. Criteria for assessment are likely to be different, depending on whether children are talking in a group, making a presentation to the class, engaged in a drama-related activity, discussing ideas in citizenship, etc. The relative formality/informality of the context and the intended audience needs to be taken into account.

There are some aspects of evaluating children's talk where great sensitivity is needed. The ways people talk can be closely related to their identities and teachers need to be careful about making evaluations of some aspects of a child's way of speaking such as their accent (→ Chapter 5). As we have previously argued, teachers need to embrace the diversity of language within their classroom.

Practice points

- Ensure your classroom promotes a rich speaking and listening environment.
- Model talk in a variety of contexts and activities to scaffold children's talk.
- Integrate a process of continuous assessment into children's language experiences.

Glossary

Transcription – the written form of a recorded conversation.

References

Baddeley, G. (ed.) (1992) *Learning Together through Talk: Key Stages 1 and 2.* London: Hodder & Stoughton.

Bearne, E. (1998) *Making Progress in English.* London: Routledge.

Department for Education (DfE) (2012) *Statutory Framework for the Early Years Foundation Stage.* London: DfE.

Department for Education and Skills (DfES) and Qualifications and Curriculum Authority (QCA) (2003) *Speaking, Listening, Learning: Working with Children in Key Stages 1 and 2. Handbook.* London: DfES Publications.

Grugeon, E., Hubbard, L., Smith, C. and Dawes, L. (2005) *Teaching Speaking and Listening in the Primary School*, 3rd edn. London: David Fulton.

Qualifications and Curriculum Authority (QCA) (2000) *A Language in Common: Assessing English as an Additional Language*. Sudbury: QCA Publications.

Annotated bibliography

Assessment of Pupil Progress
  The national archive has examples of APP speaking and listening collections.
  http://webarchive.nationalarchives.gov.uk/20090707073355/http://
  nationalstrategies.standards.dcsf.gov.uk/node/20005,
  L1 ★

Department for Education and Skills (DfES) and Qualifications and Curriculum Authority (QCA) (2003) *Speaking, Listening, Learning: Working with Children in Key Stages 1 and 2. Handbook*. London: DfES Publications.
  Guidance on speaking and listening work in primary schools.
  L1 ★

Grugeon, E., Hubbard, L., Smith, C. and Dawes, L. (2005) *Teaching Speaking and Listening in the Primary School*, 3rd edn. London: David Fulton.
  Excellent book which gives a thorough and perceptive overview of the teaching of speaking and listening and a useful chapter on monitoring and assessing.
  L2 ★★

Johnson, S. (2011) *Assessing Learning in the Primary Classroom*. London: Routledge.
  Comprehensive guide to assessment from pupil to statutory test to international survey.
  L2 ★★★

Part III

Reading

Chapter 9

The development of reading

Helping children learn to read is one of the most important roles that early years and primary teachers carry out. In order to support children effectively, it is necessary to be aware of the ways children might develop. This chapter begins with an analysis of interaction in an early years setting. New research on reading development across languages is surveyed. The second half of the chapter explores the most effective ways to teach reading and why policy makers frequently propose practice that lack a sufficient research base.

How children learn to read and – of particular significance to this chapter – how they can most effectively be taught to read is a concern for researchers, teachers, policy makers, and societies in general. If a child does not learn to read, they cannot play a full part in society once they reach adulthood, nor during childhood can they access the full school curriculum. In an ideal world, these different groups of people with an interest in the teaching of reading would have sufficient shared understanding of how it is best taught. A shared understanding could allow people to act in ways that complemented rather than contradicted each other in the best interests of supporting children's reading. It appears that this is indeed an ideal world because while theory and research have much to tell us about reading pedagogy, the route from research evidence to policy and practice is one that is far from smooth.

Learning to read is not simply a matter of acquiring knowledge about written language and skills in decoding, but becoming involved in cultural practices of meaning-making (Hall, 2003; Heath, 1983; Street, 1984). Socio-cultural theory has much to offer our understanding of reading teaching, and particularly learning to read, but in addition to some socio-cultural considerations we wish to advance the theory of contextualisation. This is explained in relation to phonics teaching.

The following extract of children talking with an adult took place in an early years setting for children aged three to four in England. The transcript of dialogue was part of a project carried out in the early years centre. Taking an ethnographic approach, the research analysed the ways that the children engaged with print and texts, and what the implications were for practitioners. One of the children was working in the 'writing area' in his classroom. He had been folding a piece of sugar paper into an irregular structure to which he added some marks with felt pen. He turned to show the adult what he had done. In seeking to ensure that the photograph of a child's writing was appropriately oriented, the adult was drawn into a pedagogic role that centred on the children's good-natured disagreement about letters and phonemes.

Adult: Oh that's good, a parcel for Ben [*Mark's friend who did not attend the same early years centre*], I like that. I'll take a picture of it like that.

Mark: I want to hold it like that.

Adult: Do you, that makes the writing upside down, is that alright? OK. You want to hold it. Well tip it back a bit so that I can get the writing. Look at the camera, you can see it . . . That looks like a letter M.

Michael: No it's a /m/ [*Michael voices the sound*].

Adult: It's a /m/ is it?

Michael: /m/ for mummy. It's for my mummy.

Neil: No it's M for mummy.

Adult: That's right, M is the name of the letter isn't it, and /m/ is the sound.

Neil: No M! [*spoken very firmly*]

Adult: M's the name yes. They're both right . . . Is that mummy?

Neil: Yes.

Pedagogy is revealed in many ways through this short extract. The teacher had organised a writing area with a range of resources to support children's mark-making, and the children were encouraged to use the area in a similar way to the other play-based areas in the classroom. The children were able to exercise choice over the kind of mark-making that they carried out. Mark had chosen to construct a parcel for his friend Ben, so in other words he had decided who the audience for his text was. Purposeful activity determined by the children, with, in Mark's case, a real audience in mind for his writing, was affected on occasion by the interaction of more expert language users – the adults who worked in the centre, including the researcher, but also the children's peers whose development of literacy varied due to their different home backgrounds.

The adult used the term M (the letter name) rather than the sound /m/, in part because of their view that learning about the distinction between letter names and the sounds associated with letters is an important feature of early years literacy learning. The ensuing discussion about letter names and sounds arguably represents significant learning about complex ideas, through a discussion led in a spirited way by children because they were interested in the topic. As a way of resolving the dispute, and to help the children's understanding, the adult intervened to offer some information to the children. The role of the adult as a more expert language user was a facilitative one, but also one that involved a kind of direct teaching informed by ongoing formative assessment of the children's discussion.

To sum up, a series of understandings about reading and writing were addressed in the course of the interaction: a) texts can communicate meaning to specific audiences; b) text has to be oriented in a particular way; c) the letter M can be called M or /m/; d) the letter M is the first letter of the word 'mummy'; e) there is a complex relationship between letters and the sounds that they represent in English. The children's knowledge of this relationship was in the early stages but it is likely that such conversations would support their emerging understanding. From a socio-cultural perspective, the example highlights some key features of pedagogy: a) children having some control over their learning within frameworks established by teachers; b) learning located in scenarios that are meaningful to children; c) the interaction of the adult as expert language user extending children's learning by responding to the children's interests with a clear understanding of, and high expectation of, the knowledge to be developed.

The scenario above represented a snapshot in time that gives a glimpse into children's learning. The consideration of longer periods of time takes us into the realms of reading development.

Reading development

Descriptions of stages of development for reading and writing are an important feature of educational curricula. In England, this feature is revealed in the National Curriculum levels of attainment. The National Literacy Strategy in England attempted to do this through the sequencing of objectives and guidance papers on progression. It is reasonable to assume that reading and writing curricula should reflect research evidence on development but it is often unclear whether such evidence has been considered.

Tierney (1991: 180) observed that although there were a large number of longitudinal studies ☞ about children's encounters with print, too many of them focused narrowly on decoding skills. Tierney also argued that reading was represented in longitudinal work more than writing and that the writing research tended to be dominated by 'cross-sectional comparisons of students varying in age or ability rather than studies that have looked at the same children at different ages' (ibid.: 189). This kind of cross-sectional comparison can be seen in Loban's (1976) data on language development which was acquired mainly through sentence-level and word-level tests. The concluding chart of sequences and stages strongly emphasised grammatical development consistent with the kind of tests that were used.

Later work, such as that by Harste, Woodward and Burke (1984), convincingly portrayed the active and constructive nature of children's meaning-making. Wells (1986) confirmed such findings, and additionally concluded that listening to stories was more significantly correlated with children's literacy acquisition than looking at picture books and talking about them; drawing and colouring; or playing at writing. Ferreiro and Teberosky's influential semi-longitudinal study (1982: 263) concluded that by the age of four, most children understand the main principle that 'writing is not just lines or marks but a substitute object representing something external to the graphics themselves'.

One feature of the research evidence focusing on the development of reading and writing has been the analysis of stages of development that are common to most children. Often these syntheses are derived from case-study data. For example, the Centre for Language in Primary Education (CLPE, 1989) developed reading scales through their work trialling the primary language record with teachers in London. Bearne (1998) worked closely with a group of 80 teachers to identify their expectations for children's development at the beginning and end of each school year.

Another important strand of case-study research, and longitudinal work, has been the use of individual child case studies; a methodology which, like Brooker (2002), we consider to be significant in the goal to better understand early childhood literacy. Seminal work ☞ in the field includes White (1954) and Butler (1975). The most important study of this kind, because of the richness of the data and its close link with other research evidence, is that by Bissex (1980) of her son Paul's development as a reader and writer between the ages of 5 and 11. Dyson (1983) cited the significance of the Bissex study arguing that it was unusual because it provided evidence of the purposes which writing serves in children's lives, something that she argued many studies had neglected because of their narrow focus.

A common criticism of individual child case studies is that their findings cannot be reliably generalised because of such small sample sizes. However, the Bissex study has shown that some generalisation is possible. Gentry (1982) carried out an analysis of the examples of Paul Bissex's spelling. Gentry identified five stages of spelling development which subsequently Ellis (1994: 156) confirmed: 'it is now generally agreed that children move through five distinct stages of spelling, viz: "precommunicative", "semi phonetic", "phonetic", "transitional", and "correct".'

The early 1980s saw a number of individual child case studies from Australia, the US and the UK which provided further data about children's development as readers and writers (those by Lass, 1982; Baghban, 1984; Kamler, 1984; Payton, 1984; Schmidt and Yates, 1985). In addition to the descriptions of developmental progression that these studies offered, a range of general conclusions was put forward. The most common themes of these conclusions were the need to alleviate the disjunction between home and school literacy learning, and the important part that appropriate social interaction played in literacy learning. However, one of the limitations of these studies was their lack of references to other similar case studies in order to build more reliable evidence about developmental progression. The lack of reference to other similar studies was something that continued in subsequent decades. Minns (1997) identified six key areas that the children in her study developed:

1 understanding that print carries a message;
2 the ability to predict key phrases and memorise chunks of book language;
3 familiarity with book handling and directionality;
4 understanding and use of metalanguage;
5 understanding that there was a correspondence between letters and sounds;
6 the ability to discriminate between letter shapes and recognise individual words.

However, like Fadil and Zaragoza (1997), there was no reference to other case studies, not even to the seminal work of Bissex. Campbell (1999) concluded that children's learning is supported when they are actively involved and interested and that story reading and the opportunity to choose books are beneficial. Although Campbell did make reference to other case studies, it is not clear from his analysis how previous studies informed his reflections on developmental progression. Kress (2000) similarly did not explicitly build on previous developmental studies in his interesting thesis that pointed to the multiple meanings of children's spelling attempts.

The rich data that has been portrayed in case studies and syntheses provides useful insights into the development of reading and writing. The milestones presented in Tables 9.1, 9.2, and 9.3 below were built from a synthesis of the case studies reviewed so far in this chapter and from case studies of two other children (see Wyse (2007) for examples from the data).

Knowledge about rich pictures of children's development is important because it can influence the way we teach our children. By knowing developmental milestones, it is possible to anticipate these and provide teaching at the appropriate level. This influence means that our pedagogy ☞ is related to what we know about how children develop. However, although milestones of development can be useful for thinking about progress, the detail of reading development is rather more complicated that such linear models suggest.

Wyse and Goswami (in press) summarise new thinking arising from research on reading development. A key understanding is the child's awareness of larger features of language preceding awareness of smaller features of language, in a trajectory that begins at birth. At word-level this begins with experiencing objects and their names through talk and interaction. But even at this stage, the syllable is the primary perceptual linguistic unit, something that is true across languages. Following awareness of syllables, children become aware of intra-syllabic features such as onsets and rimes.

Recent research on development has looked across different languages. Differences in reading development across languages are revealed when

Table 9.1 Expectations for a child's reading at age 4

What you can expect	What you can do to help
Understands distinction between print and features	Talk about pictures and talk about print. Encourage children to point to print or point to pictures.
Can recognise and understand some words and signs in the environment	Encourage children to read food packets and to play 'shop'. Read signs, logos, and labels with them. Comment on text that appears on TV. Talk about greetings cards.
Understands that text has specific meaning	Read stories and other books with children. When reading a text that is at the child's level read all the words as written. Talk about what particular words and sentences mean.
Plays at reading	Make sure that children have easy access to a really good range of books. Encourage their playing with the books and their pretend reading. Encourage them to pretend to read to others or even to cuddly toys.
Uses words and phrases from written language when retelling stories	Respond to children's requests to hear favourite stories. Encourage children to predict what is coming next in a story. Suggest that they join in with repetitive phrases. Celebrate when they remember phrases from favourite stories.
Needs other people to help with reading aloud	Read aloud daily with children. Encourage discussion and always be looking to develop children's independence to read words.
Will choose favourite picture books to be read aloud	Encourage daily reading. Give easy access to books. Read children's favourites but introduce them to new books as well.
Uses picture cues and memory of texts	Once children are familiar with a book, encourage them to to tell the story by looking at the pictures as prompts for their memory of the text.
Understands orientation of print and books	Talk about the front and back covers of books, where the print is and, where the print starts on a page. Comment on books that play with these conventions.
Salient visual cues used to remember some familiar words like own name	Give frequent opportunities to read, write and play games with words such as names.

Table 9.2 Expectations for a child's reading at age 7

What you can expect	What you can do to help
Silent reading established	Provide time, space, opportunities and resources to encourage children to read regularly.
Can accurately read increasing number of unknown texts independently	Ensure that children have access to 'new' books on a regular basis.
Uses expression when reading aloud	Have fun with using expression when you are reading to children. Encourage children to read at a good speed and with expression when they share books with you. If children are involved in any kind of performance where they have to read out loud, such as an assembly, help them with expression and clarity.
Uses a range of word-reading strategies appropriately	Help children to use semantic, phonological and orthographic knowledge to work out tricky words. Praise them for good guesses and supply the correct word if necessary but give them time to think.
Stronger individual preferences for particular texts	Encourage children to develop preferences for particular topics and types of text. Talk to them about their preferences and those of the class.
Likes reading longer stories in addition to returning to picture books	Provide access to books with more text and fewer pictures.
Sight-word reading for rapidly increasing bank of familiar words	The more children read the more sight words they will acquire.
Phonological knowledge fully established. Growing awareness of irregularities of English spelling	Phonics teaching will have taken place. Help children to see that the one-letter-makes-a-sound idea is not accurate. Discuss the irregularities of English spelling.

phoneme awareness is studied. One of the main challenges for children and their teachers is that English is one of the hardest languages to learn to read and write. The reason that it is easier to learn to read in some languages than others is to do with their linguistic complexity. As Goswami (2005) has shown, there are two key factors in this. The first is the way that consonants and vowels are linked together. Some languages, such as Italian, Spanish and Chinese, are based on a simple consonant–vowel syllable structure (like *panini* [pa-ni-ni] in Italian or *tapa* [ta-pa] in Spanish). This makes them less complex than English. English has very few consonant–vowel syllables. Words such as 'baby' and

Table 9.3 Expectations for a child's reading at age 11

What you can expect	What you can do to help
Reflective reader with strong preferences	Discuss texts that children are reading and seek to extend their understanding of the issues raised.
Uses different reading styles for different texts	Encourage children to become involved with things like map-reading or locating information on the internet through cross-curricular work.
Can follow instructional texts	Do some cooking together which requires use of a recipe book. Involve children in following instructions to assemble things including instructions that their peers have written.
Can sort and classify evidence	Encourage reading and writing of a range of formats for summarising information.
Varies pace, pitch and expression when reading aloud and varies for performance purposes	Discuss occasions when children have to perform. Encourage involvement in dramatic activities at home and at school.
Can adopt alternative viewpoints	The starting point for this might be the ability to empathise with others. Encourage consideration of evidence from different sides of an argument.
Recognises language devices used for particular effects	Enjoy the imagination of authors who like to play with text effects. Reread texts like poetry to discover effects.
Can discuss different author styles	Encourage children to read a series of books by the authors that they like and to think about their style.
Enjoys selecting and reading appropriate adult texts	Encourage access to newspapers and magazines.

'cocoa' are examples that do exist (see Table 9.4). The most frequent syllable type in English is consonant–vowel–consonant, as in words like 'dog' and 'cat'.

The second key factor is the consistency of how the written symbols represent sounds. In some languages, such as English and Dutch, one letter or one cluster of letters can have many different pronunciations. In other languages, such as Greek, Italian and Spanish, the letters and clusters are always pronounced in the same way no matter which word they appear in, which is simpler to learn. A large study of 14 European languages clearly showed the dramatic differences by measuring the reading of real words and made-up words in different languages, with English right at the bottom of the list (see Table 9.5).

Table 9.4 Examples of words in English with consonant/vowel syllables

Word	Syllable	Consonant	Vowel(s)	Syllable	Consonant	Vowel(s)
baby	ba	b	a	by	b	y
cocoa	co	c	o	coa	c	oa

Table 9.5 Data (% correct) from the large-scale study of reading skills at the end of grade 1 in 14 European languages

Language	Familiar real words	Pseudo-words
Greek	98	92
Finnish	98	95
German	98	94
Austrian German	97	92
Italian	95	89
Spanish	95	89
Swedish	95	88
Dutch	95	82
Icelandic	94	86
Norwegian	92	91
French	79	85
Portuguese	73	77
Danish	71	54
Scottish English	34	29

Source: Goswami (2005: 275)

The teaching of reading

The history of the debates about approaches to the teaching of reading has repeatedly hinged on fundamental disagreements related to different theories of learning to read. Until the early 1800s, there was no distinction between the teaching of reading and the teaching of spelling in England. Therefore, evidence on reading teaching at this time can be found in the hundreds of different spelling textbooks that were published. Michael (1984) argued, on the basis of an analysis of the spelling books, that reading teaching was for most teachers a bottom–up approach. As early as 1610 this was clear, for example:

'Therefore let the scholler, being thus traded (i.e. schooled) from letters to syllables of one Consonant: from syllables of one Consonant, to syllables of many Consonants: from syllables of many Consonants, to words of many syllables; proceede to sentences.' (1984: 57) Michael suggests that the approach was a consequence of the prevailing view that complex things could be learned by children only if they were first broken down into their component parts (a theory that still informs some current opinions of how children learn to read). In his chapter that examines the growth of whole-word methods, Michael also identifies what he sees as the first published reference to whole-word teaching. Charles Hoole, in his translation of the preface to Comenius' *Orbis Sensualium Pictus* (1659) said, 'reading cannot but be learned; and indeed too, which thing is to be noted, without using any ordinary tedious spelling, that most troublesome torture of wits, which may be wholly avoyded by this Method [the whole word method]' (1984: 60).

The seminal text in the debate of the modern era was Jean Chall's (1983) book *Learning to Read: The Great Debate*, which was first published in the 1960s. In it she defines the differences between two models:

> The top-down models relate . . . to the meaning-emphasis approaches of beginning reading and stress the first importance of language and meaning for reading comprehension and also for word recognition . . . The reader theoretically samples the text in order to confirm and modify initial hypotheses.
>
> The bottom-up models – those that view the reading process as developing from perception of letters, spelling patterns and words to sentence and paragraph meaning – resemble the code-emphasis, beginning reading approaches.
>
> (Chall, 1983: 28–29)

Chall's use of the term reading 'model' is perhaps better replaced with 'approach' because reading models generally seek to account for reading development rather than approaches to teaching. The classic example of a top-down approach to reading would be the 'real book approach' or the 'whole language approach' and the contrasting bottom-up approach would be 'phonics'.

Reading models are important because they can efficiently summarise complex areas of knowledge. However, an important consideration is the relationship between the model and approaches to the teaching of reading. For example, one model that accounts for word recognition is the parallel distributed processing model (see Figure 9.1).

Parallel distributed processing (PDP) models are based on the idea of the brain establishing 'sets of distributed, sub-symbolic codes representing the attributes of the words we know' (op. cit.). The word recognition system involves three types of mental representations: orthographic, phonological and semantic. The appropriate connections between the representations have to be

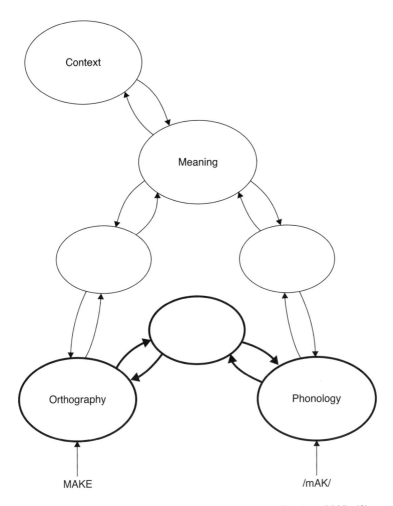

Figure 9.1 A parallel distributed processing model of reading (Lupker, 2005: 49).

learned. When presented with a word, the units at all levels begin to activate. Activation patterns are initially quite inaccurate but through experience weights between units become adjusted in order to make processing more accurate the next time.

An important aspect of this model is the *interaction* between the four main elements that leads to word recognition. This idea of interaction between elements is shared by models that have in the past informed the teaching of reading. For example, the three-part model of word recognition that featured semantic, syntactic and graphophonic *cueing* that came out of the work of Goodman (1967) and in the UK from Arnold's synthesis (Arnold, 1982) of

Goodman's ideas. This three element model was also similar to Clay's model (1979) and the *searchlights* model that underpinned the National Literacy Strategy in England from 1998 to 2006 (DfES, 1998). However, by 2007 the searchlights model had been replaced by Stuart and Watson's interpretation of the *simple view of reading* (Figure 9.2) that featured as an appendix to the controversial government-commissioned Rose Report on the teaching of early reading (Rose, 2006).

Stuart and Watson's case for the simple view was more complex, research-informed and nuanced than that of the main text of the Rose Report yet, like the Rose Report, it had some fundamental flaws. Stuart and Watson rightly saw Clay's model of reading strategies as an influence on the NLS searchlights model, but were unduly critical of Clay's work as a result of failing to take into account the substantial international evidence base supporting Clay's approach. One of their key warrants was that: 'The case for change that we discuss below [i.e. further into the text of the appendix to the Rose Report] rests on the value of explicitly distinguishing between word recognition processes and language comprehension processes.' (Rose, 2006: 74 – Appendix 1, Stuart and Watson) While the authors attempted to say that they didn't necessarily mean that phonics teaching should be separate from other language elements, the clear direction of their recommendations overall was just that (for a more extensive critique of the model, see Harrison, 2010). Rose's recommendations, informed by the simple view of reading, resulted in synthetic phonics being imposed throughout England.

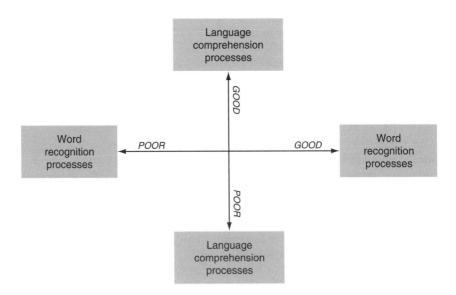

Figure 9.2   The simple view of reading.

Stuart and Watson based their model to a certain extent on Gough and Tunmer's (1986) seminal paper outlining another *simple view of reading*: Reading = Decoding × Comprehension (R = D × C). Gough and Tunmer's model has been subject to numerous interpretations, so it is important to register that there would be almost unanimous agreement with their statement that both 'decoding and comprehension are essential to reading' (p. 9). It is also important to remember that Gough and Tunmer claimed that their model was not about reading teaching, although they did refer to the reading debates in the introduction to their seminal article and suggest that reading models and teaching are interconnected, which is true.

Gough and Tunmer accepted that 'if there is no comprehension then reading is not taking place' (p. 7) so although they also concede that 'comprehension is not sufficient, for decoding is also necessary' (p. 7), the logical opposite to their first statement is, 'if there is no decoding then reading is not taking place'. This requires a precise definition of decoding. Although their definition ranges somewhat, they seem to finalise it as 'knowledge of letter–sound correspondence rules'. This reveals a flaw in the logic. Children younger than three years of age can read words such as their name or words in their environment that are part of packaging, without knowledge of letter–sound correspondence rules. Similarly the young child's ability to memorise large chunks of story texts and 'read' these in sync with the turning of the pages in a picture book involves a form of reading comprehension. Contrary to the simple view, in these cases comprehension is being demonstrated without decoding. The main limitations of the simple view are: a) the lack of fit between the model and early reading development; b) the lack of accommodation in the model for the transactions (Rosenblatt, 1985) of reading; c) the lack of accommodation of reading of visual elements such as pictures.

We would argue that a more appropriate logic is as follows. If R = Reading, U = Understanding, Mg = Meaning and → is the process of understanding written language in order to establish meaning, then

$$R = (U \twoheadrightarrow Mg)$$

Reading requires understanding of visual symbols (VS) and their relationship to phonology (P – units of sound), but VS ↔ P is only a component part of (U → Mg), as is comprehension (C) (psychologists separate linguistic comprehension and reading comprehension; in the model below C = reading comprehension because wider concepts of comprehension are represented by U → Mg).

$$R = (U \twoheadrightarrow Mg)/(C + (VS \leftrightarrow P))$$

But reading includes visual image interpretation (VII) so

$$R = (U \twoheadrightarrow Mg)/(C +/- VII + (VS \leftrightarrow P))$$

The basis for some items and relationships in the formula above is built on psycholinguistic grain size theory (Ziegler and Goswami, 2005) with the addition of visual image interpretation (a fuller account of TELL theory where the formula was first published can be found in Wyse, 2011a). Psycholinguistic grain size theory accounts for the developmental sequence of learning across languages. In spite of differences in the phonological structure of languages being learned, for example, the transparency of the orthography, the developmental sequence is the same: shallow sensitivity of large phonological units to a deep awareness of small phonological units, i.e. syllables, onset-rime, nucleas coda, phoneme and phone.

Research evidence and effective phonics teaching

One of the most significant contributions to debates about research evidence and the teaching of reading was the report of the US National Reading Panel (NRP) on reading instruction, carried out by the National Institute of Child Health and Human Development (National Institute of Child Health and Human Development, 2000). This extensive work addressed a number of questions including: 'Does systematic phonics instruction help children learn to read more effectively than non-systematic phonics instruction or instruction teaching no phonics?' (p. 3) As far as differences between analytic and synthetic phonics are concerned, the NRP concluded that 'specific systematic phonics programs are all significantly more effective than non-phonics programs; however, they do not appear to differ significantly from each other in their effectiveness although more evidence is needed to verify the reliability of effect sizes for each program' (ibid.: 93).

The NRP also concluded that reading teaching should not focus too much on the teaching of letter–sound relations at the expense of the application of this knowledge in the context of reading texts. And that phonics should not become the dominant component in a reading programme, so educators 'must keep the end in mind and insure that children understand the purpose of learning letter-sounds' (2000: 2–96). The importance of the cautions about phonics becoming a dominant component is given added weight if we consider the findings of Camilli, Vargas and Yurecko (2003). Camilli *et al.* replicated the meta-analysis from the NRP phonics instruction report and found a smaller but still significant effect for systematic phonics ($d = 0.24$) than the NRP but also found an effect for systematic language activities ($d = 0.29$) and an effect for individual tutoring ($d = 0.40$). Hence the effect for individual tutoring was larger than the effect for systematic phonics and that the effect for systematic language activities was slightly larger but comparable with that for systematic phonics. These findings resulted in their conclusion that 'systematic phonics instruction when combined with language activi ties and individual tutoring may *triple* the effect of phonics alone' (Camilli *et al.*, 2003).

In 2006, the UK Department for Education and Skills (DfES) commissioned a systematic review of approaches to the teaching of reading. The methodology of the NRP was refined to produce a meta-analysis that included only Randomised Controlled Trials (RCTs) ☞. On the basis of their work, Torgerson *et al.* conclude, once again in direct contrast to the Rose Report, that 'There is currently no strong RCT evidence that any one form of systematic phonics is more effective than any other' (2006: 49). This finding supports their pedagogical recommendation that 'Since there is evidence that systematic phonics teaching benefits children's reading accuracy, it should be part of every literacy teacher's repertoire and a routine part of literacy teaching, *in a judicious balance with other elements*' (ibid.: 49, italics added). One of the difficulties of forming policy recommendations for reading pedagogy is that this judicious balance can easily be disrupted by policy thrusts that lack a sufficient evidence base.

This work in the US and the UK was complemented by an Australian government report recommending that:

> teachers [should] provide systematic, direct and explicit phonics instruction so that children master the essential alphabetic code-breaking skills required for foundational reading proficiency. Equally, that teachers [should] provide an integrated approach to reading that supports the development of oral language, vocabulary, grammar, reading fluency, comprehension and the literacies of new technologies.
>
> (Australian Government, Department of Education,
> Science and Training, 2005: 14)

The Australian report also appropriately cautioned that:

> While the evidence indicates that some teaching strategies are more effective than others, no one approach of itself can address the complex nature of reading difficulties. An integrated approach requires that teachers have a thorough understanding of a range of effective strategies, as well as knowing when and why to apply them.
>
> (ibid.: 14)

Early years educators have been particularly concerned about the dangers of an inappropriate curriculum being imposed on young children. The research evidence on this matter was quite clear and once again contradicted the report. The majority of evidence in favour of systematic phonics teaching referred to children aged six and older. Some 20 out of the 43 studies covered in the Torgerson *et al.* (2006) and NRP reviews were carried out with children aged six to seven. Only nine studies were carried out with children aged five to six. No studies were carried out with four-year-olds. The idea that children younger than five will benefit from synthetic phonics is not supported by evidence and is arguably one of the most controversial recommendations of the

Rose Report. In spite of all the powerful evidence, policy makers in England have consistently, and with increasing emphasis over many years, promoted phonics teaching at the expense of other more important aspects of reading (Wyse and Styles, 2007).

Wyse and Goswami (2008) carried out a review of research internationally in response to the Rose Report. Part of their analysis included establishing categories for the effective phonics instruction pedagogy that was part of the experimental trials included in the two systematic reviews featured above (Torgerson, Brooks and Hall, 2006; National Institute of Child Health and Human Development (NICHD), 2000). One category of studies was 'contextualised phonics instruction'. Further analysis of the pedagogy of these studies provides insights into effective teaching (it is important to remember that these experimental trials were only the ones that addressed phonics teaching. If other areas of reading research were taken into account, such as reading comprehension, an even stronger case is likely).

Table 9.6 summarises the key features of contextualised phonics teaching revealed in a series of studies (further information about the methods used in the studies can be found in Wyse and Goswami, 2008). The key feature of the effective approach in the study by Berninger et al. (2003) was the combination of word recognition activities with comprehension teaching including language cueing at text-level as part of the lessons, although the word recognition training was contextualised in words rather than whole texts. The combination of phonics teaching with comprehension teaching was also a feature of the studies by Umbach et al. (1989) and Vickery et al. (1987). Similarly, Blachman et al.'s (1999) study featured the reading of connected text as a part of the lesson. Brown and Felton (1990) found that reinforcement of skills through use of whole texts was beneficial. Evans and Carr (1985) recognised the importance of using word analysis skills in combination with other tasks such as predicting meaning when using relatively unfamiliar reading materials. The studies by Foorman (Foorman et al., 1997 and 1998) were set in the context of language arts lessons which included literature activities. Phonics teaching was embedded in the reading of texts in the Martinussen and Kirby (1998) study in addition to the less common use of global and bridging tasks.

The studies by Santa and Hoien (1999), Tunmer and Hoover (1993), and Greaney et al. (1997) all based the pedagogy of the effective intervention on Clay's (1979) *Reading Recovery* approach with modifications. Reading Recovery teaching is well specified by Clay and also has the benefit of a particular high number of research evaluations (Brooks, 2002) which enable in-depth understanding of the pedagogy. Although Reading Recovery has attracted some debate about its effectiveness, research continues to show its benefits, as in the meta-analysis by D'Agostino & Murphy (2004). Reading Recovery lessons begin and end with the use of whole texts. In summary, the teaching of sub-word-level features such as phonemes, and the decoding of words, appears to be effective when embedded in whole texts.

Table 9.6 The pedagogy of contextualised phonics teaching

Study	Overall teaching context	Key features of contextualised phonics teaching
Berninger et al. (2003)	Combination of explicit word recognition and reading comprehension was most effective. Reading comprehension training included language cueing at text level: e.g. 'Tell the plot or main events in the story so far.'	Combination of word recognition and comprehension teaching in reading lesson.
Blachman et al. (1999)	This study covered kindergarten through to, and including, grade one. Overall sequence: 1. Review of sound-symbol associations learned previously; 2. Phoneme analysis and blending skills; 3. Automatic recognition of words. 4. Ten to 15 minutes of reading connected text.	High-frequency word selected from stories that the children would be reading and that are introduced as part of sessions. Reading of connected text. Writing to dictation so teacher could assess students' progress. Vocabulary development and comprehension not neglected. Children's understanding of words and their understanding of stories was supported.
Brown and Felton (1990)	The selection of reading programmes was based on those which were 'complete instructional programmes which emphasised both word identification and comprehension'.	Mastery of the skills taught was reinforced through the use of controlled readers and the coordination of reading and spelling.
Evans and Carr (1985)	General analysis of 20 classrooms. In these classrooms, reading was instructed primarily through basal readers and workbooks rather than student-generated stories, phonics drill rather than sight-word banking, and supervised practice at cloze-type prediction from context, using relatively unfamiliar reading materials.	Recognised the importance of helping pupils understand how to coordinate dual task performance such as word analysis with predictive context use.

(Continued overleaf)

Table 9.6 (Continued)

Study	Overall teaching context	Key features of contextualised phonics teaching
Foorman et al. (1997)	Synthetic phonics group did activities including reading practice: 'Language, Alphabet, Reading, spelling decks, New Concept, Reading practice, Handwriting, Spelling, Review, Verbal expression, Listening', p. 260.	The more successful phonics intervention is characterised as 'synthetic' but this was integrated as part of the daily lesson format which included reading practice.
Foorman et al. (1998)	Carried out during 90-minute language arts period. Direct instruction in letter–sound correspondences practised in decodable text . . . emphasis on phonemic awareness, phonics . . . and literature activities.	The more successful direct code approach mixed phonemic awareness and phonics with literature activities. The phonics rules are introduced using alliterative stories and controlled vocabulary text in order to practice. Skills in oral language comprehension and motivation for stories are developed.
Greaney et al. (1997)	Reading Recovery-type lessons but with more flexibility.	The reading of familiar and less familiar books is an integral part of the programme.
Martinussen and Kirby (1998)	Programmes included broader features such as work with shapes, matrices, and sequential analysis. The reading of picture books by instructors was part of the programmes.	Phonics teaching was embedded in the reading of texts.
Santa and Hoien (1999)	The Early Steps programme has a particular emphasis on story reading, writing and phonological skills. Similar to Reading Recovery. The programme evaluated is Early Steps, an intervention with one-to-one tutoring and with particular emphasis on story reading, writing, and phonological skills . . . 'the program emphasises real book reading' (p. 62).	The programme represents what the researcher considers to be a balanced approach and one that fitted well philosophically with programmes already in place in the district. Included reading connected text and daily writing.

Tunmer and Hoover (1993)	Reading Recovery approach.	Work on phonological and visual similarities of words was used in the context of lessons to learn strategies about how and when to apply such knowledge. Wherever possible, the teachers chose clear and memorable examples from texts that had been read. Children were encouraged to identify unfamiliar words in their reading, using strategies they had been taught and to help with spelling words in writing.
Umbach et al. (1989)	Broad approach which included teaching of text orientation, sounding-out, comprehension and problem-solving skills.	Argues for combined phonics and comprehension teaching.
Vickery et al. (1987)	Broader programme: multisensory teaching approach for reading, spelling and handwriting (MTARSH).	Comprehension is part of programme. Attention to broader areas of learning is included.

Contextualised phonics teaching is likely to be effective because new under-standings can be applied in real contexts in order to consolidate what are often complex areas of learning for pupils. The use of whole texts also enables systematic comprehension teaching to be very closely linked with phonics teaching. In addition, although the focus may be the teaching of reading, writing is frequently a part of the lessons. This enables pupils to understand the links between the decoding and encoding of language, something that once again consolidates their understanding.

Conclusions

Wyse, Andrews, and Hoffman (2010) summarise what they see as a pattern in the kinds of policy responses to the teaching of reading described above. First, a dubious characterisation by politicians that education is failing, followed by 'decisive' action giving a reason for greater centralisation as the government 'takes responsibility' for improving performance; then the inevitable increase in a battery of measures to gauge progress and the impact of curricular interven-tions ('high-stakes testing'); a gradual seeping in of pedagogical control as well as curricular control, leading to loss of teacher autonomy and agency. Such control eventually becomes unworkable, uninspiring, and ceases to provide the results it is intended to deliver; and so a reaction sets in, freeing up teachers to have more agency within what and how they teach; allowing more space for creativity across the whole English and language curriculum; making the curriculum more closely related to the outside world. Perry, Amadeo, Fletcher, and Walker's (2010) work confirms the gap between evidence and policy making, the politi-cisation of decisions on pedagogy, the speed of policy change, and the role of the media in exacerbating some of these problems. Moss and Huxford (2007) suggested that a focus by researchers on understanding the contexts of policy enactment, more than 'finding new content for policy to convey' (2007: 72), would be a helpful way forward, yet in spite of some researchers' direct engage-ment with government on policy implementation and their understanding of the contexts of policy enactment, the problems with politicisation and lack of attention to the full range of evidence remain, suggesting different problems such as increasing political control of education (see Wyse, 2011b).

The Rose Report resulted in unprecedented levels of direct political involve-ment in the work of teachers and teacher trainers. Its conclusions about synthetic phonics did not adequately reflect the evidence that was available. It missed an opportunity to take forward the debate about reading in a construc-tive way opting instead for its more controversial approach and findings. This meant that the reading wars were once again ignited. It may well take another ten years of fighting to ensure that the reading curriculum is returned to one that is more balanced. This will require all involved in education, including parents, to work for a more democratic approach to the early years and primary curriculum and its reform.

Practice points

- A truly objective and balanced approach to the teaching of reading is vital.
- Work on your observation skills and extend your understanding of children's reading development.
- Phonics teaching should be regular, brief and as enjoyable as possible.

Glossary

Longitudinal studies – research that looks at development over several years rather than a year or less.

Pedagogy – approaches to teaching and learning.

Randomised Controlled Trial – a particular kind of research which analyses the effect of an intervention on experimental groups and a control group to which the participants have been randomly allocated.

Seminal work – classic (often old) academic work that continues to be referenced by large numbers of writers.

References

Arnold, H. (1982) *Listening to Children Reading*. London: Hodder & Stoughton.

Australian Government, Department of Education, Science and Training (2005) *Teaching Reading. Report and Recommendations: National Enquiry into the Teaching of Literacy*. Barton, Australia: Department of Education, Science and Training.

Baghban, M. (1984) *Our Daughter Learns to Read and Write: A Case Study from Birth to Three*. Newark, DE: International Reading Association.

Bearne, E. (1998) *Making Progress in English*. London: Routledge.

Berninger, V. W., Vermeulen, K., Abott, R. D., McCutchen, D., Cotton, S., Cude, J., *et al.* (2003) 'Comparison of three approaches to supplementary reading instruction for low-achieving second-grade readers', *Language, Speech, and Hearing Services in Schools*, 34: 101–116.

Bissex, G. L. (1980) *GNYS AT WRK: A Child Learns to Write and Read*. Cambridge, MA: Harvard University Press.

Blachman, B., Tangel, D., Ball, E., Black, R., and McGraw, D. (1999) 'Developing phonological awareness and word recognition skills: A two-year intervention with low-income, inner-city children', *Reading and Writing: An Interdisciplinary Journal*, 11: 239–273.

Brooker, L. (2002) 'Five on the first of December!: What can we learn from case studies of early childhood literacy?', *Journal of Early Childhood Literacy*, 2(3): 291–313.

Brown, L. and Felton, R. (1990) 'Effects of instruction on beginning reading skills in children at risk for reading disability', *Reading and Writing: An Interdisciplinary Journal*, 2: 223–241.

Butler, D. (1975) *Cushla and Her Books*. Auckland: Hodder & Stoughton.

Camilli, G., Vargas, S. and Yurecko, M. (2003) 'Teaching children to read: The fragile link between science and federal education policy', *Education Policy Analysis Archives*, 11(15). Retrieved 1 March 2006, from http://epaa.asu.edu/epaa/v11n15/.

Campbell, R. (1999) *Literacy from Home to School: Reading with Alice*. Stoke-on-Trent: Trentham Books.

Centre for Language in Primary Education (CLPE)/Inner London Education Authority (ILEA) (1989) *The Primary Language Record Handbook for Teachers*. London: Centre for Language in Primary Education.

Chall, J. S. (1983) *Learning to Read: The Great Debate*, updated edn. New York: McGraw-Hill.

Clay, M. (1979) *The Early Detection of Reading Difficulties*, 3rd edn. Auckland: Heinemann Education.

D'Agostino, J. and Murphy, J. (2004) 'A meta-analysis of reading recovery in United States schools', *Educational Evaluation and Policy Analysis*, 26(1): 23–38.

Department for Education and Employment (DfEE) (1998) *The National Literacy Strategy Framework for Teaching*. Sudbury: DfEE Publications.

Department for Education and Employment (DfEE) and The Qualifications and Curriculum Authority (QCA) (1999) *The National Curriculum: Handbook for Primary Teachers in England. Key Stages 1 and 2*. Norwich: Her Majesty's Stationery Office (HMSO).

Dombey, H. (2006) 'How should we teach children to read?', *Books for Keeps*, 156: 6–7.

Dyson, A. H. (1983) 'Individual differences in emerging writing', in M. Farr (ed.) *Advances in Writing Research*, Vol. 1: *Children's Early Writing Development*. Norwood, NJ: Ablex.

Ellis, N. C. (1994) 'Longitudinal studies of spelling development', in G. D. A. Brown and N. C. Ellis (eds) *Handbook of Spelling: Theory, Process and Intervention*. Chichester: John Wiley and Sons.

Evans, M. and Carr, T. (1985) 'Cognitive abilities, conditions of learning, and the early development of reading skill', *Reading Research Quarterly*, 20: 327–350.

Fadil, C. and Zaragoza, N. (1997) 'Revisiting the emergence of young children's literacy: one child tells her story', *Reading*, 31(1): 29–34.

Ferreiro, E. and Teberosky, A. (1982) *Literacy Before Schooling*. Portsmouth, NH: Heinemann.

Foorman, B. R., Francis, D. J., Winikates, D., Mehta, P., Schatschneider, C. and Fletcher, J. M. (1997) 'Early interventions for children with reading disabilities', *Scientific Studies of Reading*, 1: 255–276.

Foorman, B. R., Francis, D. J., Fletcher, J. M., Schatschneider, C. and Mehta, P. (1998) 'The role of instruction in learning to read: Preventing reading failure in at-risk children', *Journal of Educational Psychology*, 90: 37–55.

Gentry, J. R. (1982) 'An analysis of developmental spelling in *GNYS AT WRK*', *The Reading Teacher*, 36: 192–200.

Goodman, K. (1969) 'Analysis of oral reading miscues: applied psycholinguistics', *Reading Research Quarterly*, 5(1): 9–29.

Goswami, U. (2005) 'Synthetic phonics and learning to read: a cross-language perspective', *Educational Psychology in Practice*, 21(4): 273–282.

Gough, P. B. and Tunmer, W. E. (1986) 'Decoding, reading and reading disability', *Remedial and Special Education*, 7(1): 6–10. DOI: 10.1177/074193258600700104

Greaney, K., Tunmer, W. and Chapman, J. (1997) 'Effects of rime-based orthographic analogy training on the word recognition skills of children with reading disability', *Journal of Educational Psychology*, 89: 645–651.

Hall, K. (2003) *Listening to Stephen Read: Multiple Perspectives on Literacy*. Buckingham: Open University Press.

Harrison, C. (2010) 'Why do policy-makers find the "simple view of reading" so attractive, and why do I find it so morally repugnant?', in K. Hall, U. Goswami, C. Harrison, S. Ellis and J. Soler (eds) *Interdisciplinary Perspectives on Learning to Read: Culture, Cognition and Pedagogy*. London: Routledge.

Harste, J. C., Woodward, V. A. and Burke, C. L. (1984) *Language Stories and Literacy Lessons*. Portsmouth, NH: Heinemann Educational Books.

Heath, S. B. (1983) *Ways with Words: Language, Life and Work in Communities and Classrooms*. Cambridge: Cambridge University Press.

Her Majesty's Inspectorate (HMI) (1990) *The Teaching and Learning of Reading in Primary Schools*. London: Department of Education and Science (DES).

House of Commons Education and Skills Committee (2005) *Teaching Children to Read: Eighth Report of Session 2004–2005. Report, together with Formal Minutes, Oral and Written Evidence*. London: The Stationery Office.

Kamler, B. (1984) 'Ponch writes again: a child at play', *Australian Journal of Reading*, 7(2): 61–70.

Kress, G. (2000) *Early Spelling: Between Convention and Creativity*. London: Routledge.

Lass, B. (1982) 'Portrait of my son as an early reader,' *The Reading Teacher*, 36(1): 20–28.

Loban, W. (1976) *The Development of Language Abilities, K-12*. Urbana, IL: National Council for Teachers of English.

Lupker, S. (2005) 'Visual word recognition: theories and findings', in M. Snowling and C. Hulme (eds) *The Science of Reading: A Handbook*. London: Blackwell.

Martinussen, R. and Kirby, J. (1998) 'Instruction in successive and phonological processing to improve the reading acquisition of at-risk kindergarten children', *Developmental Disabilities Bulletin*, 26: 19–39.

Michael, I. (1984) 'Early evidence for whole word methods', in G. Brooks and A.K. Pugh (eds) *Studies in the History of Reading*. Reading: Centre for the Teaching of Reading, University of Reading.

Minns, H. (1997) *Read It to Me Now! Learning at Home and at School*, 2nd edn. Buckingham: Open University Press.

Moss, G. and Huxford, L. (2007) 'Exploring literacy policy making from the inside out', in L. Saunders (ed.) *Educational Research and Policy-Making: Exploring the Border Country between Research and Policy*. London: Routledge.

National Institute of Child Health and Human Development (2000) *Report of the National Reading Panel. Teaching Children to Read: An Evidence-Based Assessment of the Scientific Research Literature on Reading and its Implications for Reading Instruction: Reports of the Subgroups* (NIH Publication no. 00–4754). Washington, DC: US Government Printing Office.

Payton, S. (1984) *Developing Awareness of Print: A Young Child's First Steps Towards Literacy*. Birmingham: University of Birmingham, Educational Review.

Perry, P., Amadeo, C., Fletcher, M. and Walker, E. (2010) *Instinct or Reason: How Education Policy Is Made and How We Might Make It Better*. Reading: CfBT Education Trust.

Reimer, J. (2006) 'Developmental changes in the allocation of semantic feedback during visual word recognition', *Journal of Research in Reading*, 29(2): 194–212.

Rose, J. (2006) *Independent Review of the Teaching of Early Reading*. Nottingham: DfES Publications.

Rosenblatt, L. (1985) 'Viewpoints: Transaction versus Interaction: A Terminological Rescue Operation', *Research in the Teaching of English*, 19(1): 96–107.

Santa, C. and Hoien, T. (1999) 'An assessment of early steps: A program for early intervention of reading problems', *Reading Research Quarterly*, 34: 54–79.

Schmidt, E. and Yates, C. (1985) 'Benji learns to read naturally! Naturally Benji learns to read', *Australian Journal of Reading*, 8(3): 121–134.

Street, B. (1984) *Literacy in Theory and Practice*. Cambridge: Cambridge University Press.

Tierney, R. J. (1991) 'Studies of reading and writing growth: longitudinal research on literacy development', in J. Flood, J. M. Jenson, D. Lapp and J. R. Squire (eds) *Handbook of Research on Teaching the English Language Arts*. New York: Macmillan.

Torgerson, C. J., Brooks, G. and Hall, J. (2006) *A Systematic Review of the Research Literature on the Use of Phonics in the Teaching of Reading and Spelling*. London: Department for Education and Skills (DfES).

Tunmer, W. and Hoover, W. (1993) 'Phonological recoding skill and beginning reading', *Reading and Writing: An Interdisciplinary Journal*, 5: 161–179.

Umbach, B., Darch, C. and Halpin, G. (1989) 'Teaching reading to low performing first graders in rural schools: A comparison of two instructional approaches', *Journal of Instructional Psychology*, 16: 22–30.

Vickery, K., Reynolds, V. and Cochran, S. (1987) 'Multisensory teaching approach for reading, spelling, and handwriting, Orton-Gillingham based curriculum, in a public school setting', *Annals of Dyslexia*, 37: 189–200.

Wells, G. (1986) *The Meaning Makers: Children Learning Language and Using Language to Learn.* Sevenoaks: Hodder & Stoughton.

White, D. (1954) *Books Before Five.* Auckland: New Zealand Council for Educational Research.

Wray, D. (1995) 'Reviewing the reading debate', in D. Wray and J. Medwell (eds) *Teaching Primary English: The State of the Art.* London: Routledge.

Wyse, D. (2003) 'The National Literacy Strategy: a critical review of empirical evidence', *British Educational Research Journal,* 29(6): 903–916.

Wyse, D. (2007) *How to Help Your Child Read and Write.* London: Pearson/ BBC Active.

Wyse, D. (2011a) 'Towards a theory of English, Language and Literacy Teaching', in D. Wyse (ed.) *Literacy Teaching and Education: SAGE Library of Educational Thought and Practice.* London: Sage.

Wyse, D. (2011b) 'Control of language or the language of control? Primary teachers' knowledge in the context of policy', in S. Ellis and E. McCartney (eds) *Applied Linguistics and the Primary School.* Cambridge: Cambridge University Press.

Wyse, D. and Goswami, U. (2008) 'Synthetic phonics and the teaching of reading', *British Educational Research Journal,* 34(6): 691–710.

Wyse, D. and Goswami, U. (in press) 'The development of reading', in J. Marsh, N. Hall and J. Larson (eds) *Handbook of Early Childhood Literacy,* 2nd edn. London: Sage.

Wyse, D. and Styles, M. (2007) 'Synthetic phonics and the teaching of reading: The debate surrounding England's "Rose Report" ', *Literacy,* 47(1): 35–42.

Wyse, D., Andrews, R. and Hoffman, J. (2010) 'Introduction', in D. Wyse, R. Andrews and J. Hoffman (eds) *The Routledge International Handbook of English, Language and Literacy Teaching.* London: Routledge.

Ziegler, J. and Goswami, U. (2005) 'Reading acquisition, developmental dyslexia and skilled reading across languages: A psycholinguistic grain size theory', *Psychological Bulletin,* 131(1): 13–29.

Annotated bibliography

Hall, K., Goswami, U., Harrison, C., Ellis, S. and Soler, J. (eds) (2010) *Interdisciplinary Perspectives on Learning to Read: Culture, Cognition and Pedagogy.* London: Routledge.
    Powerful, evidence-based contribution to understanding the teaching and learning of reading.
    L2 ★★★

Rose, J. (2006) *Independent Review of the Teaching of Early Reading.* Nottingham: DfES Publications.
    The Rose Report. It controversially concluded that synthetic phonics should be the preferred phonics approach. Also includes the rationale for the simple model of reading.
    L2 ★★

Wyse, D. and Goswami, U. (2008) 'Synthetic phonics and the teaching of reading', *British Educational Research Journal*, 34(6): 691–710.
Put forward a new analysis of high-quality research in relation to the teaching of early reading in order to offer a strong critical response to the Rose Report. This was the most read BERJ article in 2009–2011.
L3 ★★★

National Institute of Child Health and Human Development (2000) *Report of the National Reading Panel. Teaching Children to Read: An Evidence-Based Assessment of the Scientific Research Literature on Reading and its Implications for Reading Instruction: Reports of the Subgroups* (NIH Publication no. 00–4754). Washington, DC: US Government Printing Office.
An extremely important and extensive contribution to the reading debates although the findings on phonics were not without critics.
L3 ★★★

Weaver, C. (1994) *Reading Process and Practice from Socio-psycholinguistics to Whole Language*, 2nd edn. Portsmouth, NH: Heinemann.
The classic account of whole language teaching from the perspective of research, theory and practice.
L3 ★★★

Chapter 10

Listening to children read

Listening to children read plays a key role in understanding children's reading ability for teachers. The chapter addresses this in the context of one-to-one and paired reading. It concludes with thoughts about the kinds of conversations that take place with more experienced readers.

The teacher's ability to interact with a small group or a whole class can be greatly enhanced if they understand the subtleties of reading with an individual child. In the early years in particular, the supportive, personal context of one-to-one reading is very important. The strategy can provide a natural link with the kinds of reading that many children experience at home with parents and other family members. In addition, if teachers are to advise parents on effective ways of working with their children, they need to be knowledgeable and effective at one-to-one reading themselves. One-to-one reading is also important because of its significant value to struggling readers. Teachers who work with struggling readers themselves, or who delegate this responsibility to teaching assistants, need to fully understand the possibilities of one-to-one reading.

Listening to children read on a one-to-one basis

Historically, teachers have always listened to children read. Campbell (1995: 132) originally called this practice *shared reading*: 'shared reading involves a child and a teacher (or other adult) reading together, in a one-to-one interaction, from a book.' Since then, shared reading as a term has been used to mean a whole class sharing an enlarged version of a book (→ Chapter 13, 'Routines for reading'). The following example from Campbell (1990) is indicative of the original definition. The extract is from a one-to-one reading session that took place over a period of approximately five minutes and which ended with the teacher and the child discussing the story for a few minutes more and the child telling of her own pet's adventures.

Five-year-old Kirsty was sharing a new book with her teacher. First, the teacher read the story while Kirsty looked at the pictures. Then they read through the story again with the teacher asking Kirsty questions that drew her into conversation about different incidents in the story. Then, when the teacher felt Kirsty was ready, she asked her to read aloud:

Teacher: Your turn to read it, All right, let's see.
Kirsty: The dog sees a box.
Teacher: Mmmh.
Kirsty: He sniffs in the box.
Teacher: He sniffs it, doesn't he?
Kirsty: He kicks the box. He climbs in the box.
Teacher: Oh, now what happens?
Kirsty: He falls down the stairs. The dog falls out the box. The (hesitates)
Teacher: The (pauses)
Kirsty: The dog falls over.
Teacher: He does, doesn't he?
              Then what does he try to do?

Original text:

> The dog sees the box.
> The dog sniffs the box.
> The dog kicks the box.
> The dog gets in the box. The dog gets out of the box.
> The dog falls over.
>
> (Campbell, 1990: 29–30)

Although Kirsty was not reading every word accurately, the meaning of the text had largely been retained, so the teacher did not correct the child, although she did make several interjections to support and encourage Kirsty's reading. When the child hesitated, the teacher simply restarted the sentence, then paused, prompting Kirsty to respond appropriately. Such one-to-one interactions can effectively take place with all levels and ages of children learning to read in the primary school. The level of text may change, but the principles of encouragement, support, discussion, instruction and enjoyment will not.

Key pointers for reading with children on a one-to-one basis include selecting a book that you think will engage the child's interest, or being guided by the child's own choice. If the child is already reading texts with minimal support, try to select one which the child is able to read without support, but choose one which you consider to be of high quality (→ Chapter 3, 'Children's literature'). Read alongside the child, reading to them if necessary but allowing them to take the lead whenever possible. Discuss the book with the child, noting, for example, interest, understanding, awareness of bibliographical features and genre. If appropriate, focus on semantic, syntactic and grapho-phonic cueing strategies ☞ (and consider where and how these strategies could be developed, explicitly or implicitly, throughout the child's day; → Chapter 13, 'Routines for reading').

Another strategy when working with children on a one-to-one basis is to conduct a reading 'interview' or 'conference'. The purpose of this strategy is to find out about the child's reading interests and attitudes. Questions might include:

- Which books do you like to read/look at?
- What is your favourite book? Why?
- What do you like to read at home?
- Do you go to the library?
- What do you like to read? Why?
- Who reads to you at home?
- What do you think about reading?
- Where do you do most of your reading?

You will need to frame your reading interview questions to reflect the age and ability of the child, but it is important to remember that children should not equate reading solely with books, but also a range of different texts (non-fiction texts, poetry, magazines, comics, film, TV and computer games to name but a few).

Reading with more experienced readers

As children's reading becomes more fluent, the priorities for one-to-one reading change. For the majority of children, efficient use of teachers' time can be made by gradually moving towards more emphasis on group reading and literature circles (→ Chapter 13, 'Routines for reading'). Overall there is less of a need for one-to-one sessions for fluent readers, but this does not mean that they should be completely abandoned. One of the most important things that can be discovered by talking to a child about their reading in the one-to-one session is their motivation for reading. Do they read for pleasure? If so, what kinds of texts are they interested in? A motivated reader is surely one who is likely to progress further in their understanding of English than one who is not motivated. The one-to-one session also allows for a more in-depth exploration of children's understanding of and response to particular texts.

Another thing that one-to-one sessions can help with is the identification of struggling readers. Although guided group reading enables the teacher to work with individuals there is some risk that children with reading difficulties might not be identified during a guided group read. A one-to-one session is an ideal opportunity to assess a child's understanding of a text, their ability to decode the words, and any problems in these areas.

The links between reading at home and reading at school

Early years settings and primary schools have encouraged parents/carers to read with their children by sending home a range of texts that the child has chosen to share. Parents/carers are also encouraged to listen to their children read their 'reading books' and to make records in reading diaries (→ Chapter 24). In this way, parents/carers can support their children on a one-to-one basis. Teachers can also scaffold this process by sending home comments and key questions to prompt response and discussion. Holdaway's (1979) developmental approach recognised and built upon children's prior reading experiences, for example acknowledging the importance of the 'pre-school bedtime story learning cycle':

1   The parent introduces a new story. The child is curious so they ask questions and predict the things that are likely to happen next.
2   If the child likes the story, they ask for it to be reread immediately and/or later on. They participate more each time they hear the story. The number of questions they ask increases.
3   If the book is stored somewhere accessible, they use it later to play at reading and to re-enact the story independently which gives them additional satisfaction.
4   Further rereadings result in the child becoming more familiar with the book.
5   Play-reading and re-enactment become closer to the language of the text.
6   The concepts, language and attributes of the story are extended into play.
7   The book may become an 'old favourite' and/or attention turns to the beginning of the cycle with a new book.

Paired reading

A more structured method that research has shown to be effective is paired reading, developed by Keith Topping (1987). Although the approach is structured, it is not overly technical; a pragmatic consideration that has to be taken into account with any method for parents. Paired reading involves the following stages:

1   Ideally, the child chooses the book or text to be read.
2   The book should be briefly discussed before reading aloud commences.
3   The adult and the child begin by reading the text aloud together.
4   The child may follow the text with a finger.
5   When the child wants to read alone, they indicate this by tapping the table or arm of the adult.
6   The adult ceases reading immediately and praises the child for signalling.
7   The child continues alone.
8   When a child makes a miscue, the adult supplies the word.
9   The child then repeats the word.

10 Praise is given for the correct reading of difficult words and for self-corrections ☞.

11 If a child is unable to read a word or correct an error in about five seconds, the adult and child return to reading in unison.

12 The child makes the signal when they feel confident enough to resume reading alone.

13 Further praise and encouragement are given at the end of the session.

One important feature of paired reading is that the adult provides a model of appropriate reading behaviour for the child alongside the child's own attempts at reading satisfactorily.

Topping has since developed the strategy of paired reading for the school setting, as he colourfully describes in the following extract:

> What is that noise? It is like a buzz. Let us go investigate. Down the corridors of the school we go. Getting nearer. It does indeed sound like a beehive. But louder! By the classroom door now – and what do we find? Instead of the regular similar-age children, there is a mix of older and younger pupils, a couple of years between them. They are all matched up in pairs, older with younger. Each pair has their own book, each quite different to any other pair in the class. And each pair is reading – sometimes one out loud, sometimes both. That is where the buzz is coming from! How is the teacher coping with this chaos? Actually, where is the teacher? Oh, there she is – down low with a pair. Coaching, I guess – then she moves on to another pair. Seems unflustered. But there is more buzz than just one classroom – sure enough, the next classroom is at it as well. And the next! So many children reading at the same time, in an interactive way, without the expense of additional resources.
>
> (Topping *et al.*, 2011: 3)

In paired reading, pairs of children (either same age or cross age groups), choose their own books (or other reading materials) which are of high interest to themselves. The materials must be above the independent readability level of the tutee but not of the tutor. Both members of the pair should be able to see the book equally easily in a quiet, comfortable place. They are encouraged to talk about the book to develop shared enthusiasm and ensure the tutee really understands (comprehends) the content. Tutors support tutees through difficult text by reading together and by giving praise.

Practice points

- Make time for one-to-one reading with individual children.
- Allow time for children to respond to the text they are reading, for example, by asking questions to elicit their comprehension.

- Note the strategies children use to decode texts when they are reading aloud to you.
- Provide opportunities for parents/carers to be involved with their children's reading.

Glossary

Graphophonic cueing strategies – the reader understands the relationship between letters and phonemes. They 'sound out' words using their knowledge of the alphabetic code.
Self-corrections – a child's oral correction of a word they mis-read..
Semantic cueing strategies – the reader understands the centrality of meaning to reading. They check the meaning of a word showing awareness that the word makes sense within the sentence as a whole.
Syntactic cueing strategies – the reader understands the relationship between words and word order. They use their grammatical knowledge to predict the words in a sentence.

References

Campbell, R. (1990) *Reading Together*. Buckingham: Open University Press.
Campbell, R. (1995) *Reading in the Early Years Handbook*. Buckingham: Open University Press.
Holdaway, D. (1979) *The Foundations of Literacy*. Portsmouth NH: Heinemann Educational Books Ltd.
Topping, K. (1987) 'Paired reading; a powerful technique for parent use', *The Reading Teacher*, 40(7): 608–614.
Topping, K., Miller, D., Thurston, A., McGavock, K. and Conlin, N. (2011) 'Peer tutoring in reading in Scotland: thinking big', *Literacy*, 45(1): 3–9.

Annotated bibliography

Campbell, R. (1995) *Reading in the Early Years Handbook*. Buckingham: Open University Press.
Sixty different topics relating to reading are presented alphabetically and succinctly. Each of these is followed by suggestions for further reading in the very useful form of annotated bibliographies. A number of interesting classroom examples are included to focus on specific concerns.
L2 ★★
Hall, K. (2003) *Listening to Stephen Read: Multiple Perspectives On Literacy*. Buckingham: Open University Press.
A wonderful example of different perspectives on a child's reading.
L2 ★★
Singleton, C. (2005) 'Dyslexia and oral reading errors', *Journal of Research in Reading*, 28(1): 4–14.
Makes the case that the study of oral reading is still of value to the teacher and researcher alike.
L3 ★★★

Chapter 11

Reading comprehension

Reading comprehension is the essence of reading because it entails readers understanding the written word expressed in texts. In this chapter, we discuss the nature of reading comprehension and some of its components. We argue that it is a vital component of reading development from the earliest stages and throughout the primary phase, and one that should not be separated from other important elements such as phonological understanding.

Children are naturally predisposed to make sense of life, and this includes making sense of texts. This meaning-making has been explained socio-culturally as a *transaction* between text and reader 'an event involving a particular individual and a particular text, happening at a particular time, under particular circumstances, in a particular social and cultural setting, and as part of the ongoing life of the individual and the group' (Rosenblatt, 1985: 100). At the cognitive level, this is explained as *reading comprehension*. Where the two perspectives have something in common is in the idea that interpretation of texts requires the ability to extract and construct meaning.

One of the first important studies in relation to understanding reading comprehension skills was published by Thorndike (1917). His article analysed the errors made by elementary school pupils in writing the answers to simple questions based on short paragraphs. Thorndike found that even when the pupils understood the meaning of the individual words in a paragraph, many of them made errors in answering questions about it. The nature of these errors led him to conclude that the pupils were unable to use relational words and phrases (such as *but* or *on the contrary*) to fit together the separate ideas expressed, or to give to the individual words or word groups the proper amount of emphasis with respect to one another. Thorndike maintained that comprehension in reading is much the same as reasoning in mathematics: comprehending a printed paragraph involves selecting the right elements of the situation and placing them together in the right relationship with the right amount of weight, influence, or force for each.

The RAND Reading Study Group (RRSG, 2002) define reading comprehension as follows:

> the process of simultaneously extracting and constructing meaning through interaction and involvement with written language. We use the words *extracting* and *constructing* to emphasise both the importance and insufficiency of the text as a determinant of reading comprehension. Comprehension entails three elements:
>
> • The *reader* who is doing the comprehending
> • The *text* that is to be comprehended
> • The *activity* in which comprehension is a part.
>
> (RRSG, 2002: 11)

It is important to distinguish between literal comprehension and inferential comprehension. Literal comprehension indicates the understanding of text at a surface level, whereas inferential comprehension indicates the understanding of a text at a much deeper level where the reader is able to pick up nuances implied – but not actually stated – by the text. It is perhaps unfortunate that reading comprehension 'skills' have often been described as 'higher-order' or 'advanced', with the associated implication that they are only relevant to the oldest or most able children (Wray, 1981). We now know that children engage with comprehension from a young age onwards. For example, the nursery children in Levy's (2011) study who described themselves as 'readers' perceived reading to be many different things. As well as saying letters and employing elements of print decoding, reading for these children included looking at books, enjoying books, reading pictures, guessing what printed words said and using context. Reception-aged children in the study similarly recognised that reading was more than just being able to decode print. One child, Imogen, claimed that reading was about 'understanding' words. She used a variety of strategies to make meaning from texts including phonetic strategies, picture, and contextual clues. As Levy argues; 'she recognised she could derive meaning from many different sources . . . all of which could help her to understand what the words were "saying" ' (2011: 49). If children from the earliest age are naturally reading for meaning, then there is all the more reason for the teacher to support comprehension skills alongside accurate decoding of text.

There is evidence that some explicit teaching of comprehension is important. A number of strategies have been identified that support children's reading comprehension in the hands of skilful teachers. These include: summarising texts; children generating questions about texts; clarifying meanings; children verifying their predictions by analysing texts; summarising;

visualising scenes; using context clues in the text to support discussion about issues related to the text; linking texts with children's background knowledge; distinguishing main issues from minor issues; etc. When teachers combine some of these strategies, they seem to be more effective than using the strategies in isolation (Snow and Sweet, 2003; National Institute of Child Health and Human Development, 2000).

In England, a particular interpretation of the simple view of reading (→ Chapter 9) has informed the view that children should be exposed to synthetic phonics teaching before they will be able to move onto reading comprehension. In thinking about reading comprehension in this chapter, we challenge the notion that these two important areas of reading should be decontextualised from each other. The importance of not neglecting reading comprehension at any stage is underlined by the finding that children who have poor reading comprehension skills are at risk of not only poor reading development but also generally poor educational attainment (Cain and Oakhill, 2006). Such children need to be identified and additional reading support put in place (→ Chapter 14).

Comprehension, then, is an active process that children engage with from the earliest stages and throughout the primary age phase. It involves the following elements:

- engaging with the text;
- understanding the text;
- making connections with existing knowledge;
- critically evaluating the text;
- reflecting upon children's responses;
- self-regulating the comprehension process through making decisions about which strategies will help to clarify understanding.

Cognitive strategies

Chapter 13 outlines two routines for reading, including shared and guided reading, that are commonly used in English schools as ways to develop children's comprehension of texts. These practices support children to think carefully and in greater depth about the texts they are exposed to. Cognitive features of reading comprehension that could be built on in one-to-one, shared and guided reading practice include prediction and hypotheses; visualisation; making connections; questioning; inference; and anaphor.

Prediction involves encouraging children to think about how a text, or part of a text, might develop. Particularly with younger children, this might involve scrutinising the title, the front cover, the endpapers or the blurb, and thinking about what these might suggest to gain clues about the content. The teacher's role here is to offer open-ended questions to prompt responses. Pausing during the reading of a text, for example, to review events, to discuss character, plot, themes and setting can also allow children to consider what might happen next. Here are some examples of the kind of open-ended questions that can be used to support prediction and hypothesis:

- 'What do you think this book is about? Why/what makes you say that?'
- 'I wonder why ...?'
- 'What do you think might happen next?'
- 'Why do you think the author/illustrator ...?'
- 'What does this page/image tell you?'

Of course it is important to model how to respond to these types of questions, and also to encourage personal responses so that children understand there is usually not one right answer.

Visualisation involves constructing mental images suggested by the text that will deepen children's understanding by encouraging them to return to interrogate the text more thoroughly, and to check or look for more details. Visualisation can be elicited through asking children to create a picture in their mind, using drawing or through employing drama techniques (→ Chapter 7).

Through activating prior knowledge, children's understanding can be developed, thus helping them to make links between what they already know and new information they encounter within a text. A starting point could be a key word from the title or text, or an artefact associated with a book. For example, the book *Traction Man* could prompt the teacher to ask the children to suggest what kinds of Christmas presents might be appropriate (→ Chapter 3). It can also be helpful to give children sentence starters to frame their responses such as, 'This reminds me of . . .'; 'It makes me think of . . .'; or 'this is a bit like . . .'.

Questions operate at different levels and can take children deeper into texts. Different types of questions demand different levels of thinking, from lower- to higher-order, making increasing cognitive demands on children. Another way of thinking about questions is in terms of developing children's understanding of the text to promote thinking at three levels:

1   Literal questions involve simple recall questions designed to help children recall/revise material already covered as well as simple comprehension questions to elicit their understanding of main points and as a description of what they know.
2   Deductive or inferential questions ask children to become text detectives, deducing from the lines from the text and reading between the lines of the text (inference).
3   Evaluative or response questions ask children to evaluate a text, asking children to think about whether the text achieves its purpose, for example, or to make connections with other texts.

Questions can be initiated either by the teacher or the children, to support their literal and higher-order thinking skills. Questions initiated by the children evolve from the content of the text before, during and after reading. This type of questioning is self-initiated. The reader might ask questions in relation to the following: to clarify meaning; to think about the text yet to be read; to show doubt about an idea in the text; to determine the author's intent, style and content of format; to locate a specific answer in a text; or to take their understanding deeper into the text. Younger children or less experienced readers could be asked what questions they would like to find the answers to in the context of a guided reading session and supported to develop strategies to find the answers leading to being able to generate questions independently.

Inference

Inference is such an important area to develop in children's comprehension that it deserves further mention in its own right. Inference involves filling in the 'gaps' that are not explicitly stated by the author. Several types can be found in the literature:

- *Bridging inference,* where the reader semantically or conceptually relates the sentence being read to previous content.
- *Explanation-based inference,* where the reader infers that the cause of the event being read can be related to previous content found within the text.
- *Process inference,* where understanding increases as the reader reads further into the text – unearthing the steps of an event, for example.
- *Predictive inference,* where the reader predicts or forecasts possible upcoming events in the text.
- *Goal inference,* where the reader infers the motives for an action of a character.
- *Elaborative inference,* where the reader infers the facts of an event or the characteristics of a character not explicitly explained in the text.
- *Anaphoric inference* (see below).

Anaphoric inference is reference to a previously mentioned concept in consecutive sentences or within the same sentence. Anaphors can be explicit, for example, involving the repetition of key words, or implicit, for example, through the use of pronouns, synonyms and repeated nouns. An example of an explicit anaphor would be the repeated chorus which begins 'We're going on a bear hunt' in Michael Rosen's classic children's picture book of the same name. The chorus serves the purpose of regularly drawing the audience back to the main theme of the story.

Practice points

- Practise developing literal and higher-order comprehension questions as you read children's literature.
- Develop children's reading comprehension skills alongside their developing phonic knowledge, from even the earliest stages.
- Practise devising comprehension questions across a range of genres.

References

Cain, K. and Oakhill, J. (2006) 'Profiles of children with specific reading comprehension difficulties', *British Journal of Educational Psychology*, (76): 683–696.

Levy, R. (2011) *Young Children Reading at Home and at School*. London: Sage.

National Institute of Child Health and Human Development (2000) *Report of the National Reading Panel: Teaching children to read: An evidence-based assessment of the scientific research literature on reading and its implications for reading instruction*. Washington, DC: US Government Printing Office.

Rosenblatt, L. (1985) 'Viewpoints: Transaction versus interaction: A terminological rescue operation', *Research in the Teaching of English*, 19(1): 96–107.

RRSG (2002) *Reading for understanding. Toward an R & D program in reading comprehension*. Santa Monica, CA: RAND.

Snow, C. E. and Sweet, A. P. (2003) 'Reading for comprehension', in A. P. Sweet and C. E. Snow (eds) *Rethinking Reading Comprehension*. New York: The Guilford Press.

Thorndike, E. L. (1917) 'Reading as reasoning: a study of mistakes in paragraph reading', *Journal of Educational Psychology* (8): 323–332.

Wray, D. (1981) *Extending Reading Skills*. Lancaster: University of Lancaster.

Annotated bibliography

For additional ideas and teaching approaches to support the development of children's reading comprehension skills, useful sources are CLPE's Bookpower publications. See http://www.clpe.co.uk/publications for more information.

Duffy, G. D., Miller, S., Howerton, S. and Williams, J. B. (2010) 'Comprehension instruction: merging two historically antithetical perspectives', in D. Wyse, R. Andrews and J. Hoffman (eds) *The Routledge International Handbook of English, Language and Literacy Teaching*. London: Routledge.

Overview (see pp. 58–73) of the way that our understanding of reading comprehension has developed.

L3 ★★★

National Institute of Child Health and Human Development (2000) *Report of the National Reading Panel: Teaching children to read: An evidence-based assessment of the scientific research literature on reading and its implications for reading instruction.* Washington, DC: US Government Printing Office.
One of the reports from this major initiative in the US was on reading comprehension.
L3 ★★★

Chapter 12

Phonics

Phonics teaching is one of the key aspects of early reading. This chapter outlines ways of developing phonological awareness ☞ and examines statutory guidance that you need to be aware of as you start teaching phonics. We discuss examples of phonics teaching schemes in the context of a systematic phonics programme.

The English language has 26 graphemes ☞ which are used to represent approximately 44 phonemes ☞ (the exact number continues to be an area of debate). All the words in the English language are spoken using combinations of phonemes, and written using combinations of graphemes. One of the challenges of teaching children this alphabetic code is the lack of consistency between grapheme to phoneme correspondence in English (as opposed to languages such as Finnish or Italian which feature a 1:1 letter mapping to sound). An important concept therefore is the way that different groups of letters represent the same sound. For example, if you look at the vowel phoneme /ie/ which is the long I sound, it can represent the words tried, light, my, shine and mind. The idea that the letters 'igh' represent the /ie/ sound can be counter-intuitive for some people. The old-fashioned way would be to say that these letters sound as /i/ /g/ /h/. But if we said this, it would mean that we would pronounce the word 'light' as 'liguhut' which of course would be ridiculous (although this can be one useful strategy to remember spellings)! So, it is quite accurate to say that the /ie/ sound in the spoken word can be represented in the written word by the letters 'ie' or 'igh' or 'y' or 'i-e'.

Children's early awareness of the phonemic principle of alphabetic writing 'plays a central role in becoming a skilled reader of English and other alphabetic systems' (Shankweiler and Fowler, 2004: 483). Sensitivity to larger phonological units including words, rhymes and syllables occurs at an early age and before awareness of individual phonemes. In all languages so far studied, children develop syllable and onset–rime awareness prior to literacy whilst phoneme awareness develops as literacy is taught (Goswami, 1995).

One of the ideas that has emerged from the research on phonics is the significance of onsets ☞ and rimes ☞, the beginnings and ends of syllables. An understandable mistake is to confuse 'rime' and 'rhyme': the following poem helps to illustrate this:

Spellbound

I have a spelling chequer
It came with my PC
It plainly marks four my revue
Miss takes I cannot sea.
I've run this poem threw it
I'm shore your pleased too no;
It's letter perfect in it's weigh
My chequer tolled me sew.
(Vandal, 1996: 14)

The *rhymes* in lines 2 and 4, and 6 and 8, are present because the 'rime' of the words 'C' (letter names are also words, in this case spelled 'cee') and 'sea', and 'no' and 'sew' are the same. This poem nicely illustrates the problems that we can have when representing phonemes with letters.

Using the concept of onset and rime, Goswami (1995: 139) emphasised the importance of reading by analogy: 'Analogies in reading involve using the spelling-sound pattern of one word, such as *beak*, as a basis for working out the spelling-sound correspondence of a new word, such as *peak*.' Children's development of phonological understanding tends to proceed from the ability to identify syllables, then onsets and rimes, and finally the ability to segment phonemes. The use of analogies draws on children's early recognition of onsets and rimes.

In order to see further potential for analogies, it is necessary to briefly look at the irregularity of English. It has often been pointed out that the links between sound and symbol in the English language are notoriously irregular and Frank Smith (1978) raised this in his controversial chapter 'The fallacy of phonics'. For example, what is the sound of the vowel phoneme in the following word: 'read'? You may have assumed that it was /ee/. However, if we explained that the sentence context is 'Yesterday I read a good book', then it is clear that not just the meaning of the word but the meaning of the sentence as a whole has an impact on the particular vowel phoneme. This perhaps reached the height of irregularity in the name of the university department, 'The Centre for Reading in Reading'. Also, consider the way that the /sh/ phoneme is represented in the following words: appreciate, ocean, machine, moustache, stanchion, fuchsia, schist, conscious, extension, pressure, admission, sure, initiate, attention, and luxury.

A short anecdote helps us to explore further the irregularities of sounds and symbols. A child in one of the classes we were teaching was writing a book with the following joke:

Saima:	Will you remember me tomorrow?
Dominic:	Yes.
S:	Will you remember me in a week?
D:	Yes.
S:	Will you remember me in a month?
D:	Yes.
S:	Will you remember me in a year?
D:	Yes.
S:	Knock, knock.
D:	Who's there?
S:	You've forgotten me already!

Saima was stuck on the spelling for 'remember' and Dominic was about to suggest that she sound out the word, when it struck him that each time the letter 'e' is used in 'remember' it represents a different phoneme.

One of the important aspects of onset and rime is that when young children learn nursery rhymes and simple songs, their awareness of sounds is raised and it is often their attention to the rime of the words that is strong. Because this is the case, it has been argued that teaching which emphasises onset and rime can be beneficial, particularly if it is linked to the different ways that onsets and rimes can be written down. Children's understanding of rime seems to be part of a normal developmental process whereas the ability to segment phonemes does not come so naturally.

Teaching phonics

As you saw in Chapter 9, the teaching of reading – and particularly the teaching of phonics – continues to arouse intense debate. Most countries for whom English is the main language include some phonics teaching as part of their reading curriculum. However, the trend in recent years has been for governments to require a particular form of phonics teaching called *synthetic phonics*. Synthetic phonics programmes emphasise teaching pupils to convert letters (graphemes) ☞ into sounds (phonemes) ☞ and then to blend the sounds to form recognisable words. *Analytic phonics*, on the other hand, is taken to refer to larger-unit phonics programmes which introduce children to whole words as a context for analysing their component parts, with an emphasis on the larger subparts of words (i.e. onsets, rimes, phonograms and spelling patterns) as well as phonemes.

In England, systematic synthetic phonics (SSP) is viewed by the government as the prime strategy for teaching children to read. SSP is a misnomer as all phonics programmes are systematic to different degrees. Statutory guidance lays out core criteria for systematic synthetic phonics programmes, including recommended examples, and changes to the school timetable have been made to include daily phonics teaching sessions for children in the early years of primary schooling. Synthetic phonics consists of:

- identifying sounds (phonemes) in spoken words;
- recognising the common spellings of each phoneme;
- blending phonemes into words for reading;
- segmenting words into phonemes for spelling.

The 'synthetic' part of the term 'synthetic phonics' comes from the part played by synthesising (blending) in reading as outlined below. Children are taught grapheme–phoneme (letter–sound) correspondences and how to use their phonological knowledge to work words out.

Synthetic phonics teaching emphasises that when children are reading, they are taught to look at the graphemes (letters) of a word from left to right, convert them into phonemes and blend the phonemes to work out the spoken forms of the words. For example, if children see the word *hat*, they need to know what phoneme to say for each grapheme (/h/ – /a/ – /t/) and then to be able to blend those phonemes together into a recognisable word. Once words have been read this way often enough, they become known and can then be read without sounding out and blending. For spelling, children are taught to segment spoken words into phonemes and write down graphemes for those phonemes. For example, if children want to write *hat*, then they need to be able to split it into the phonemes /h/ – /a/ – /t/ and write the appropriate graphemes.

There is an increasing number of synthetic phonics teaching programmes available for schools to use. A programme originally approved by government is Letters and Sounds (DfES, 2007a), a six-phase programme which builds first and foremost on children's early speaking and listening skills:

> Letters and Sounds is designed as a time-limited programme of phonic work aimed at securing fluent word recognition skills for reading by the end of Key Stage 1, although the teaching and learning of spelling, which children generally find harder than reading, will continue . . . it enables children to see the relationship between reading and spelling from an early age.
>
> (DfES, 2007b: 3)

Tables 12.1 to 12.4 outline progression through the phases showing how a systematic approach goes from the simple to the more complex. Starting at the simplest level means that learning to read and spell can be as easy in English at this stage as in other languages which are alphabetically written. Children can thus grasp the basic workings of alphabetic writing before they have to start dealing with the complexities which are unavoidable in English:

Table 12.1 Phonemes to graphemes (consonants)

	Correspondences found in many different words		High-frequency words containing rare or unique correspondences (graphemes are underlined)
Phoneme	**Grapheme(s)**	**Sample words**	
/b/	b, bb	bat, rabbit	
/k/	c, k, ck	cat, kit, duck	s<u>ch</u>ool, mos<u>qu</u>ito
/d/	d, dd, -ed	dog, muddy, pulled	
/f/	f, ff, ph	fan, puff, photo	rou<u>gh</u>
/g/	g, gg	go, bigger	
/h/	h	hen	<u>wh</u>o
/j/	j, g, dg	jet, giant, badge	
/l/	l, ll	leg, bell	
/m/	m, mm	map, hammer	la<u>mb</u>, autu<u>mn</u>
/n/	n, nn	net, funny	<u>gn</u>at, <u>kn</u>ock
/p/	p, pp	pen, happy	
/r/	r, rr	rat, carrot	<u>wr</u>ite, <u>rh</u>yme
/s/	s, ss, c	sun, miss, cell	<u>sc</u>ent, li<u>s</u>ten
/t/	t, tt, -ed	tap, butter, jumped	<u>Th</u>omas, dou<u>bt</u>
/v/	v	van	o<u>f</u>
/w/	w	wig	peng<u>u</u>in, <u>one</u>
/y/	y	yes	on<u>i</u>on
/z/	z, zz, s, se, ze	zip, buzz, is, please, breeze	sci<u>ss</u>ors, <u>x</u>ylophone
/sh/	sh, s, ss, t (before -ion and -ial)	shop, sure, mission, mention, partial	spe<u>ci</u>al, <u>ch</u>ef, o<u>ce</u>an
/ch/	ch, tch	chip, catch	
/th/	th	thin	
/th/	th	then	brea<u>the</u>
/ng/	ng, n (before k)	ring, pink	ton<u>gue</u>
/zh/	s (before -ion and -ure)	vision, measure	u<u>s</u>ual, bei<u>ge</u>

Table 12.2 Phonemes to graphemes (vowels)

Phoneme	Grapheme(s)	Sample words	High-frequency words containing rare or unique correspondences (graphemes are underlined)
			Correspondences found in many different words
/a/	a	ant	
/e/	e, ea	egg, head	said, says, friend, leopard, any
/i/	i, y	in, gym	women, busy, build, pretty, engine
/o/	o, a	on, was	
/u/	u, o, o-e	up, son, come	young, does, blood
/ai/	ai, ay, a-e	rain, day, make	they, veil, weigh, straight
/ee/	ee, ea, e, ie	feet, sea, he, chief	these, people
/igh/	igh, ie, y, i-e, i	night, tie, my, like, find	height, eye, I, goodbye, type
/oa/	oa, ow, o, oe, o-e	boat, grow, toe, go, home	oh, though, folk
/oo/	oo, ew, ue, u-e	boot, grew, blue, rule	to, soup, through, two, lose
/oo/	oo, u	look, put	could
/ar/	ar, a	farm, father	calm, are, aunt, heart
/or/	or, aw, au, ore, al	for, saw, Paul, more, talk	caught, thought, four, door, broad
/ur/	ur, er, ir, or (after 'w')	hurt, her, girl, work	learn, journey, were
/ow/	ow, ou	cow, out	drought
/oi/	oi, oy	coin, boy	
/air/	air, are, ear	fair, care, bear	there
/ear/	ear, eer, ere	dear, deer, here	pier
/ure/			sure, poor, tour
/ə/	many different graphemes		corner, pillar, motor, famous, favour, murmur, about, cotton, mountain, possible, happen, centre, thorough, picture, cupboard . . . and others

Table 12.3 Graphemes to phonemes (consonants)

Grapheme	Phoneme(s)	Correspondences found in many different words — Sample words	Correspondences found in some high-frequency words but not in many/any other words
b, bb	/b/	bat, rabbit	lamb, debt
c	/k/, /s/	cat, cell	special
cc	/k/, /ks/	account, success	
ch	/ch/	chip	school, chef
ck	/k/	duck	
d, dd	/d/	dog, muddy	
dg	/j/	badge	
f, ff	/f/	fan, puff	*of*
g	/g/, /j/	go, gem	
gg	/g/, /j/	bigger, suggest	
gh	/g/, /-/	ghost, high	rough
gn	/n/	gnat, sign	
gu	/g/		guard
h	/h/	hen	honest
j	/j/	jet	
k	/k/	kit	
kn	/n/	knot	
l	/l/	leg	half
ll	/l/	bell	
le	/l/ or / l/	paddle	
m, mm	/m/	map, hammer	
mb	/m/		lamb
mn	/m/		autumn
n	/n/, /ng/	net, pink	
nn	/n/	funny	
ng	/ng/, /ng+g/, /n+j/	ring, finger, danger	
p, pp	/p/	pen, happy	
ph	/f/	photo	

qu	/kw/	quiz	mosquito
r, rr	/r/	rat, carrot	
rh	/r/		rhyme
s	/s/, /z/	sun, is	sure, measure
ss	/s/, /sh/	miss, mission	
sc	/s/	scent	
se	/s/, /z/	mouse, please	
sh	/sh/	shop	
t, tt	/t/	tap, butter	listen
tch	/ch/	catch	
th	/th/, **/th/**	thin, then	Thomas
v	/v/	van	
w	/w/	wig	answer
wh	/w/ or /hw/	when	who
wr	/r/	write	
x	/ks/ /gz/	box, exam	xylophone
y	/y/, /i/ (/ee/), /igh/	yes, gym, very, fly	
ye, y-e			goodbye, type
z, zz	/z/	zip, buzz	

Table 12.4 Graphemes to phonemes (vowels)

			Correspondences found in some high-frequency words but not in many/any other words
	Correspondences found in many different words		
Grapheme	**Phoneme(s)**	**Sample words**	
a	/a/, /o/, /ar/	ant, was, father	water, any
a-e	/ai/	make	
ai	/ai/	rain	*said*
air	/air/	hair	
al, all	/al/, /orl/, /or/	Val, shall, always, all, talk	half
ar	/ar/	farm	war
are	/air/	care	*are*

(continued overleaf)

Table 12.4 (Continued)

	Correspondences found in many different words		Correspondences found in some high-frequency words but not in many/any other words
au	/or/	Paul	aunt
augh			caught, laugh
aw	/or/	saw	
ay	/ai/	say	says
e	/e/, /ee/	egg, he	
ea	/ee/, /e/	bead, head	great
ear	/ear/	hear	learn, heart
ed	/d/, /t/, /∂d/	turned, jumped, landed	
ee	/ee/	bee	
e-e	/ee/	these	
eer	/ear/	deer	
ei	/ee/	receive	veil, leisure
eigh	/ai/	eight	height
er	/ur/	her	
ere	/ear/	here	were, there
eu	/yoo/	Euston	
ew	/yoo/, /oo/	few, flew	sew
ey	/i/ (/ee/)	donkey	they
i	/i/, /igh/	in, mind	
ie	/igh/, /ee/, /i/	tie, chief, babies	friend
i-e	/igh/, /i/, /ee/	like, engine, machine	
igh	/igh/	night	
ir	/ur/	girl	
o	/o/, /oa/, /u/	on, go, won	do, wolf
oa	/oa/	boat	broad
oe	/oa/	toe	shoe
o-e	/oa/, /u/	home, come	
oi	/oi/	coin	

oo	/oo/, /oo/	boot, look	blood
or	/or/, /ur/	for	work
ou	/ow/, /oo/	out, you	could, young, shoulder
our	/ow ∂/, /or/	our, your	journey, tour
ow	/ow/, /oa/	cow, slow	
oy	/oi/	boy	
u	/u/, /oo/	up, put	
ue	/oo/, /yoo/	clue, cue	
u-e	/oo/, /yoo/	rude, cute	
ui			build, fruit
ur	/ur/	fur	
uy			buy

Another popular scheme is the commercially produced 'Jolly Phonics'. The example from this series shown in Figure 12.1 is from *The Phonics Handbook* which provides photocopiable worksheets with each sheet covering one phoneme. Like some other programmes, multi-sensory ☞ approaches are used; each phoneme is accompanied by an action that the children carry out to act as an aide memoire when articulating the phoneme. The phonemes are linked to a storyline to help the children remember them.

There are a number of more questionable ideas. The sheets include a picture related to the suggested storyline which is left blank for children to colour in; something that is not particularly educationally valuable. Additionally, a handwriting exercise is offered which encourages the children to write two letters that represent the phoneme. The problem here is a confusion of learning objectives (handwriting and learning phonemes) and the fact that most phonemes can be represented by a range of letter combinations, not just the ones that are offered.

One of the most controversial ideas of synthetic phonics programmes is the recommendation that books are withheld. In 'Jolly Phonics':

> During the first 8–9 weeks the aim is to prepare the children for reading books. Stories and poems are read to them, but the children are not expected to try and read books for themselves . . . Teachers and parents may find it difficult not to give children books to read in the first few weeks.
>
> (Lloyd, 1998: 25–26)

An example of another synthetic phonics teaching programme that was praised by the Rose Report also denies children books during the programme: 'This

th th

voiced and unvoiced th

ACTION
Child pretends to be a little rude by sticking out tongue a little and saying *th* (as in them), and very rude by sticking tongue further out and saying *th* (as in thumb).

that   **thin**

then   thumb

this   thick

feather thunder

with   moth

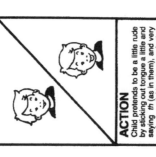

Figure 12.1 A page from the 'Jolly Phonics' scheme.

is a very accelerated form of phonics that does not begin by establishing an initial sight vocabulary. With this approach, before children are introduced to books, they are taught letter sounds.' (House of Commons Education and Skills Committee, 2005: Ev 61).

There is a wealth of evidence pointing to the fact that pre-school children acquire a range of sophisticated understandings. Many two-year-old children, for example, enjoy choosing books from their bookshelves in the home and flicking through the pages or sharing the books with siblings or parents. The idea that when children come to school this opportunity to read books should be denied for eight to nine weeks seems extraordinary and is not supported by research evidence.

Whilst debate continues over the efficacy of a purely synthetic phonics approach, research shows that a systematic approach (not necessarily synthetic) to the teaching of phonics will support the development of children's reading. Any phonics programme should be contextualised in language as a whole for real purposes. As discussed in Chapters 3 and 6, this context should be rich in literature and opportunities for talk.

Practice points

- Practise articulation of phonemes.
- Make a clear distinction between sounds and letter names. Help children to understand that various letter combinations can produce the same sound.
- Phonics teaching should be carefully contextualised in real texts, sentences and words.
- Remember that learning to read is a complex process that requires a broad range of teaching strategies, of which phonics is one important part.

Glossary

Grapheme – written representation of a sound, e.g. a letter of the alphabet.
Multi-sensory – approaches that use sight, sound and touch to reinforce language learning.
Onset – any consonant sounds that come before the vowel in a syllable.
Phoneme – the smallest unit of sound in a word.
Phonological awareness – understanding of the links between sounds and symbols.
Rime – the vowel and any consonants that follow the onset in a syllable.

References

Alexander, R. (ed.) (2010) *Children, Their World, Their Education: Final Report and Recommendations of the Cambridge Primary Review*. London: Routledge.

Department for Education and Skills (DfES, 2007a) *Letters and Sounds*. London: DfES Publications.

Department for Education and Skills (DfES, 2007b) *Letters and Sounds: Notes of Guidance for Practitioners and Teachers*. London: DfES Publications

Goswami, U. (1995) 'Phonological development and reading: what is analogy, and what is not?', *Journal of Research in Reading*, 18(2): 139–145.

Lloyd, S. (1998) *The Phonics Handbook (3rd ed.)*. Chigwell: Jolly Learning Ltd.

National Institute of Child Health and Human Development (2000) *Report of the National Reading Panel: Teaching Children to Read: An Evidence-based Assessment of the Scientific Research Literature on Reading and its Implications for Reading Instruction. Reports of the Subgroups* (NIH publication no. 00-4754). Washington, DC: US Government Printing Office.

Shankweiler, D. and Fowler, A. E. (2004) 'Questions people ask about the role of phonological process in learning to read', *Reading and Writing: An Interdisciplinary Journal*, 17: 483–515.

Smith, F. (1978) *Reading*. Cambridge: Cambridge University Press.

Vandal, N. (1996) 'Spellbound', in J. Foster (compiler) *Crack Another Yolk and Other Word Play Poems*. Oxford: Oxford University Press.

Annotated bibliography

Dombey, H., Moustafa, M. and the staff of the Centre for Language in Primary Education (CLPE) (1998) *Whole to Part Phonics: How Children Learn to Read and Spell*. London: CLPE.
A practical alternative to standard phonics approaches. This book shows how phonological understanding can be successfully developed in the context of whole texts first and foremost.
L1 ★★

Goouch, K. and Lambirth, A. (eds) (2011) *Teaching Early Reading and Phonics*. London: Sage.
A theory-based practical approach to teaching early reading and phonics with many examples of suggested activities.

Lewis, M. and Ellis, S. (eds) (2006) *Phonics: Practice Research and Policy*. London: Paul Chapman Publishing.
A very strong contribution to the debate on phonics teaching. This book clearly shows the complexities of phonics teaching and in the process reveals the inadequacies of a one-size-fits-all model.
L2 ★★

Torgerson, C. J., Brooks, G. and Hall, J. (2006) *A Systematic Review of the Research Literature on the Use of Phonics in the Teaching of Reading and Spelling*. London: Department for Education and Skills (DfES).
This review is restricted to research studies which were randomised controlled trials which the authors claim are most important kinds of studies for judging teaching effectiveness.
L3 ★★★

Chapter 13

Routines for reading

The aim of reading teaching is to develop enthusiastic and independent readers. This chapter illustrates some of the practical techniques that teachers need to adopt to support this aim. Thoughts on classroom organisation are followed by outlines of two significant strategies: shared and guided reading. We consider the value of literature circles, reading journals and reading aloud to children.

In Chapter 3, the importance of teachers reading widely in order to choose texts to inspire children was underlined. A teacher's knowledge of texts for children influences many of the decisions to be made about the teaching of literacy. It will enable, for example, selection of a class reader ☞ (or readers) which will motivate and interest the children. A teacher's reading and interaction with children provides a powerful model of the reading process. In addition to more structured routines for reading – for example, shared and guided reading – opportunities for 'story time' should be a part of daily classroom practice.

An initial consideration in any teacher's classroom is how space for reading resources is utilised to the best possible effect. There are many advantages to a comfortable and attractive carpeted area which allows the class to sit together and share ideas. It has to be acknowledged, however, that the size of many classrooms makes this difficult to achieve. Whether there is a carpeted area or not, classroom organisation needs to accommodate a range of teaching including discussion, shared reading and word work, such as phonics. In the early years, designated classroom areas that support language and literacy work are common. These include a reading area with comfortable seating such as cushions; listening points with CD players/computers and headphones; display areas such as 'author of the week'; message boards; and role-play areas. These areas are also very valuable for older children, although these tend to be equated with early years and infant practice.

Whether you have a carpeted reading area or not, the display and storage of books are important considerations. Teachers need to know about the books in their reading area and to display them in a way that will entice children. Practical issues such as how often books will need to be changed should also be considered. There should be a wide range of fiction ☞, non-fiction ☞ and poetry, including books made by the class. Multiple copies of reference books such as atlases, dictionaries and thesauri should also be clearly labelled and accessible. Magazines, comics and newspapers should also be featured from time to time; many children read these at home, particularly those who show reluctance to read fiction at school. For that reason, children can be encouraged to bring any reading materials from home to school on a regular basis. This can serve a number of purposes: it shows that you value children's own reading choices; it motivates many children; as the teacher you get an insight into their reading interests; and the children share their interests with their peers who may read more as a consequence. An open mind about the quality of reading materials coupled with a critical appreciation of the qualities of different texts is a good foundation for teaching reading.

A whole class session when each child in the class reads a text of their choice used to be called *quiet reading*. This has attracted a number of acronyms over the years, such as ERIC (Everyone Reads in Class); USSR (Uninterrupted Silent Sustained Reading); and DEAR (Drop Everything and Read), and was sometimes characterised by the teacher modelling the process of individual reading by reading their own book alongside the class. In some schools, however, quiet reading in this way has been interpreted as a time when individual children read *to* the teacher whilst the remainder of the class read independently. The main advantage of the quiet reading approach is that children can make *choices* over the texts that they read which can motivate them to read more, and is therefore a valuable part of the routine of a reading classroom.

Shared reading

The term *shared reading* or *shared read* is now associated with a whole class objective-led lesson which features a text that a whole class can access, such as one that is enlarged electronically or a *big book*. It is used throughout the primary phase, but this was not the original idea of shared reading.

Don Holdaway developed a system called 'shared book experience' in 1979. Although he was one of the first to recommend the use of big books, because they enabled the group of children to see the print clearly, his approach had other aspects that are not part of the version of shared reading that evolved from the late 1990s onwards. Holdaway's approach was cross-curricular; for example, it involved the children in the making of enlarged versions of favourite picture books with an emphasis on the artwork required for the pictures. Phonics teaching was included as part of the shared book experience rather than as a separate session. Similarly, Campbell (1995: 132) defined shared reading as an experience which 'involves a child and a teacher (or other adult) reading together, in a one-to-one interaction, from a book'.

Shared reading is now a term used to describe a whole class reading experience designed to form a bridge between the teacher reading to pupils and independent reading by children. Its main feature is that the teacher and pupils read a single text together as a whole class where the teacher is the 'expert' modelling what it means to be a reader. Shared reading provides a wide range of opportunities for teachers to model effective strategies, explicitly teaching a skill or approach and drawing children into the process through questioning, paired talk, drama and other response activities. The key features of shared reading are as follows:

- a text pitched at or above average reading attainment level of the class;
- a shared text, such as a *big book* or other enlarged text, or multiple copies of the text in normal size;
- high-quality teacher–pupil interaction;
- discussions about the text focusing on meanings and on words and sentences;
- the modelling of reading processes;
- teaching which is informed by lesson objectives;
- preparation for main activities.

Books chosen for shared reading can be a little above the attainment level of the class because the teacher is reading the text for them. This is an opportunity to extend children's thinking and knowledge. If it is the first time that you have shared the book, it is normal for you to read it without comment from the children. This gives them the opportunity to hear the text as a whole. If the text is a story or poem, it gives you the opportunity to offer a dramatic reading to highlight the memorable features and to motivate the class. On subsequent readings, which may or may not happen on the same day, you will engage the children in discussion about a range of things that are of interest in the text.

An enlarged text, which could be a big book, is particularly helpful to discuss features of the text and the subtleties of the illustrations. However, just because it is a big book does not mean that it is a good book. It is far better that you share a normal size version of a really good text than an enlarged version of a poor text. Some of the so-called 'interactive' texts available on the internet which are convenient to use on whiteboards are examples of very poor texts. As with any teaching resource you need to critically evaluate them to assess their value in supporting learning. An example of a good big book to use in KS1 is *Where's My Teddy?*, written and illustrated by Jez Alborough.

Ideas for using picture books during a KS1 shared read

Where's My Teddy? (Written and illustrated by Jez Alborough)

- Discuss cover features. Discuss pictures, author/illustrator, title, predicting what the book is about. Read the blurb.
- Read the book and ask questions to encourage prediction throughout: e.g. page that says 'WHAT'S THAT?' waits for page turn for answer.
- Ask specific questions related to the children's lives/experiences: e.g. do you ever feel scared in the dark?
- Post-it notes to cover key words, e.g. rhyming words. Ask for suggestions.
- Re-enact Teddy's actions from the text in sequence.
- Dialogue pairs: try and remember what Eddy and the giant teddy say to each other when they first meet. Think of different versions.
- Think about story structure.
- Write a sentence on card and rearrange the words. Do a similar activity using the IWB (Interactive White Board).
- Find the rhyming words in the text. Make a list.
- This is a great text for looking at some basic punctuation.
- Do read the book for enjoyment and general discussion on one or more occasions!

Some suggestions for follow-up activities:

- Take a trip to a wood and get the children to bring their teddies. Record some of the children's thoughts about the wood (organisation for writing). Take photographs.
- Write a letter from Eddy to the Big Bear asking him or her to become friends.
- Take children into the ICT suite to write their own stories, experimenting with different fonts, lower case and upper case letters, etc. for effect.
- Design a 'Lost Teddy' poster to be stuck in the neighbourhood.

Our advice for successful shared reading is to keep sessions relatively brief. Fifteen minutes should be ample time to engage the children in a text. It is also important that you remember to elicit the children's responses to texts, not just require them to answer the questions that you have planned in relation to your lesson objectives.

Shared reading has a number of specific functions in the teaching of early reading:

- inducting children into the world of literature, meaning and response;
- providing rich opportunities for increasing children's stock of words and teaching early reading behaviours;
- serving as a vehicle for extending children's understanding of what is being read; that is, their language comprehension;
- providing opportunities to apply acquired decoding skills in context, reinforcing children's developing phonic knowledge and skills gained from discrete, daily phonic sessions.

(Primary National Strategy, 2006: 9)

By the time children enter their later primary years, the focus of a shared read moves to focus on comprehension. This includes predicting/hypothesising, visualising, making connections, questioning, clarifying, inferring, synthesising and exploring vocabulary in relation to meaning. However, it is also vital that comprehension is a focus of all reading teaching, ranging from literal comprehension towards increasingly inferential forms of comprehension.

Another feature of the shared read is that it can be used to introduce a main lesson activity. It is our view that this works best if the activity involves further active engagement with the text, exploration of the issues that the text raises, and active practical work to extend understanding (refer to the Follow-up Activities above for *Where's my Teddy?*)

Guided reading

Effective teaching of reading requires work with individual children (→ Chapter 10), the whole class and with small groups of children. Small group reading is often called *guided reading*, where the teacher leads the session but this time with a maximum of six children, usually of similar ability. In Chapter 2 we address socio-cultural theory that has shown the vital importance of interaction to children's learning. The goal of guided reading is to enable children to become independent readers who are able to read, understand and appreciate texts on their own without the teacher's help. Guided reading is a collaborative experience which enables children to talk about their learning, and share explorations and approaches. The teacher manages the group in such a way that children read independently, with the teacher monitoring progress and interacting with the group and individual children as appropriate. The teacher will have identified a clear learning objective and outcome for the session which will extend the range of pupils' reading strategies. As children become more proficient, guided reading sessions may shift towards a greater emphasis on response and discussion. The children are encouraged to apply strategies learned in guided reading in their independent reading. One of the positive features of small group work such as guided reading is that children often find it easier to contribute to discussions in that context as opposed to the whole class.

Many schools operate guided reading as a separate lesson. The class is frequently organised into five guided reading groups. Whilst the guided group are working with the teacher, the other groups could be: reading independently; preparing for/following up from the next/previous guided session, e.g. writing a character analysis, examining setting; having a supported reading session with a teaching assistant (not necessarily the lowest ability children); reading from a variety of other texts; listening to story tapes; and playing word games on computers.

The main features of guided reading are as follows:

- Multiple copies of texts are used, one for each pupil in the small group.
- Books are matched to the achievement levels of the group.
- It involves introduction to a new text or reflections on a known text, or section of text, read previously.
- Following discussion, the teacher supports the children as they read independently.
- The other groups of the class are engaged in independent group work.
- At lower primary, the emphasis is on helping children learn to read (→ Chapter 10 outlines examples of interaction strategies).
- At upper primary, the objectives are to analyse and discuss the text although some children will still require help in learning to read.
- The teacher works with a different group on each day of the week.

Generic teaching sequence for guided reading

The teaching sequence for guided reading is designed in three phases: Starting Points, Reading and Responding, and Reflecting and Evaluating.

Phase 1: Starting Points

SELECTING OBJECTIVES

When selecting objectives for the group, consider both curriculum *and* learning objectives. In addition, consider:

- which reading strategies are established;
- which reading strategies need to be practised and consolidated;
- which reading strategies need demonstration and development;
- what the next steps are for the group to develop their understanding of text.

SELECTING A TEXT

- Teachers need to make informed choices about the texts they select for guided reading. Texts should be of high quality, should interest and excite children, and should offer opportunities to work towards specific objectives.

- The teacher should select a text at the children's instructional level; children should be able to read the text at between 90% and 95% accuracy and with understanding. A guided reading text should not present too many difficulties because otherwise both meaning and motivation may be lost.
- The choice of text must be considered carefully as difficulties may lie in the concepts, the language structures, the vocabulary, cultural references and organisation.
- If a text is too easy, there will be insufficient challenge for the group.
- Texts can be cross-curricular; for example, guided reading could be taught as part of a science topic.
- Decide on the objectives for the group. Select these objectives in the context of the group's reading ability.

INTRODUCE THE TEXT AND CARRY OUT THE STRATEGY-CHECK

During the introduction and *strategy-check* the teacher:

- sets a purpose for reading;
- encourages links with previous experience and draws attention to important ideas;
- gives opportunities for children to discuss new vocabulary;
- reminds children of the repertoire of strategies they can use. Depending on the reading fluency of the children, examples of strategies might be sounding out a word from left to right, one-to-one pointing, rereading to check sense, identifying the main points in a sentence or paragraph, and skimming and scanning.

This ensures that by the time the children read the text they:

- know that the reading will inform and interest them;
- have certain questions in mind which they will expect to answer;
- have some knowledge of how to solve problems within the text.

Phase 2: Reading and Responding

INDEPENDENT READING

- All guided reading sessions should include independent reading.
- Following the introduction and strategy-check, each child reads the text independently.
- The teacher may intervene to deepen a child's understanding, ask questions or focus on a teaching point, giving praise for use of specific strategies where appropriate.

RETURNING TO THE TEXT

- This is an opportunity to review the use of particular strategies and to revisit the questions discussed at the start of the session. Encourage the children to identify issues requiring clarification or discussion.

RESPONDING TO THE TEXT

- Allow time for the children to respond to the text, develop and justify opinions, and explore personal preferences.

Phase 3: Reflecting and Evaluating

- Assessment of the children's learning during guided reading will inform the next steps for your planning. This will involve the selection of appropriate objective(s) for the next session in the context of the reading targets.
- Children may follow up their guided reading with further reading of the text during independent reading time.

Literature circles and reading journals

Literature circles are another way to explore children's understanding of text, improve their reading skills, and encourage the development of positive attitudes towards reading. Harste, Short and Burke (1989) first used the term 'literature circle', which is seen as a way of encouraging enjoyment of reading and talking about books. In a literature circle, a group of children all read the same text and, sometimes with the support of reading journals and/or their teacher, come together to talk about their reading and to read more of the text together. For older children, literature circles are similar to adult reading groups in that the text is read independently and most of the circle time is spent discussing the group members' responses. Younger children (aged five to seven) are encouraged to read the text aloud around the group and then talk about it. Literature circles are therefore an active and creative way for to give children time to read and to talk about the texts with each other, and with adults.

Reading journals provide children with the opportunity to document their reading experiences and responses and can be used in a variety of ways. They can take the form of a book or folder but might also be kept as an audio diary or on a computer. Journals can provide space for reflection and evaluation as well as speculation and exploration of ideas. They can provide teachers with information about pupils' thinking and comprehension skills as they engage with text. There are many formats for reading journals. Much will depend on the age and ability of the children, personal preference and how reading is organised. It is important to be clear about how the journal is to be used and its purpose. The teacher could model how to use a journal during shared and guided reading. With younger children or less confident writers, the journal could be a whole class book where the teacher takes responsibility for the writing process and children can concentrate on articulating ideas and responses. In some classes, each guided group could have its own collaborative journal. This is useful when children are being introduced to journals or have not yet developed confidence to maintain individual journals.

Practice points

- Selecting texts of the highest quality is a vital first step in your reading teaching.
- Give plenty of opportunities for independent reading including choice over reading materials.
- Draw on a range of reading experiences and routines with the children in your class.

Glossary

Class reader – a text, usually fiction, which the teacher reads aloud to the class. This is normally carried out as a regular session outside of the main English teaching.
Fiction – text which is invented and in the main is not factual; novels are described as fiction.
Non-fiction – texts which are factual. Information books are non-fiction.

References

Campbell, R. (1995) *Reading in the Early Years Handbook*. Buckingham: Open University Press.
Harste, J., Short, K. and Burke, C. (1989) *Creating Classrooms for Authors: the Reading–Writing Connection*. Portsmouth, NH: Heinemann Educational.

Annotated bibliography

Centre for Language in Primary Education (CLPE) Barrs, M. and Thomas, A. (eds) (1991) *The Reading Book*. London: CLPE.
An important practical guide based on close work with London teachers. It introduces the idea of a 'core' selection of high-quality books to support reading. Equal opportunities is a strong strand to the work.
L1 ★
Graham, J. and Kelly, A. (2007) *Reading Under Control: Teaching Reading in the Primary School*, 3rd edn. London: David Fulton.
A very useful account with a particularly strong section on 'Reading Routines' which develops a number of the points about reading that we touch on in this book.
L1 ★★

Hobsbaum, A., Gamble, N. and Reedy, D. (2006) *Guided Reading: A Handbook for Teaching Guided Reading at Key Stage 2*, 2nd edn. London: The Institute of Education.

An excellent resource which includes an overview of guided reading and recommended texts for different year groups.

L2 ★

Skidmore, D., Perez-Parent, M. and Arnfield, D. (2003) 'Teacher–pupil dialogue in the guided reading session', *Reading Literacy and Language*, 37(2): 47–53.

Important research evidence about how teacher–pupil dialogue can help or hinder during guided reading.

L2 ★★★

Chapter 14

Reading difficulties

Children who struggle with literacy are a major concern to teachers, parents and governments around the world. The point is made in this chapter that we have strong evidence to suggest that Reading Recovery is a tried and tested, evidence-based approach that works with most children who struggle with reading. Some of the main factors that are part of the more complex needs of children with dyslexia ☞ are also briefly addressed.

One of the main concerns for early years and primary school teachers is how to help children who struggle with their reading. The ability to read gives access to so many areas of learning. First and foremost, it is important to remember that the reasons for struggling with reading are many and complex. Some people would suggest that the quality of teaching is the main reason why children struggle. However, factors such as confidence, self-esteem and motivation can all be part of the picture. It is also important to remember that there may be contributory physiological problems, such as those affecting eyesight and hearing.

To illustrate aspects such as the importance of building relationships with children, their confidence, their motivation, and collaboration with parents, consider this comment offered by an experienced teacher who was also the special needs coordinator:

Darren had struggled with his reading throughout the school. I asked if I could read with him one day. It was an uncomfortable experience. His intonation and expression were very low. He stopped and stared when he didn't know a word. If he was stuck on a word, he would sound out every letter. The result of this often didn't give him enough of a clue to the word because he wasn't using the other cueing strategies to support his reading. When I asked him about sections that he had read, he would only offer minimal information. The class teacher felt that I should give him more phonics practice and that perhaps we should try earlier books in the reading scheme. My heart sank because I knew that the boy had had phonics and reading schemes throughout the school. It was clear to me that he already had enough phonic knowledge. Knowing that my daughter had learnt to read at the age of three simply by sharing and discussing books and other texts, I wondered whether a variation on this would work with Darren.

The following academic year he joined my own class having progressed very little. I decided that the first thing I had to tackle was his motivation. I collected ten picture books that I thought he might be interested in which I labelled with green stickers. These books were kept for him alone. The next thing I knew I had to do was to start talking to him about why he didn't like reading. At the time I was in contact with his mum who was quite sceptical that this would work after so many years. I followed these two main ideas of talking to the child and trying to find texts that would motivate him for the best part of the year. When it came to his next assessment, the educational psychologist gave Darren a standardised reading test and was astonished.

I wondered if some extra tuition that he had at home had contributed but his father said that until his motivation changed Darren wasn't prepared to work with a tutor. That child had gone through repeated systematic phonics programmes in the past and they had simply not worked.

Understanding reading difficulties, including dyslexia

The example above illustrates how reading difficulties can be attributed to a range of social and physiological factors. A child with reading difficulties can be defined as one whose reading achievements are significantly below the expected reading development of most children. But the definition of dyslexia is more precise than this: 'Developmental dyslexia is defined as specific and significant impairment in reading abilities, unexplained by any kind of deficit in general intelligence, learning opportunity, general motivation or sensory acuity (Critchley, 1970; World Health Organization).' (Habib, 2000: 2374) The important aspect to remember here is the fact that a child who is dyslexic is not regarded as having problems of the general kinds listed, for example IQ, hence the more specific term of dyslexia (children who have low IQ *and* reading difficulties are given the unfortunate name 'garden variety' poor readers by psychologists).

Although children are tested and registered as dyslexic, research has still not determined the precise nature of dyslexia. Goswami (2010) provides a useful overview of current understandings. From very early in life, babies begin to learn the auditory patterns of speech such as pitch, duration, rhythm, and dynamics. Using this auditory information and their articulatory practice through, for example, babbling, they begin to make sense of the ways that these acoustic patterns represent meaning. In other words, they develop 'phonological representations' of the language or languages that they will eventually speak. Later, phonological awareness – an awareness of the component sounds of words – develops. Once children learn to read an alphabetic script, phonological awareness is refined to the point that the phonemes of individual words can be identified. The quality of the phonological representations that children develop is correlated with later acquisition of literacy. So, both articulatory and auditory processing are important precursors to learning to read. Brain imaging studies have shown that children with phonological difficulties rely more on articulatory networks than other children, probably as a result of compensation for poorer perceptual networks. Goswami (op. cit.) suggests that activities that emphasise rhythm and rhyme, such as nursery rhymes and songs, are likely to help support the development of phonological awareness. She suggests that because appropriately efficient ways of testing for dyslexia (that genuinely account for current research knowledge) are not yet available, all children should experience enriched linguistic and phonological environments. Consequently she does not recommend trying to identify individual children for special programmes. However, as you will see below this recommendation could be at odds with the success that one-to-one programmes have had, although this success may be with struggling readers more generally as opposed to those with the particular problem of dyslexia.

Supporting children with reading difficulties

As a result of Marie Clay's work as early as the 1980s, we have known for many years that sensitive identification of children before the age of six who struggle with reading is one important element. Sensitivity is required not least because the damaging effects on self-esteem for children who are inappropriately labelled are also understood. Clay (1979) outlined a diagnostic survey that includes a range of assessments. One of these is the 'running record': it is important to remember that this is a specific strategy for recording children's ability to read words (→ Chapter 15, 'Assessing reading') rather than the more general meaning suggested by the term. Once identification has taken place the most effective way to support children is through additional support in one-to-one sessions with a knowledgeable and skilled educator. Research evidence of the vital importance of one-to-one support can be seen in the work by Camilli *et al.* (2003) whose reanalysis of a meta-analysis from the National Reading Panel (NRP) in the US also questioned the strength of support for systematic phonics found by the NRP. Further evidence in relation to the importance of skilled one-to-one support can be found in relation to the international success of Marie Clay's approach called 'Reading Recovery', an approach that has been led for many years by the outstanding work of the European Centre for Reading Recovery team at the Institute of Education,

University of London (http://www.ioe.ac.uk/research/4399.html). Robust evidence can also be seen in the meta-analysis by D'Agostino and Murphy (2004) and see also Wyse and Goswami (2008), who found significant experimental trials that had included Reading Recovery as the experimental group in the comparison with control groups and other approaches to reading.

Reading recovery is an early intervention programme for children with reading difficulties and it is important to point out that: 'Most children (80–90%) do not require these detailed, meticulous and special reading recovery procedures or any modification of them. They will learn to read more pleasurably without them.' (Clay, 1979: 47) The teaching procedures for Reading Recovery include a range of ideas for enhancing children's reading. As far as the use of text is concerned, although Clay is critical of the controlled vocabulary of reading schemes (she emphasises the importance of natural language), she does not particularly emphasise the significance of the particular texts that children read.

Clay's procedures include: learning about direction of text and pages; 'locating responses' that support one-to-one correspondence ☞ (e.g. locating words and spaces by pointing or indicating); spatial layout; writing stories; hearing the sounds in words; cut-up stories (i.e. cutting up texts and reassembling them); reading books; learning to look at print; linking sound sequences with letter sequences; word analysis; phrasing and fluency; sequencing; avoiding overuse of one strategy; memory; and helping children who are hard to accelerate.

Another procedure that Clay emphasises is the importance of 'teaching for operations or strategies' (ibid.: 71). Within this is the idea that readers need to be able to monitor their own reading and solve their own problems. It is suggested that teachers should encourage children to explain how they monitor their own reading. The process of explanation helps to consolidate the skills. Clay offers useful examples of language that teachers might use:

Teacher:	What was the new word you read?
Child:	Bicycle.
Teacher:	How did you know it was bicycle?
Child:	It was a bike (semantics).
Teacher:	What did you expect to see?
Child:	A 'b'.
Teacher:	What else?
Child:	A little word, but it wasn't.
Teacher:	So what did you do?
Child:	I thought of bicycle.
Teacher:	(reinforcing the checking) Good, I liked the way you worked at that all by yourself.
Teacher:	You almost got that page right. There was something wrong with this line. See if you can find what was wrong.

Child:	(child silently rereads, checking) I said Lizard but it's Lizard's.
Teacher:	How did you know?
Child:	'Cause it's got an 's'.
Teacher:	Is there any other way we could know? (search further)
Child:	(child reruns in a whisper) It's funny to say 'Lizard dinner'! It has to be Lizard's dinner like Peter's dinner, doesn't it?
Teacher:	(reinforcing the searching) Yes, that was good. You found two ways to check on that tricky new word.

(Clay, 1979: 73–74)

The government's approach in England

Governments in England have fully engaged with Reading Recovery ☞ in the past. In the late 1980s and early 1990s, reading recovery was rolled out nationally. However, in spite of the evidence of success, the national programme was discontinued due to the claim that it was too expensive – although a comprehensive cost–benefit analysis that includes the negative cost of children who continue to struggle is unlikely to have been carried out. Up until 2012, the Department for Education in England was still providing some funding for the International Centre for Reading Recovery but tensions began to emerge with the change to a Conservative-led coalition government in 2010.

The main reason for the tension was the approach to reading imposed by one of the Education Ministers, Nick Gibb, that also resulted in the introduction of the phonics screening check (see Chapter 1, 'The history of English, language, and literacy') as the main means of holding teachers and schools to account. The rationale for the introduction of the test, similar to the rationale for most of the changes to reading policy post-2010, was that synthetic phonics first and foremost was the best way to both ensure that all children learned to read well, and that testing for children's knowledge of phonemes was the best way to identify those children who are struggling with reading. The 'answer' for those children was of course yet more phonics, something that was unlikely to achieve the desired effect, the reasons for which are perhaps evident in the example at the beginning of this chapter, and clearly known from the kind of research evidence that we have addressed in this chapter.

Practice points

- Identify children who are struggling as early as possible.
- Improve the relationship with the child and try to understand and empathise with their particular problems.
- Decisions should be made in terms of time and resources for extra support, including the use of classroom assistants.

Glossary

Dyslexia – a formally recognised condition that results in specific difficulties with reading and writing.

One-to-one correspondence – the understanding that one word on the page corresponds with one spoken word. Evidence comes from finger pointing at words and numbers.

Reading Recovery – a set of techniques developed by Marie Clay designed to eradicate children's reading problems.

References

Camilli, G., Vargas, S. and Yurecko, M. (2003) 'Teaching children to read: The fragile link between science and federal education policy', *Education Policy Analysis Archives*, 11(15). Retrieved 1 March 2006, from http://epaa.asu.edu/epaa/v11n15/.

Clay, M. M. (1979) *The Early Detection of Reading Difficulties*, 3rd edn. Auckland, New Zealand: Heinemann.

D'Agostino, J. and Murphy, J. (2004) 'A meta-analysis of reading recovery in United States schools'. *Educational Evaluation and Policy Analysis*, 26(1): 23–38.

Goswami, U. (2010) 'Phonology, reading, and reading difficulties', in K. Hall, U. Goswami, C. Harrison, S. Ellis and J. Soler (eds) *Interdisciplinary Perspectives on Learning to Read: Culture, Cognition and Pedagogy*. London: Routledge.

Habib, M. (2000) 'The neurological basis of developmental dyslexia: An overview and working hypothesis', *Brain*, 123: 2373–2399.

Wyse, D. and Goswami, U. (2008) 'Synthetic phonics and the teaching of reading', *British Educational Research Journal*, 34(6): 691–710.

Annotated bibliography

Burroughs-Lange, S. (2006) 'Evaluation of reading recovery in London schools: every child a reader 2005–2006'. Retrieved 12 December 2006, from http://ioewebserver.ioe.ac.uk/ioe/cms/get.asp?cid=9263&9263_0=9261
Important evidence on the impact of reading recovery. Includes helpful review of literature. Part of the Institute for Education Reading Recovery site.
L3 ★★

Clay, M. M. (1979) *The Early Detection of Reading Difficulties*, 3rd edn. Auckland, New Zealand: Heinemann.
This gives a full account of how to implement the reading recovery approach. One of the many useful aspects includes information on what a typical tutoring session looks like.
L2 ★★

D'Agostino, J. and Murphy, J. (2004) 'A meta-analysis of reading recovery in United States schools', *Educational Evaluation and Policy Analysis*, 26(1): 23–38.
In-depth analysis of the impact of reading recovery. Carries out statistical analysis of effects of a large number of relevant studies.
L3 ★★★

Chapter 15

Assessing reading

Assessment of children's reading is built on an understanding of reading development. This chapter starts with the importance of one-to-one interaction in assessing reading. It evaluates the importance of understanding children's reading errors (or miscues) and the continuing influence of Goodman's theories. We discuss strategies for assessing reading in group situations. The chapter concludes with some reflections on statutory and standardised tests.

The perceptive assessment of children's reading is built on a strong knowledge of children's likely reading development (→ Chapter 9) and the teacher's ability to observe carefully and interact appropriately. Children's reading can be assessed during one-to-one interaction and small group work (e.g. guided reading). Shared reading in whole class situations (→ Chapter 13) also provides opportunities for the teacher to assess children's reading through the use of differentiated questioning.

There are a variety of strategies that can be used to assess individual readers; we consider reading interviews, observations of children reading, reading with children on a one-to-one basis, observing individuals within a group and using running records and miscue analysis.

Reading interviews

Through conducting reading interviews, the teacher can find out about the child's perceptions of themselves as a reader, their reading habits and interests and general attitude towards reading. When conducting an interview, make sure your pupil is relaxed and comfortable and somewhere where you can both concentrate. You can now find out about their reading in general, for example, where and when they read; likes and dislikes; experience of comics, media and ICT texts; reading at home and school. The questions to ask might include:

Do you like reading? Which books do you like to read/look at? What is your favourite book? What do you have to read at home? Do you go to the library? What kind of books do you choose? Do you read with anyone at home? Do you prefer comics? Why?

Observations of a child reading

Observations are an essential tool for gathering assessment data on a child's current reading ability. An individual child can be observed reading, or being read to individually; in a group; with the class (for example, during shared and guided reading time or when the teacher is reading to the class); reading texts in all curriculum areas; reading work that they have written.

Questions to ask when observing children's reading behaviour include:

- Do they actively seek out books to look at or to be read to them?
- What texts do they choose?
- Do they read intently or flick through texts to avoid engagement?
- Do they spend time in the reading area?
- Do they try to retell a favourite story?
- What strategies do they use to interpret the text?

It is important not to forget early reading behaviours, such as looking at a book the right way round, turning the pages one at a time and retelling a favourite story whilst 'pretending' to read the text, which will be evident in early years settings.

In addition, consider the following points to help focus your observations.

- Is the child reading for enjoyment/information?
- When is the child engaged, confident?
- Can the child read independently or are they dependent on support? Do they prefer reading with an adult?
- Can the child talk with interest and understanding about what has been read?
- In a small group context, does the child take a lead or wait for others? Are they engaged with the text? Do they feel comfortable in a group situation? How do they engage with the group?
- In a whole class context, how does the individual child respond when they are being read to?

Reading with a child one-to-one (→ Chapter 10)

Although it is hard to find time in a busy classroom schedule to read with children on a one-to-one basis, this is still an important strategy in assessing where a child is in their reading. Having selected a book that you think will engage the child's interest, or one that the child has chosen, consider the following:

- Note positive and negative strategies, specific difficulties, understanding of the text, pleasure, etc.
- Discuss the book with the child, noting interest, understanding, awareness of bibliographical features, genre, etc.
- If appropriate, focus on semantic, syntactic and graphophonic cueing strategies. Note how these are used, and where they could be developed, explicitly or implicitly, throughout the child's day. When planning your work within English and other curriculum areas, find opportunities to support and develop these strategies.

Running records and miscue analysis

Running records were a method of assessment devised by Marie Clay as part of her highly successful Reading Recovery programme. They can also be used as a method to assess the reading of children in your class who are not decoding with fluency. Conducting a running record will enable you to discover with individual children:

- which reading strategies are established;
- which reading strategies need to be practised and consolidated;
- which reading strategies need demonstration and development.

A book should be selected that a child can decode at approximately 95% accuracy. As the child reads aloud from the text, the teacher records the reading on a photocopy of the text using a specified coding system, as devised by Clay (1979: 18):

- Tick words read correctly.
- Write incorrect guesses above the word in the text.
- If there is more than one guess, record each of them even if only one letter.
- Write 'SC' (Self Correction) if child corrects previous error.
- If the child makes no response put a dash – above the word.
- If the child has to be told the word, write 'T' above it.
- If the child asks for help, write 'A'. The teacher says 'you try it' first and then enters 'T' for told if the child still can't work out the word.

Here is a short example of how this works in practice: Helen, aged seven, read the following text, 'There was soup for dinner. Chicken soup for all the children' as, 'There is soup for dinner. Children . . . Chicken soup for all the children'. The teacher duly coded this as ✓ 'is' ✓ ✓ ✓ SC ✓ ✓ ✓ ✓ ✓, indicating that the child read the piece accurately apart from substituting the word 'is' for 'was'. Also, when Helen substituted 'children' for 'chicken', she immediately corrected herself when she realised that 'children soup' was very unlikely (except perhaps in a Roald Dahl story!).

Once a child has finished reading for the running record, the teacher might discuss with them some of the miscues made, particularly the substitutions ☞, to determine which cueing strategies the child is currently employing and how they might be taken forward in their reading development.

The great advantage of a running record is that it is immediate, in the sense that special materials are unnecessary (although there are published schemes available with ready made materials). Provided you remember the codings, you can complete one or more records during one-to-one reading, or at any other suitable times of the day. There are limitations, however. Instant coding by the teacher is likely to be inaccurate from time to time, because some utterances by children need greater reflection or at least need to be listened to more than once or twice. The running record is one of the techniques used for teacher assessment at Key Stage 1 for determining children's National Curriculum levels for reading.

An important part of assessing children's reading is how we respond to their mistakes, or miscues ☞. This will be affected by our understanding of the reading process and our understanding of models of how children read. In a seminal paper, Ken Goodman argued that children's reading errors should 'be called miscues, rather than errors, in order to avoid the negative connotation of errors (all miscues are not bad) and to avoid the implication that good reading does not include miscues' (Goodman, 1969: 12). In the paper he put forward a 28-item taxonomy of the kinds of miscues that children frequently made when reading aloud. He also suggested that the reader uses three basic kinds of information: *semantic, syntactic* and *graphophonic* ☞. These three basic kinds of information have in some ways overshadowed the taxonomy of cues and miscues that were the more important aspect of Goodman's paper (→ Chapter 9).

Subsequently, other researchers combined Goodman's taxonomy with different ways of assessing children's miscues such as the Neale Analysis of Reading Ability which is still used today as a standardised reading test. Goodman's theory that children's miscues can tell us useful things about their reading is accepted by many people, but some of his other theory has been more heavily criticised. The most serious of the criticisms is about his assumption that skilled readers are more likely to be influenced by context than less skilled readers. Research has now shown that the reverse is true: *less skilled* readers are more likely to be influenced by context. This is probably because their knowledge of the links between letters and phonemes is underdeveloped.

The three basic kinds of information that Goodman identified are subject to another problem. It is very difficult to identify a clear distinction between the influence of syntactic information and semantic information, and contextual information more generally. It seems to us that appropriate use of contextual information when reading requires use of both syntax, or grammar, *and* meaning (→ Chapter 9 for our thinking on models of reading).

For further information about miscue analysis and Ken and Yetta Goodman's seminal work, refer to http://www.u.arizona.edu/~kgoodman/ where you will find examples of running records.

Assessing reading during small group work

As we explained in Chapter 13, the aim of guided reading sessions is to encourage and extend independent reading skills. Groups of children work together on the same text which is selected to match the reading ability of the group. The teacher leads the session, aiming to address the teaching objectives and the Assessment Focuses for Reading. When deciding on objectives for the group, consider:

- which pupil reading strategies are established (based on your prior assessment);
- which reading strategies need to be practised and consolidated;
- which reading strategies need demonstration and development;
- what the next steps are for the group to develop their understanding of text?

Assessing reading with parents

Observations of children's reading completed during one-to-one reading sessions, or when noteworthy things occur at other times, are sometimes collected in what are called 'reading diaries' (or 'reading journals' or 'logs'). Teachers usually write brief observational jottings, appropriately dated, noting significant features of the child's reading as they occur. Over time, patterns of development and areas for further support become evident.

Reading diaries can be sent home to help parents support their children's reading. If parents are able to write comments, then the diary can offer an even richer picture of the child's reading development. Children too can contribute or keep their own reading diaries. Periodically teachers and other adults may participate in a written dialogue with the child about their reading, the books they like to read in and out of school and even problems they are having with their reading. Some of the comments by children taken from actual diaries read like this: 'I enjoyed this book because it was in English as well as Gujerati' (sic); 'I found the story quite difficult because there were some very long words and lots of names that were a bit hard'; and 'I wish I could read like you, Miss. I enjoy it when you read to us because it makes the stories even better'.

Assessing Pupils' Progress (APP)

APP is the national approach to periodic assessment. APP materials are available for reading, writing, and speaking and listening. APP is a tool used to refine judgements made using assessment for learning strategies, and combines a range of outcomes (written, oral, and observed) to inform a judgement about pupils' levels of attainment. The APP process involves teachers selecting a sample of pupils (usually six: two pupils from each ability group). Each term, teachers review the full range of evidence for each Assessment Focus (AF), usually about six pieces of work including different written genres and curriculum areas. They then refer to the APP assessment criteria and arrive at judgements using the *assessment guidelines* sheet. You may find further information created during the development of APP at http://webarchive.nationalarchives. gov.uk

The Assessment Focuses (AFs) for Reading are:

- **AF1:** use a range of strategies, including accurate decoding of text, to read for meaning.
- **AF2:** understand, describe, select or retrieve information, events or ideas from texts and use quotation and reference to text.
- **AF3:** deduce, infer or interpret information, events or ideas from texts.
- **AF4:** identify and comment on the structure and organisation of texts, including grammatical and presentational features at text level.
- **AF5:** explain and comment on the writers' use of language, including grammatical and literary features at word and sentence level.
- **AF6:** identify and comment on writers' purposes and viewpoints, and the overall effect of the text on the reader.
- **AF7:** relate texts to their social, cultural and historical traditions.

Whereas AF1 and AF2 assess children's ability to decode and their literal understanding of texts, AFs 3 to 7 are helpful in assessing children's reading comprehension (→ Chapter 11). One of the intentions of APP is to be able to identify which AFs children are struggling with and to modify planning accordingly. It also enables teachers to establish where there is insufficient evidence to make a judgement and therefore to again modify planning accordingly.

Statutory tests

The statutory tests (known as SATs) have become an increasingly dominant feature of the curriculum in England. Although they are carried out in Years 2 and 6, their influence stretches far beyond these years because of the target-setting that is required throughout schooling. Teachers of all years in the primary school have increasingly felt pressurised into focusing more and more on key areas that are required by the tests. We include a short analysis of a reading test.

The Key Stage 2 reading test consists of a booklet that children have to read and a series of questions they have to answer. In 2006, the booklet was called *Heart Beat* and was an information text about drumming that included: a short introduction; a short biography of Evelyn Glennie, the world-famous classical percussionist; some information about drumming around the world; and a section on skills needed to become a drummer. The booklet was in full colour, including photos of drums, other percussion instruments and a variety of performers from around the world; as a text, it was something that could interest many children. However, despite the picture of a young person playing kit drums on the front cover, the main information was all about Evelyn Glennie, whose work was less likely to appeal to the majority of children than information focusing, say, on pop music. This highlights a big problem with a national testing system as opposed to a system based on teacher assessment. In the national tests, *one* text has to be chosen for all children, whereas children could be assessed reading and responding to a text of their choice if the teacher were undertaking the assessment. The nature of children's reading differs according to the text they are reading.

As with Key Stage 2 SATs papers in all other years, having read the text in the booklet, pupils then had to write answers to questions. The answers had four different formats: short answers of a word or phrase (these include ticking a box as part of multiple choice); several line answers; longer answers which required a more detailed explanation of the pupil's opinion; and other answers which had different requirements. Question 13 was a question which required inference and a higher level of thought. The teacher booklet explaining the marking criteria included examples of answers from pupils who trialled the tests. The quote below is taken from the guidance. You will see that it starts with the test question followed by the assessment focus that is linked to the question. Examples are then given of answers to the question that would attract different marks.

13. Why do you think many people admire Evelyn Glennie?

up to 3 marks

Assessment focus 3: deduce, infer or interpret information, events or ideas from texts (complex inference).
Possible points might refer to Evelyn's:

- musical ability
- sensory ability
- determination/perseverance
- professional success
- inspiration to others

Award **3 marks** for answers which provide substantial coverage of at least two points, e.g.:

- *I think many people admire her because she is such a talented person and she can sense the notes through her body and it is very interesting, almost as if she is psychic. Also many people may just learn from her example* (sensory ability and inspiration)

Award **2 marks** for answers which **either** explore one of the points above in more detail / with textual support **or** explore two of the points superficially, e.g.:

- *because she is a great musician and also because she can't hear but she still performs and plays successfully* (musical ability and determination)

Award **1 mark** for answers which are **either** very general **or** refer to a very specific detail relating to one of the points above, e.g.:

- *she gives around 110 concerts a year* (success)

It is worth noting that requirements for statutory assessing and reporting arrangements do change on an annual basis. At Key Stage 1, reading assessments are no longer externally marked but provide part of teachers' overall assessment. There is a paper for children working at Level 2 and a separate test for children working towards Level 3.

The Year 1 phonics screening check

In line with the government's strategy of teaching early reading through systematic synthetic phonics (→ Chapter 12), the new statutory phonics screening check for all pupils in Year 1 was introduced in 2012. The purpose of the screening check is to confirm whether individual pupils have learnt phonic decoding to an appropriate standard. Pupils who have not reached this standard should receive support from their school to ensure they can improve their phonic decoding skills. The check consists of a list of 40 words, half of which are non-words, to be read by pupils one-to-one with a teacher they know. The rationale for including non-words is to ensure that pupils are being assessed for their phonic decoding rather than their vocabulary knowledge or visual memory (→ Chapter 1 for a critique of the politics of the screening check).

A note on standardised reading tests

At times it is important to know how well the children in your class read in comparison to others of the same age. Although in theory the statutory assessments should be able to do this, the fact that they change from year to year makes this difficult. Reading tests are standardised by trialling them with large samples of children (typically thousands from a range of backgrounds) in order to identify the typical score that a child of a particular age will score. This enables teachers to compare the children in their class with other children of the same age. Once standardised, the tests remain the same for a number of years. An example of a popular standardised reading test is the NFER-NELSON Group Reading Test II. It is called a group reading test because it can be administered to a whole class or groups of smaller sizes. A sentence completion test consists of 48 items which require the child to fill in the gap in a sentence, for example:

36. He had a _____ cold and stayed indoors.

sight

sling

night

slight

stream

The child has to shade in a small rectangular box next to the word suitable for reading by an optical mark reader. A context comprehension test features a passage of text written in paragraphs, once again with words missing from the sentences (the numbers in the quote below are question numbers):

Charlotte and Emma were sisters. One day they went to see ___ 1 Aunt Susan. The girls were interested in their aunt's sun-room. It had two chairs ___ 2 out of bamboo.

There have been many criticisms of reading tests over the years. Some criticisms have resulted in continuing improvements of reading tests. However, most of the problems with standardised tests can be avoided if the teacher bears in mind that there are acknowledged limitations to their use. Standardised tests offer a summative judgement about a child's reading. They are rarely diagnostic in character. One thing that they *can* help with is in assessing whether a particular approach to the teaching of reading has been successful, particularly if the test information is collected over a period of years.

Practice points
- Ensure your classroom promotes a rich reading environment.
- Carry out reading observations of all the children in your class very early in the year in order to identify those who need help. Talk to the previous class teacher to confirm your judgements.
- Decide the kinds of assessment strategies you will use throughout the year and plan for when they will happen. Adjust your planning regularly based on frequent analysis of the results of your assessments.

Glossary

Miscues – examples of mistakes where children's reading differs from the words in the printed text.

Semantic, syntactic and graphophonic reading cues – mental strategies that people use to read texts. Most commonly described as semantic (using meaning), syntactic (using grammar) and graphophonic (using sound and symbol correspondences).

Substitutions – words guessed in place of unknown printed words.

References

Clay, M. M. (1979) *The Early Detection of Reading Difficulties*, 3rd edn. Auckland, New Zealand: Heinemann.

Goodman, K. (1969) 'Analysis of oral reading miscues: applied psycholinguistics', *Reading Research Quarterly*, 1(3): 9–30.

Reimer, J. (2006) 'Developmental changes in the allocation of semantic feedback during visual word recognition', *Journal of Research in Reading*, 29(2): 194–212.

Annotated bibliography

Clay, M. M. (1979) *The Early Detection of Reading Difficulties*, 3rd edn. Auckland, New Zealand: Heinemann.
Marie Clay created the running record and she shows how its use can feed directly into teaching decisions.
L2 **

Coles, M. and Jenkins, R. (eds) (1998) *Assessing Reading 2: Changing Practice in Classrooms: International Perspectives on Reading Assessment*. London: Routledge.
One of two substantial books that look at the theory and practice of assessment. This book uses case studies to focus on practice and serves as a reminder that assessment is a complex process.
L2 ***

The European Centre for Reading Recovery (ECRR) http://www.ioe. ac.uk/research/4399.html
The impressive results of research internationally into Reading Recovery are backed up by the research and outstanding practice of this home of reading recovery. There should be no doubt in any politician's mind about what is clearly the most effective way to help children who struggle with reading.
L1 ***

Johnson, S. (2011) *Assessing Learning in the Primary Classroom*. Abingdon: Routledge.
Comprehensive guide to assessment from pupil to statutory test to international survey.
L2 ***

Marshall, B. and Wiliam, D. (2006) *English Inside the Black Box*. Glasgow: Letts.
Offers practical ideas for improving formative assessment in the English classroom, including questioning techniques, asking the right questions and listening carefully to how pupils respond.
L2 ★★★

Part IV

Writing

Chapter 16

The development of writing

Historically, the teaching of writing has been much less of a focus than the teaching of reading. However, just as we illustrated for reading, in order to teach writing effectively it is necessary to be aware of how children learn. We return to the evidence from case studies of children (→ Chapter 9, 'The development of reading') in order to look at writing development. This picture of development is followed by a large section on the teaching of writing, including some of the different views that have been expressed in relation to the importance of creativity, expression and choice.

It is important to understand the typical stages of development that children pass through in their writing. This knowledge helps you to pitch your planning and interaction at an appropriate level for the children you are teaching. People who have already experienced such development as teachers and parents are in an advantageous position. However, teachers who are inexperienced need to grasp the fundamental aspects of such development. One of the reasons for this is that it heightens your awareness of what to look for when you have the opportunity to interact with young writers.

As we showed in Chapter 3, there are a number of in-depth case studies of individual children that can help in acquiring knowledge about children's development. Studies of individual children do not act as a blueprint for all children: one of the important things that such case studies show us is that children's experiences vary greatly. However, if we focus on certain key concepts and significant milestones, these can be applied to larger groups of children. These milestones are likely to happen at roughly the same age for many children but there will be significant numbers of children whose development is different. Once again, the stages of development are based on our analysis of case studies of children's writing development which more frequently feature young children's development than older children.

Tables 16.1 to 16.3 illustrate the development of children's writing through the primary school.

Table 16.1 Expectations for a child's writing at age 4

What you can expect	What you can do to help
Understands distinction between print and pictures	Talk about the differences between pictures and print. Show what you do when you write and tell children that you are writing.
Plays at writing	Provide a range of accessible resources. Encourage the use of writing as part of role play.
Assigns meaning to own mark-making	Ask children about their writing and discuss its meaning with them. Set them challenges to write things for you, such as little notes.
Often chooses to write names and lists	Help children to write their name properly. Encourage them to sign their name on greetings cards.
Uses invented spelling	Encourage children to have a go at writing and spelling in their own way. Once they have this confidence help them move towards conventional spellings.
Has knowledge of letter shapes particularly those in child's name	Teach children how to form the letters properly. Teach them how to write their name.
Recognises some punctuation marks	Help them to recognise the difference between letters and punctuation marks.
Knows about direction and orientation of print	Talk to children about left and right, top and bottom. Use your finger to point as you read from time to time. Ask questions to encourage children to show you their knowledge about orientation of print.

Table 16.2 Expectations for a child's writing at age 7

What you can expect	What you can do to help
Occasional interest in copying known texts	Encourage this provided it does not become the main form of writing over time. Use the opportunity to help with letter formation and whole word memory.
Range of genres of chosen writing more limited reflecting specific interests and motivation	Encourage children to explore the things that they are interested in and to write about those topics.

Able to write longer texts such as stories	Children's stamina for writing improves as the conventions like handwriting and spelling get a little easier. They will still need help with structuring their texts as they try to control these longer forms.
Understands the need to make changes to writing	Help children to see how redrafting writing can help them to get better outcomes.
Understands that writing is constructed in sentences	Explain that a sentence is something that makes complete sense on its own.
Word segmentation secure and all phonemes represented in invented spellings	Help children by engaging them with the visual aspects of words. Word games, word chunks, etc. should be the focus to help them understand English spelling.
Use of punctuation for meaning. Full stops used conventionally	Help children to organise their writing in sentences and to remember to check for capital letters and full stops.
Handwritten print of lower and upper case letter shapes secure	Keep an eye on letter formation and remind children from time to time if they are not forming letters conventionally.

Table 16.3 Expectations for a child's writing at age 11

What you can expect	*What you can do to help*
Using information sources and writing to learn	Support the skills of note-taking and/or tabulating information, etc.
Will redraft composition as well as transcription elements	Help children to see the value of redrafting to improve the final product. Support their proof reading skills.
Able to successfully control a range of text forms and have developed expertise in favourites	Encourage experimentation to find types of writing that they enjoy.
Length of writing increasing	Help children to control the larger structural elements such as headings and paragraphs.
Growing understanding of levels of formality in writing	Discuss differences between things like emails to friends and family as opposed to formal letters.
Standard spelling most of the time. Efficient use of dictionaries and spell checking.	Help children to enjoy the wealth of information contained in dictionaries. Show them how to use standard adult dictionaries.
Basic punctuation secure. Aware of a range of other marks	Encourage use of full range of punctuation. Enjoy spotting things like the 'grocer's apostrophe', e.g. apple's and pears.
Presentation and fluency of handwriting differentiated for purpose	Support handwriting with good-quality pens and other implements. Encourage proper typing when using computer keyboard.

We explained in Chapter 9 that linear models of development are necessary but not sufficient models for understanding reading development, the same is true for writing development as the next section reveals.

Cognitive models of writing

Universal patterns of behaviour reflecting a common set of cognitive processing decisions on the part of children have been identified, as is evident from children making marks which reflect the written language of their culture when asked to write, and composing 'signs' when they first start to make associations between the making of marks and the representation of personal meanings (Borzone de Manrique and Signorini, 1998; Levin and Bus, 2003; Scheuer *et al.*, 2006a; Yamagata, 2007; Yang and Noel, 2006). Children's early writing also displays the features of form common to writing in almost any language such as linearity, directionality and presence of distinguishable units.

Working memory is increasingly seen as an important function of the brain which has contributed to our understanding of language processing. It has been proposed that working memory consists of three parts: a phonological loop for storing verbal information; a visuospatial sketchpad for visual information; and a central executive which regulates the other two parts (Hayes, 2006). There is disagreement as to whether some parts of working memory are not involved in the basic decisions of writing processing such as planning, reading and editing, or whether all three parts of working memory are involved at all times (Hayes, 2006). An attractive feature of Hayes' theory is the representation of the individual's cognitive resources as part of 'the task environment' (see Flower and Hayes, 1981).

Neuroscience has enabled us to think further about the potential role of working memory. Berninger and Winn's (2006) model, informed by neuroscientific research, portrays text generation as the two elements of 'transcription' and 'executive functions' both controlled by a third element, working memory. Berninger and Winn (op. cit.) portray working memory as activating long-term memory during planning, composing, reviewing and revising, and activating short-term memory during reviewing and revising output. However, they appropriately caution that most neuroscientific research has addressed transcription processes, with a few studies tackling word generation with and without the constraints of sentence context, but studies have not been undertaken at discourse-level.

Research has also examined the extent to which the effort required by transcription can compromise other aspects of writing (McCutchen, 2006). Evidence suggests that for beginner writers in particular, the heavy demands on working memory lead to limitations of writing output. For example, when trying to compose sentences, handwriting may not be fluent enough for children to record everything they want to say before they start to forget some of their original thoughts (Graham *et al.*, 2008). Being able to write letters automatically and legibly therefore has implications for children's writing proficiency (Ritchey, 2008). Only when automaticity with basic writing skills and handwriting is achieved will children be able to fully focus cognitive resources on aspects such as spelling and compositional demands (Kellogg, 1996). This does not however imply that the teaching of basic writing skills should necessarily happen before, or to the exclusion of, the teaching of other aspects of writing.

The writing environment

Young children show natural curiosity about the nature of written language through living, observing and participating in an environment in which others use print for various purposes (Purcell-Gates, 1996; Dyson, 2001). Factors such as a print-rich environment, informal instruction and reading ability have some effect on the emergence of writing (Dyson, 2001, 2008; Neuman and Dickinson, 2002; Nunes and Bryant, 2004). Children's earliest discoveries about written language are therefore learned through active engagement with both their social and cultural worlds (Rowe, 1994; Gee, 2001; Pellegrini, 2001; Makin and Jones-Diaz, 2002; Barrat-Pugh, 2002; Compton-Lilly, 2006). Neuman and Roskos (1997) argued that participation in writing and reading practices represents an important phase of literacy learning because children come to understand that print is meaningful, and participation enables them to practise what written language is for and how it works. Embedding writing experiences in meaningful activity models several distinctive features about it for young children such as: written text conveys a message; writing is made up of separate words that correspond to spoken utterances; words are made up of individual letters; and, in English, texts are read from left to right. Several research studies have suggested that as a result of such individual and shared exploration, children are able to test their hypotheses about the forms and functions of written language in situational contexts from a very early age (Ferreiro and Teberosky, 1982; Barrat-Pugh, 2002; Rowe, 2008).

   Young children arrive at school with different understandings of what writing is because of their varying exposure to writing experiences (Barrat-Pugh, 2002). Whilst there is a regularity which characterises literacy development, children reach developmental milestones through a variety of different routes (Pellegrini, 2001); each child's pathway into literacy is a distinctive journey shaped by personal, social and cultural factors (Martello, 2002; Rowe, 2008; Scheuer et al., 2006b). Aspects of literacy that children see as most relevant will differ according to the circumstances of their upbringing: 'learning, especially learning an expressive system like written language, is not divorced from one's identity and history but, of necessity, embedded within it.' (Dyson, 2001: 139) For writing to become part of a child's communicative repertoire, children need to be in an environment that allows them opportunities to write. It is the quality and frequency of the literacy-related interactions and activities that children experience at home that makes a difference to children's short- and long-term outcomes (as shown in Wells, 1986; Dunsmuir and Blatchford, 2004).

Cognitive theory and socio-cultural theory seems to converge on the idea that young children's writing features variable mental processing during writing, dependent on the form of writing the child is attempting to use and the point in time during the writing process. This in turn is influenced by the task, and the writing experiences that are part of young children's lives outside formal educational settings.

Towards conventional writing

Drawing is an important precursor to and part of emergent writing (e.g. Ferreiro, 1986; Levin and Bus, 2003; Yamagata, 2007; Yang and Noel, 2006; Lancaster, 2003. Even if children have not learned how to write convention-ally, they are able to distinguish between the two systems of drawing and writing and are therefore able to produce marks based on and associated with the features of each. Levin and Bus (2003: 891) showed that in the early stages the child writes by *drawing* the two-dimensional object (known as 'print') until they begin to understand that writing represents meaning primarily by phonological units of language. As children explore the features of writing, the discovery that some features are distinctive helps children to organise their written materials; for example, moving from a discontinuous linear pattern to a small number of distinguishable elements. It is in this respect that the graphic patterns of writing are being reproduced. Later writing is distinguishable from early drawings in terms of properties such as linearity and segmentation into units.

Yamagata (2007) investigated the process by which representational activity and knowledge about drawing and letter and number writing emerge in Japanese children aged between 21 and 46 months. An example of representational activity in relation to writing is the child's name written in the top left-hand corner of the paper: at this stage, the meaning of what is written is perhaps determined by the place where it appears, or by the child's intention as a writer, rather than by its linguistic features. The main findings of the study were: a) the recognition of representational systems increases with age; b) representational activities corre-spondingly develop with age through several phases; and c) that while children over three can recognise each system correctly, this is not necessarily related to representational activity. By the age of four years, writing has been grasped inter-nally by the child as a particular activity that produces a specific formal output distinct from drawing, in that it is linear and discrete (Yang and Noel, 2006).

A child's knowledge of their name plays a significant role in their early writing development prior to phonological understanding (Haney, 2002). Names provide a way for children to make sense of the print world as they learn to recognise their own name; names also become a natural focus for them as they begin to explore written language (Bloodgood, 1999; Haney, 2002;

Blair and Savage, 2006; Yang and Noel, 2006). Bloodgood (1999) found that the name has the potential to enable children to connect literacy strands in a meaningful way. When faced with a writing task, the child problem-solves, typically by applying and using what they know in order to make meaning of the situation. If all or some of the letters in their name are the only letters they know how to reproduce, children will often reorchestrate that same set of letters intentionally to produce an infinite number of words. Significantly, whilst each message might look similar, children consider them to be different (Ferreiro and Teberosky, 1982).

As young children make the important transition from emergent to conventional writing (building on their knowledge of drawing and writing, and the writing of their name), they are usually receiving formal writing instruction at school. We have established that children have considerable understanding of how to communicate meaningfully via intentional marks they make on the page, and that the transcriptional demands of conventional writing are a particular challenge. One of the fundamental aspects that children must understand in order to progress to conventional writing is knowledge of the alphabetic code (Blair and Savage, 2006), which Goswami (2008) suggests develops as a result of direct teaching rather than through experience prior to schooling, a point which could beneficially be further explored through research. Once the rules of the alphabetic code are internalised, children are able to move from a preoccupation with code acquisition according to conventional grapheme– phoneme correspondence rules, to a concern with orthography (Scheuer et al., 2006b). As far as English orthography is concerned, this requires children to begin learning about the complexity of English spelling; English is a language that is uniquely difficult in this regard, especially in comparison with other languages such as Spanish (→ Chapter 9).

Tolchinsky (2006) argues that children's writing develops at many levels simultaneously and that rather than following a continuum or linear line of development, '. . . what children come to know about texts guides and constrains their knowledge of letters and words, and what they grasp about letter-sound correspondences guides and constrains their way of writing texts' (op. cit., p. 87). These findings provide a challenge to over-prescriptive linear models of development that are commonly adopted in the context of teaching policy documents and school assessment systems.

The teaching of writing

In Chapter 9, 'The development of reading', we described how the pedagogy ☞ of reading teaching had been dominated by the 'reading wars'. As far as writing is concerned, it is much more difficult to identify a central theme to the discussions about teaching. In part, this reflects the fact that writing continues to attract less attention than reading: less research is devoted to writing and there are fewer publications on the subject. Writing also seems to attract less attention in the media although standards of spelling and grammar (→ Chapters 18 and 21) recurrently hit the news. However, overall the disagreements in relation to the teaching of writing have tended to centre on the amount of creativity and self-expression that is desirable and how these should be balanced with acquiring the necessary writing skills. As we work through a number of key moments in the history of writing pedagogy, you will see that this central point about creativity and skills will recur.

Frank Smith (1982: 20) made the distinction shown in Table 16.4 between the composition of writing and transcription. As you will see, the extent to which pupils are allowed to experience the processes of 'getting ideas' is one of the battlegrounds in the teaching of writing.

One aspect of composition is the extent to which children should be required to plan their writing. The process that professional writers go through sheds light on the issue of planning. Carter (1999) collected together the thoughts of a number of fiction writers and included reflections on the routines that they used for writing. Helen Cresswell, a prolific and talented author for both children and adults, describes her way of composing:

> With most of my books I simply write a title and a sentence, and I set off and the road leads to where it finishes. All my books are like journeys or explorations. Behind my desk I used to have this saying by Leo Rosten pinned up on the wall that went 'When you don't know where a road leads, it sure as hell will take you there.' When I first read that, I thought, that's exactly it! That's what happens when I start on my books – I really don't know what's going to happen; it's quite dangerous, in a way. I often put off starting because it seems a bit scary. Yet at the end of the day, I feel that a story has gone where it's meant to have gone.
>
> (Carter, 1999: 118)

Table 16.4 The composition and transcription of writing

Composition (author)	Transcription (secretary)
Getting ideas	Physical effort of writing
Selecting words	Spelling
Grammar	Capitalisation
	Punctuation
	Paragraphs
	Legibility

Source: Reproduced from Smith (1982: 20). Used with permission.

There are other writers who carry out written plans in detail before they write a word:

> Unlike novelists like Brian Moore, who write to discover what happens to their characters, Iris Murdoch writes nothing until she knows how the story will develop:
> 'I plan in enormous detail down to the last conversation before I write the first sentences. So it takes a long time to invent it.'
> (Harthill, 1989: 87)

As you can see, professional writers have different approaches to planning, so it is logical to assume that children need a range of ways into writing. It is not a good idea to insist that every piece of writing that children do should be preceded by a written plan. Many will benefit from frequent opportunities to get stuck into their writing with the minimum of delay.

Creative writing

As a reaction against rather formal approaches, 'creative writing' flourished in the 1960s. One of the most famous texts from this time is Alex Clegg's book *The Excitement of Writing*. Clegg recognised the extensive use – and potentially damaging effect – of published English schemes. As an alternative he showed examples of children's writing

> taken from schools which are deliberately encouraging each child to draw sensitively on his own store of words and to delight in setting down his own ideas in a way which is personal to him and stimulating to those who read what he has written.
> (1964: 4)

The use of artefacts and first-hand experiences is also a well-established means of stimulating writing through a creative writing approach which the following examples illustrate.

A maths lesson was postponed for an hour when it began to hail and the children's collective attention was focused on the sudden change in light, the noise, the heightened sense of unease and danger. Standing outside, underneath a canopy, they began to write what they saw. Rebecca (aged eight) wrote:

Hail

Suddenly, the light changed
Crisp, bright, yellow
I rushed outside and stood
Waiting impatiently

Just as the hail fell
Heavy ricochets
The air smelt, strangely
And the breath was sucked
From my lips
The wind changed the weather vane
And made the bushes dance
In a moment it was gone
The air hung grey empty
The clanging flagpole signalled
All clear

Many children are not able to sustain observational writing in this way, but they should still feel their work has worth and potential. A class of children on a field trip to the Northumbrian coast sat beside the harbour watching the day developing. One girl wrote a series of unrelated observations which neither inspired nor interested her. She was asked to select two or three elements of her writing which might 'feel right' together, and to express them in the smallest space which achieved what she wanted to say. Charlotte wrote:

Soon the tide
And the birds will follow

It took Charlotte some considerable time to arrive at these two lines, and it brings to mind an anecdote from Oscar Wilde. He once said that he had spent the morning working on a piece of writing and by lunch had added a comma. In the afternoon he took it out again.

Protheroe (1978) provided a very useful summary of the impact of creative writing and his paper also signalled some of the criticisms that were emerging. Overall he felt that the creative writing movement was an important one and that 'the emphasis on personal, imaginative writing [needed] to be maintained and extended' (1978: 18). But he felt the model had some weaknesses. One of these weaknesses was the restriction on the forms of writing that were used. The teacher provided a stimulus (such as a piece of music or visual art) which was followed by an immediate response, and this implied brief personal forms of writing such as a short descriptive sketch or a brief poem. The model did not encourage the writing of other forms such as argument, plays, or even short stories. Protheroe recommended that:

the stimulated writing is to be seen *not* as the end-product, but as a stage in a process. Pupils need to be helped to develop their work, and to learn from each other as well as from the teacher.

(ibid.: 18)

Figure 16.1 Britton's categorisation of forms of writing.

Source: Reproduced from *Language and Learning*. Harmondsworth: Allen Lane/The Penguin Press, 1970, second edition 1972. Copyright © James Britton, 1970, 1972.

By the end of the 1970s, concerns were growing about the emphasis on 'feeling' in writing teaching and the fact that much of the creative stimuli required an immediate response which did not allow for suitable reworking or redrafting. Allen (1980) pointed out that too much focus on expressive writing could lead to a lack of emphasis on more 'abstract modes'. At this time it was suggested that the teaching of writing required tighter structures that were deemed to be missing from the creative writing ideas.

One of the influential thinkers of the period, James Britton, proposed that writing could be categorised into several key forms (Figure 16.1). Britton offers a scientific report as one example of transactional writing ☞. He argues that this kind of writing 'may elicit the statement of other views, of counterarguments or corroborations or modifications, and is thus part of a chain of interactions between people' (1970: 175). He contrast this with poetic writing where the reader is invited to share a particular verbal construct ☞. The sharing of the writer's thoughts in poetic writing does not 'elicit interaction' in the same way that transactional writing does.

Britton suggested that most of children's writing produced in the primary school is expressive writing. But it develops, through Britton's transitional categories (2 and 4), towards transactional and poetic forms as they gain greater experience and control over their writing. Britton argued that children's expressive writing needs to adapt to the more public writing of transactional and poetic forms. Transactional writing needs to be more explicit, for the unknown reader. Poetic writing on the other hand emphasises implicit meanings in order to create 'sounds, words, images, ideas, events, feelings' (1970: 177). At this time there was a feeling that expressive writing could and should be a foundation for other more abstract forms. However, overall, Allen (1980) maintains that the mid- to late 1970s were characterised by uncertainty and lack of consensus on approaches to the teaching of writing.

Developmental writing

The creative writing movement can be seen as linked with philosophies such as those of Rousseau who advocated that children's free expression was vital. But there was a lack of research evidence to support claims about children's 'natural' development. One of the reasons that in-depth case studies of individual children became important was that they documented children's natural development as language users. This kind of data was also collected from larger groups of children. Harste *et al.* (1984) were able to extend our knowledge of children's writing by looking at three- and four-year-olds. Their conclusions signalled concern about the lack of 'uninterrupted' writing in most early years settings. One of the striking features of their work was the researchers' ability to focus on the positive features of early writing rather than the deficits: an extract from 'Lessons from Latrice' – a chapter from their book – is shown in Figure 16.2.

The researchers initially confessed to being more unsure about Latrice's writing than any of the other children they studied: she was developmentally the least experienced child that they encountered. The researchers asked Latrice to write her name and anything else that she could write; she was then

Uninterrupted Writing

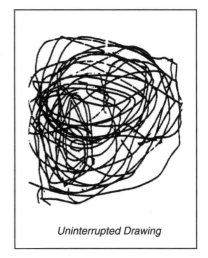

Uninterrupted Drawing

Name

Figure 16.2 Samples of Latrice's writing.

Source: Reproduced from Harste *et al.* (1984) *Language Stories and Literary Lessons*, Oxford: Heinemann. Used with permission.

asked to draw a picture of herself. By positively and actively searching for evidence of Latrice's achievements they were able to understand her writing in great depth. The following is a list of some of the knowledge that Latrice had already acquired:

- Latrice was aware of how to use writing implements and paper.
- She understood and demonstrated the difference between writing and pictures.
- She switched between writing and drawing as a strategy to maintain the flow of her writing.
- Each new mark represented a new or different concept.
- She had developed some knowledge of the importance of space in relation to text.
- She was aware of the permanence of meaning in relation to written language.

Another important point that Harste *et al.* made is that judgements about children's writing based on the final product do not give us enough information about their writing achievements. It is only by analysing the process of writing, in addition to the product, that valid information can be gathered.

The research evidence on children's natural literacy development led to new theories on writing pedagogy. It was argued that as children seemed to develop to a large extent by using their own natural curiosity and ability, perhaps formal teaching should take account of this reality. The theories of 'emergent literacy' developed alongside approaches such as 'developmental writing'. The use of the term 'emergent literacy' in education was popularised by Hall (1987) in his book *The Emergence of Literacy*. The basis of the philosophy is the notion of the child as an active and motivated learner who experiments with a wide range of written forms out of a sense of curiosity and a desire to learn. Hall described emergent literacy as follows:

> It implies that development takes place from within the child . . . 'emergence' is a gradual process. For something to emerge there has to be something there in the first place. Where emergent literacy is concerned this means the fundamental abilities children have, and use, to make sense of the world . . . things usually only emerge if the conditions are right. Where emergent literacy is concerned that means in contexts which support, facilitate enquiry, respect performance and provide opportunities for engagement in real literacy acts.
>
> (1987: 9)

The theory of emergent literacy was very closely linked with the practice of developmental writing. The following list identifies some of the key features of developmental writing and was influenced by Browne's (1996: 21) points that characterise such writing:

1   Builds on children's literacy experience prior to coming to school.
2   Encourages independent writing from day one of the nursery.
3   Modelling is provided by physical resources and the actions of the teacher.
4   Transcription errors are dealt with after the meaning has been established.
     A smaller number of errors are corrected but each one in more detail.
5   Learning to write developmentally can be slow but results in motivation
     for future writing.
6   Writing tasks emphasise purpose and real reasons.
7   Children have time to develop pieces of writing in depth.
8   The confidence to take risks is encouraged.

Developmental writing differs from the creative writing of the 1960s and 1970s
in two main ways. Both approaches share the recognition that children must
be given opportunities to carry out uninterrupted writing which uses their
previous knowledge and experience. However, with developmental writing
there is a stronger expectation that the teacher will interact, particularly with
individual children, in order to take learning forward. The second difference
relates to the first in that the teacher's interaction during developmental writing
is based on a high level of knowledge about common developmental patterns
in the children's writing and this informs the focus of their interaction. With
these clearer pictures of development came different and more realistic expectations of children's learning.

The process approach to writing

The uncertainty of the 1970s was finally transformed by the process writing of
the 1980s. The work of the New Zealander Donald Graves became very influential, culminating in international recognition for his work and great demand
for him as a keynote speaker. Czerniewska (1992: 85) described Graves as 'one
of the most seductive writers in the history of writing pedagogy'. Graves's
approach to writing became known as the 'process approach' and had a significant influence on the teaching of writing in the UK. It is difficult to assess
exactly how many schools and teachers took up the approach in the UK but,
for example, the National Writing Project and the Language in the National
Curriculum Project both involved many schools in the UK, and it is clear from
their reports of practice that the process approach was influential. Frank Smith
was also very popular at the time and although his theories on reading
have attracted some severe criticism, his theories on writing, particularly the
separation between composition and transcription, have remained largely
unchallenged.

It has been argued that writing is learned by writing, by reading, and by
perceiving oneself as a writer. The practice of writing develops interest and
with the help of a more able collaborator provides opportunity for

discovering conventions relevant to what is being written . . . None of this can be taught. But also none of this implies that there is no role for a teacher. Teachers must play a central part if children are to become writers, ensuring that they are exposed to informative and stimulating demonstrations and helping and encouraging them to read and to write. Teachers are influential, as models as well as guides, as children explore and discover the worlds of writing – or decide that writing is something they will never voluntarily do inside school or out.

(Smith, 1982: 201)

Smith expresses some of the key ideas of the process approach and particularly the notion of children being regarded as writers from the start. However, the idea of the teacher as primarily a demonstrator, as role model, and as an 'encourager' has received repeated criticism because of the perception that this does not involve direct instruction. Graves's work (which fitted with Smith's ideas) developed classroom routines which turned such theories into a practical reality for many teachers.

One of the fundamental principles of Graves's process approach was downplayed in the UK. He was quite clear that children needed to be offered choices in their writing.

Children who are fed topics, story starters, lead sentences, even opening paragraphs as a steady diet for three or four years, rightfully panic when topics have to come from them . . . Writers who do not learn to choose topics wisely lose out on the strong link between voice and subject . . . The data show that writers who learn to choose topics well make the most significant growth in both information and skills at the point of best topic. With best topic the child exercises strongest control, establishes ownership, and with ownership, pride in the piece.

(Graves, 1983: 21)

This choice was not the restricted kind offered when a teacher has decided the form of writing. Graves advocated that children should select the topic and form of the writing. Wyse (1998) carried out the first research and book-length publication about the process approach at a time when few researchers were focusing on the teaching of writing. The book *Primary Writing* included evidence of the subtly different ways that teachers in England used the process approach compared to those characterised by Graves.

Genre theory

In the late 1980s, the popularity and optimism of the process approach began to be attacked mainly by a group of Australian academics called the 'genre theorists'. The tide began to turn away from the importance of self-expression towards greater emphasis on skills and direct instruction. The three authors who perhaps have been referred to most in relation to genre theory are J. R. Martin, Frances Christie and Joan Rothery. One of the key texts from 1987 was *The Place of Genre in Learning*, in which these three authors put forward some of their ideas as a response to other authors in the book. They also offered some criticisms of the process approach.

In a section of Martin *et al.*'s chapter they examine the notion of 'freedom' during the process approach. They ask a series of important questions:

> What is freedom? Is a progressive process writing classroom really free? Does allowing children to choose their own topics, biting one's tongue in conferences and encouraging ownership, actually encourage the development of children's writing abilities?
>
> (Martin *et al.*, 1987: 77)

To answer these questions, the authors report on a school in the Australian Northern Territory with a large population of Aboriginal children. They claimed that over the course of the year the children had only written about one of four topics: '(a) visiting friends and relatives; (b) going hunting for bush tucker; (c) sporting events; (d) movies or TV shows they have seen' (ibid.: 77). This example is used to cast doubts on the effectiveness of the process approach claiming that the range of forms that children choose is limited. However, as Wyse's (1998) research showed, the process approach can have the opposite effect. The following is a snapshot of children's writing carried out during a writing workshop. It also gives a contextual background pointing to the origin of the idea and indication of the nature of teacher support given during a writing conference:

Computer Games and How to Cheat
The two pupils came up with the idea. The teacher suggested a survey of other children in the school who might be able to offer ways of getting through the levels on computer games. The teacher also suggested a format which would serve as a framework for the writing about each game.

A Book of Patterns
Self-generated idea with the teacher offering guidance on the amount of text that would be required and the nature of that text.

Tools Mania
A flair for practical design technology projects resulted in one of the pair of pupils choosing this topic which involved writing a manual for the use of tools. Both pupils found the necessary expository writing a challenge.

The New Girl
The girl herself was new to the school and this title may have provided her with a means of exploring some of her own feeling when she first arrived.

Manchester United Fanzine
This was a particularly welcome project as it involved three girls working on an interest they had in football. It was an opportunity to challenge the stereotypes connected with football. The teacher set a strict deadline as the project seemed to be growing too big and also suggested the girls send the finished magazine to the football club to see what they thought.

Football Story
The pupil worked unaided only requesting the teacher's support to check transcription.

A Book of Children's Games
Using a book from home, the pupil chose her favourite games and transcribed them in her own words.

Secret Messages
Various secret messages were included in the book which the reader had to work out. This was aimed at the younger children and involved a series of descriptions of unknown objects which the reader had to find around the school.

Kitten for Nicole
This was an advanced piece of narrative; the teacher made minor suggestions for improving the ending. Unfortunately the child decided she didn't like the text and started on a new one without publishing this.

Book for Young Children
The two boys used pop-art style cartoons for the illustrations as a means of appealing to the younger children. The teacher gave some input on the kinds of material that were likely to appeal to the younger children. One of the pair tended to let the other do most of the work and the teacher encouraged the sharing out of tasks.

Football Magazine
There had been an epidemic of football magazines and the teacher made a decision that this was to be the last one for a time in order to ensure a balance of forms. The two boys used ideas from various professional magazines combining photographs with their own text.

Information about Trains
Great interest in one of the school's information books which included impressive pull-out sections was the stimulus for this text. At the time the work in progress consisted of a large drawing of a train. The teacher had concerns that concentration on the drawing could become a strategy for avoiding writing.

The Magic Coat
An expertly presented dual-language story which had been written with help from the child's mother for the Urdu script. The home computer had also been used to create borders and titles. The teacher's role simply involved taking an interest in the progress.

Catchphrase
A pupil's doodling had given the teacher an idea for an activity which involved devising catchphrases based on the television programme. This pupil decided to compile a book of her own catchphrases.

Chinwag
Originally two pupils had been encouraged to devise and sell a school magazine. This included market research around the school, design, word processing, editing other children's contributions, selling, accounting, etc. This was a large-scale project and the original editors felt they would like to delegate the responsibility for the second issue to someone else, so two new editors took over.

Newspaper
The idea came from the two pupils but coincided fortuitously with a competition organised by the local paper encouraging students to design their own paper. The children asked various people around the school to offer stories. Layout became an important issue. The children brought in their own camera and took pictures to illustrate their text. BBC and Acorn computers were both used, necessitating understanding of two different word processors.

Modern Fairy Tale
The two pupils were struggling for an idea so the teacher suggested they contact another school to find out the kinds of books they liked with a view to writing one for them. The school was in a deprived area and had many more bilingual children than the two pupils were used to. They realised that their initial questionnaire would need modification if it was to be used again. The children at the other school expressed a preference for traditional stories so the two pupils decided to write a modern fairy tale. They were encouraged by the teacher to ask the opinion of bilingual peers on suitable subject matter and some information about India.

Joke Book
The two pupils surveyed the children in the school for good jokes. This was a popular title and had been done before in the course of the year.

Knightrider
A book based on the favourite television programme of the pupil.

It can be seen from this list that the children were involved in a large range of ideas and formats. Many of the ideas are firmly rooted in the children's interests and culture. A significant proportion of the texts involved children collaborating in twos or threes as well as those children who wrote individually. The flexibility of the workshop allowed for a range of groupings that were influenced by the piece of writing concerned and the children's social needs. This organisation also reflected the nature of language and literacy as a social phenomenon.

Writing workshops offer the potential for a much greater range of texts which are created using the children's intrinsic motivation. Another major benefit is the opportunity for study in depth over a long period of time. Set written tasks often have a deadline, too often this can be to start and finish on the same day. With writing workshops, the session is timetabled and the children decide on the task. This means that the children are thinking about their writing prior to the day itself. Often they will be working on texts at home (an important test of their interest in school activities) which they bring in to continue. Having the time to continue with a text for as long as it takes is an important principle. The result can be texts which are longer and written with more thought.

In spite of a number of significant criticisms (Barrs, 1991; Cairney, 1992), the views of the genre theorists proved to be influential. Consequently, between 1998 and 2010 genre theories were a dominant feature of the National Literary Strategy in England. There was an equal emphasis on fiction and non-fiction that had been informed by the view that there was too much story writing happening in primary schools. The goals for written composition no longer emphasised personal choice, writing to interest and excite readers, finding a vehicle for expression, writing to explore cross-curricular themes, writing as art, but were much more about the analysis of genre structures. The importance of writing for real purposes and reasons in order to communicate meaning was replaced by an emphasis on textual analysis as the main stimulus for composition.

Developing written argument

One of the characteristics of the more recent research on writing pedagogy is that much has been done by looking at non-fiction genres but less on the writing of fiction and very little on forms of writing such as poetry. Andrews *et al.*'s (2006) systematic review looked at the writing of argumentative non-fiction writing. Their main findings with regard to the context for writing teaching were that the following were important:

- A writing process model in which students are encouraged to plan, draft, edit and revise their writing.
- Self-motivation (personal target-setting as part of self-regulated strategy development).
- Some degree of cognitive reasoning training in addition to the natural cognitive development that takes place with maturation.
- Peer collaboration, thus modelling a dialogue that (it is hoped) will become internal and constitute 'thought'.

(Andrews *et al.*, 2006: 32)

They also suggested some specific interventions that were successful, including support to use the structures and devices that aid the composition of argumentative writing; the use of oral argument to inform the written argument; identification of explicit goals including the audience for the writing; teacher modelling; and the teacher coaching writing during the process. Andrews *et al.* also point out that the recommendations were not universally shared by the studies that they looked at in their systematic review of research studies.

One of the limitations of these outcomes is that the recommendations for practice cannot be related to the writing of fiction or poetry. At the heart of these and other forms is the use of imagination, and the extent of the originality and quality of ideas are paramount concerns. But these are measureable only if children are actually given choices over the topic and form of their writing. The links between genre theories, structured teaching and individuality were explicitly addressed by Donovan and Smolkin (2002). Their study examined the use of scaffolding in a range of writing tasks including story writing and non-fiction writing. One of their key findings based on evidence that writers' personal interests could result in improved writing was about the importance of 'author aim', which was explained as a keen sense of the audience for the writing linked with personal intentions and motives:

> Author aim reintroduces individuality to the writing landscape, a point with which certain Systemic Functional linguists [the theoretical tradition to which the genre theorists were linked] were not particularly comfortable . . . we are not distressed by the idea of instructing children in form. We are, however, concerned that individuals, authors, and their aims receive so little focus in considerations of structure-based instruction.
>
> (ibid.: 462)

This chapter has explored the teaching of writing from an interdisciplinary cognitive and socio-cultural perspective consistent with the book's theoretical framework (→ Chapter 2). Its theoretical ideas can also be seen supported in recent experimental trial research. Research such as that by Graham (2010) has provided trial evidence that the combination of a focus on writing processes (such as the process approach) with instruction for writing strategies is the most effective way to teach writing. As we argue in this book, pupil ownership (that is related to motivation) is the other vital aspect of such writing teaching. Is it important for children to have opportunities to make decisions? Research has addressed that question. However, this matter is also a question of values. You may feel that offering genuine choices frequently during a child's early years and primary schooling is ethically necessary and that this could result in children being more motivated to write.

Practice points

- Improve your observation and interaction skills by increasing your knowledge of writing development.
- Make decisions on how and when you will offer choices.
- Use your observations to adjust your planning for writing so that children's needs are met.

Glossary

Construct – in this context the word is a noun – as opposed to a verb – and means a specific way of thinking about something.
Pedagogy – approaches to teaching.
Transactional writing – concerned with getting things done, e.g. information, instructions, persuasion, etc.

References

Allen, D. (1980) *English Teaching Since 1965: How Much Growth?* London: Heinemann Educational Books.

Andrews, R., Torgerson, C. J., Low, G., McGuinn, N. and Robinson, A. (2006) 'Teaching argumentative non-fiction writing to 7–14 year olds: a systematic review of the evidence of successful practice', Technical report. *Research Evidence in Education Library.* Retrieved 29 January 2007, from http://eppi.ioe.ac.uk/cms/.

Barrat-Pugh, C. (2002) 'Children as writers', in L. Makin and C. Jones-Diaz (eds) *Literacies in Early Childhood: Challenging Views, Challenging Practice.* NSW: MacLennan & Petty.

Barrs, M. (1991) 'Genre theory: what's it all about?' *Language Matters,* 1991/92(1): 9–16.

Berninger, V. W. and Winn, W. D. (2006) 'Implications of advancements in brain research and technology for writing development, writing instruction, and educational evolution' in S. Graham, C. A. MacArthur and J. Fitzgerald (eds) *Handbook of Writing Research*. New York: The Guilford Press.

Blair, R. and Savage, R. (2006) 'Name writing but not environmental print recognition is related to letter-sound knowledge and phonological awareness in pre-readers', *Reading and Writing*, 19: 991–1016.

Bloodgood, J. (1999) 'What's in a name? Children's name writing and literacy acquisition', *Reading Research Quarterly*, 34(3): 342–367.

Borzone de Manrique, A. M. and Signorini, A. (1998) 'Emergent writing forms in Spanish', *Reading and Writing*, 10: 499–517.

Britton, J. (1970) *Language and Learning*. Harmondsworth: Penguin.

Browne, A. (1996) *Developing Language and Literacy 3–8*. London: Paul Chapman.

Cairney, T. (1992) 'Mountain or mole hill: the genre debate viewed from "Down Under" ', *Reading*, 26(1): 23–29.

Carter, J. (1999) *Talking Books: Children's Authors Talk about the Craft, Creativity and Process of Writing*. London: Routledge.

Clegg, A. B. (1964) *The Excitement of Writing*. London: Chatto & Windus.

Compton-Lilly, C. (2006) 'Identity, childhood culture, and literacy learning: A case study', *Journal of Early Childhood Literacy*, 6(1): 57–76.

Czerniewska, P. (1992) *Learning about Writing*. Oxford: Blackwell.

Department for Education and Employment (DfEE) (1998) *National Literacy Strategy Framework for Teaching*. London: DfEE.

Donovan, C. and Smolkin, L. (2002) 'Children's genre knowledge: an examination of K–5 students' performance on multiple tasks providing differing levels of scaffolding', *Reading Research Quarterly*, 37(4): 428–465.

Dunsmuir, S. and Blatchford, P. (2004) 'Predictors of writing competence in 4- to 7-year old children', *British Journal of Educational Psychology*, 74: 461–483.

Dyson, A. (2001) 'Writing and children's symbolic repertoires: development unhinged', in S. B. Neuman and D. K. Dickinson (eds) *Handbook of Early Literacy Research*. New York: The Guilford Press.

Dyson, A. (2008) 'Staying in the (curricular) lines: practice constraints and possibilities in childhood writing', *Written Communication*, 25(1): 119–157.

Ferreiro, E. (1986) 'The interplay between information and assimilation in beginning literacy', in W. Teale and E. Sulzby (eds) *Emergent Literacy: Writing and Reading*. Norwood, NJ: Ablex.

Ferreiro, E. and Teberosky, A. (1982) *Literacy Before Schooling*. Portsmouth, NH: Heinemann.

Flower, L. and Hayes, J. R. (1981) 'A cognitive process theory of writing', *College English*, 46(2): 99–117.

Gee, J. P. (2001) 'A sociocultural perspective in early literacy development', in S. B. Neuman and D. K. Dickinson (eds) *Handbook of Early Literacy Research*. New York: The Guilford Press.

Goswami, U. (2008) *Cognitive Development: The Learning Brain*. Hove: Psychology Press.

Graham, S. (2010) 'Facilitating writing development', in D. Wyse, R. Andrews and J. Hoffman (eds) *The Routledge International Handbook of English, Language and Literacy Teaching*. London: Routledge.

Graham, S., Harris, K. R., Mason, L., Fink-Chorzempa, B., Moran, S. and Saddler, B. (2008) 'How do primary grade teachers teach handwriting?', *Reading and Writing*, 21: 49–69.

Graves, D. H. (1983) *Writing: Teachers and Children at Work*. Portsmouth, NH: Heinemann Educational Books.

Hall, N. (1987) *The Emergence of Literacy*. Sevenoaks: Hodder & Stoughton.

Haney, M. R. (2002) 'Name writing: A window into the emergent literacy skills of young children', *Early Childhood Education Journal*, 30(2): 101–105.

Harste, J. C., Woodward, V. A. and Burke, C. L. (1984) *Language Stories and Literacy Lessons*. Portsmouth, NH: Heinemann Educational Books.

Harthill, R. (1989) *Writers Revealed. Eight Contemporary Novelists Talk About Faith, Religion and God*. New York: Peter Bedrick Books.

Hayes, J. R. (2006) 'New directions in writing theory', in C. MacArthur, S. Graham and J. Fitzgerald (eds) *Handbook of Writing Research*. New York: The Guilford Press.

Kellogg, R. T. (1996). 'A model of working memory in writing', in C. M. Levy and S. Ransdall (eds) *The Science of Writing: Theories, Methods, Individual Differences and Applications*. Hillsdale, NJ: Lawrence Erlbaum Associates.

Lancaster, L. (2003) 'Moving into literacy: How it all begins', in N. Hall, J. Larson and J. Marsh (eds) *Handbook of Early Childhood Literacy*. London: Sage.

Lancaster, L. (2007) 'Representing the ways of the world: how children under three start to use syntax in graphic signs', *Journal of Early Childhood Literacy*, 7(2): 123–154.

Levin, I. and Bus, A. G. (2003) 'How is emergent writing based on drawing? Analyses of children's products and their sorting by children and mothers', *Child Psychology*, 39(5): 891–905.

Makin, L. and Jones-Diaz, C. (2002) *Literacies in Early Childhood: Challenging Views, Challenging Practice*. NSW: MacLennan & Petty.

McCutchen, D. (2006) 'Cognitive factors in the development of children's writing', in C. A. MacArthur, S. Graham and J. Fitzgerald (eds) *Handbook of Writing Research*. New York: The Guilford Press.

Martello, J. (2002) 'Many roads through many modes: becoming literate in early childhood', in L. Makin and C. Jones-Diaz (eds) *Literacies in Early Childhood: Challenging Views, Challenging Practice*. NSW: MacLennan & Petty.

Martin, J. R., Christie, F. and Rothery, J. (1987) 'Social processes in education: a reply to Sawyer and Watson (and others)', in I. Reid (ed.) *The Place of Genre in Learning*. Victoria: Deakin University.

Neuman, S. B. and Dickinson, D. K. (eds) (2001) *Handbook of Early Literacy Research*. New York: The Guilford Press.

Neuman, S. B. and Roskos, K. (1997) 'Literacy knowledge in practice: contexts of participation in young writers and readers', *Reading Research Quarterly*, 32(1): 10–32.

Nunes, T. and Bryant, P. (2004) *Handbook of Children's Literacy*. Dordrecht: Kluwer Academic Publishers.

Pellegrini, A. D. (2001) 'Some theoretical and methodological considerations in studying literacy in social context', in S. B. Neuman and D. K. Dickinson (eds) *Handbook of Early Literacy Research*. New York: The Guilford Press.

Protheroe, R. (1978) 'When in doubt, write a poem', *English in Education*, 12(1): 9–21.

Purcell-Gates, V. (1996). 'Stories, coupons, and the TV guide: relationships between home literacy experiences and emergent literacy knowledge', *Reading Research Quarterly*, 31(4): 406–428.

Ritchey, K. D. (2008) 'The building blocks of writing: learning to write letters and spell words', *Reading and Writing*, 21: 27–47.

Rowe, D. W. (1994) *Preschoolers As Authors: Literacy Learning in the Social World of the Classroom*. New York: Hampton Press.

Rowe, D. W. (2008) 'The social construction of intentionality: two-year-olds' and adults' participation at a preschool writing center', *Research in Teaching*, 42(4): 387–434.

Scheuer, N., De la Cruz, M., Pozo, J. I., Huarte, M. F. and Sola, G. (2006a) 'The mind is not a black box: children's ideas about the writing process', *Learning and Instruction*, 16: 72–85.

Scheuer, N., De la Cruz, M., Pozo, J. I. and Neira, S. (2006b) 'Children's autobiographies of learning to write', *British Journal of Educational Psychology*, 76: 709–725.

Shayer, D. (1972) *The Teaching of English in Schools 1900–1970*. London: Routledge and Kegan Paul.

Smith, F. (1982) *Writing and the Writer*. Portsmouth, NH: Heinemann Educational Books.

Tolchinsky, L. (2006). 'The emergence of writing', in C. A. MacArthur., S. Graham and J. Fitzgerald (eds) *Handbook of Writing Research*. New York: The Guilford Press.

Wells, G. (1986) *The Meaning Makers: Children Learning Language and Using Language to Learn*. London: Hodder & Stoughton.

Wray, D. and Lewis, M. (1997) *Extending Literary: Children Reading and Writing Non-fiction*. London: Routledge.

Wyse, D. (1998) *Primary Writing*. Buckingham: Open University Press.

Yamagata, K. (2007) 'Differential emergence of representational systems: drawings, letters, and numerals', *Cognitive Development*, 22: 244–257.

Yang, H. C. and Noel, A. M. (2006) 'The developmental characteristics of four-and-five-year-old pre-schoolers' drawings: an analysis of scribbles, placement patterns, emergent writing, and name writing in archived spontaneous drawing samples', *Journal of Early Childhood Literacy*, 6(2): 145–162.

Annotated bibliography

Andrews, R., Torgerson, C. J., Low, G., McGuinn, N. and Robinson, A. (2006) 'Teaching argumentative non-fiction writing to 7–14 year olds: a systematic review of the evidence of successful practice', Technical report. *Research Evidence in Education Library*. Retrieved 29 January 2007, from http://eppi.ioe.ac.uk/cms/.
Offers conclusions on effective pedagogy for the teaching of written argument.
L3 ★★★

Bissex, G. L. (1980) *GNYS At WRK: A Child Learns to Write and Read*. Cambridge, MA: Harvard University Press.
An extremely thorough and insightful account of one child's development. A rich picture is combined with knowledgeable academic analysis: an important book.
L2 ★★

Donovan, C. and Smolkin, L. (2002) 'Children's genre knowledge: an examination of K–5 students' performance on multiple tasks providing differing levels of scaffolding', *Reading Research Quarterly*, 37(4): 428–465.
This study provides evidence in relation to the importance of pupil choice in relation to their writing.
L3 ★★★

Graham, S. (2010) 'Facilitating writing development', in D. Wyse, R. Andrews and J. Hoffman (eds) *The Routledge International Handbook of English, Language and Literacy Teaching*. London: Routledge.
A very clear account of the implications for practice that emerge from experimental trial evidence on what works in the teaching of writing.
L3 ★★★

Chapter 17

Routines for writing

> The aim of writing teaching is to develop motivated and independent writers. This chapter illustrates some of the practical techniques that teachers need to adopt to support this aim. We explore ways that writing can be stimulated using a range of approaches, including the use of writing journals.

How do we move children from having no idea of what to write to being thoroughly engaged in the writing process, like this ten-year-old child who said, following a school visit to a museum: 'I started off with no clue at all what to do, but then some thoughts came into my head and it just went down my arm to the pen and onto the page . . .' One of the key questions when planning the teaching of writing is 'what kind of stimulus should I offer?'. In other words, the teacher has to decide what kind of encouragement, activities and experiences children need in order to help them to write. These decisions should be affected by consideration of children's motivation. Most teachers make the sensible assumption that when children are not motivated, they do not learn as well as they could.

When planning activities to stimulate children's writing, it is helpful to think of a continuum between loosely structured and tightly structured approaches (see Figure 17.1).

Tightly structured approaches prescribe very clearly the kind of texts or extracts of texts that children are expected to produce. Loosely structured approaches give children much more opportunity to make choices about their writing. As an example of loosely structured approaches, the *process approach* has an enviable track record in motivating children to write and is based on establishing authorship in the classroom supported by a publishing process. The most important feature of the 'process approach' to teaching writing is that children are offered choice over what to write. This is not just choice within a genre ☞ prescribed by the teacher, but real choice over the topic and type of

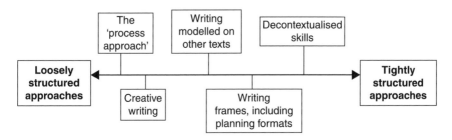

Figure 17.1 Writing approaches continuum.

writing. One of the classic techniques is to ask children to generate a list of five things that they would like to write, then for them to choose one and get writing. The key elements of the process approach are regular *writing workshops*; a publishing cycle in the classroom; writing seen as a process that requires drafting and redrafting; extended opportunities for writing to completion; writing with real audiences in mind; mini-lessons to work on writing skills and understanding; and one-to-one interaction with the teacher to support writing.

Lambirth and Goouch (2006) argue that a number of features act as motivating factors for children in preparation for writing and during writing. These include:

- authentic contexts for writing;
- choice of content, genre and audience;
- reference to 'more knowledgeable others';
- access to models for writing;
- freedom to use cultural connections;
- access to support for skills development;
- access to a range and choice of resources for writing.

This highlights the importance of preparing children for writing. Stimuli you might use include: visual images, including pictures, photographs, and film; music; children's literature; artefacts; first-hand experiences, including school trips; writing warm-ups; writing games; role play and drama; talk before writing; story boxes and bags. For example, if you were to use children's literature as a stimulus, texts that are a core focus for reading can also be used to stimulate writing. Thinking about different versions, sequels and taking the characters into a new context are all examples of ways to use high-quality texts as a stimulus (→ Chapter 3). Drama and role play are also used to stimulate writing, sometimes linked to a core text or simply as a way of generating ideas. The use of artefacts and first-hand experiences can lead to writing that is either loosely structured or tightly structured. Artefacts and other physical resources are a well-established means of stimulating writing through a creative writing approach.

Children need to be taught strategies that will help their writing. For example, learning to summarise texts that have been read helps writing because it can be used as a way to illustrate that writing requires conciseness and accuracy. Other strategies children need to be taught include how to plan, write, revise and edit writing. Structural concepts – such as headings and paragraphs – also need to be taught. The teaching of strategies for writing is supported by modelling the writing using a flipchart or board (interactive or traditional), and interacting with children on a one-to-one basis to discuss their writing and helping them improve it. For children in the earliest stages, educators can also act as *scribes* for children's ideas.

One way of fostering independence in writing is through the use of writing journals. These often take the form of exercise books given to children for the sole purpose of encouraging their independent writing. Time is allocated, as part of the school day, for the children to use them. Graham and Johnson (2003) suggest 20–30 minutes, two or three times a week. The children are given flexibility over where to work. Importantly, teachers provide no written response to the children's writing. They do not mark the children's writing in any way and indeed, in some cases, will read the writing only with the permission of the author. At the end of the session, children are invited to share their pieces of writing with others in the class. Lambirth and Goouch (2006) argue that writing journals form part of a pedagogy derived from an understanding of how children can be motivated to express themselves independently of teachers. Writing journals can also allow children to bring elements of their home cultures into the classroom through writing.

A sequence for teaching writing

During the years of the Primary National Strategy in England, a three-phase model was used to ensure that planning for writing was integrated with reading, speaking and listening. The idea of scaffolding children's learning in order for them to be able to sustain independent writing was often suggested, although this differed in key ways form the original idea of scaffolding (→ Chapter 2). Similar to effective teaching of reading, effective teaching of writing requires input with individual children, the whole class and small groups of children.

Shared writing

Shared writing is a term used to describe a whole class writing experience designed to form a bridge between the teacher demonstrating the writing process to pupils and independent writing by children. There are three levels of shared writing which provide a range of opportunities for teachers to model effective strategies, explicitly teaching a skill or approach and drawing children into the process through questioning, talk, drama and other response activities. The three levels are:

1   Demonstration, where the teacher is the 'expert', modelling how to write a particular genre of text or a particular feature, giving a running commentary on what they are doing, and why.
2   Scribing, where the teacher involves the pupils in the composition, writing down their suggestions to create a shared piece. Examples of suggestions might include word choices, sentence construction, characterisation and editing.
3   Supported writing, where the teacher gives responsibility for word choices or a sentence to the class. Children work in pairs with whiteboards and hold their whiteboards up for the teacher to see.

Guided writing

Guided writing is a small group approach for which children are grouped on the basis of ability and need. Guided writing normally follows on from shared writing and addresses the specific identified writing development needs of each group, with a specific focus at whole text, sentence or word level. As with guided reading, sessions involve groups of six children working with the teacher or teaching assistant for a period of 20 minutes. The focus may be general, for example understanding the concept of a sentence. Or it might be more specific to a particular genre, such as the use of descriptive language when writing a story, or thinking about the structure of a report. Guided writing may be used to simplify elements of the shared writing session for less confident writers or extend shared writing to challenge more able writers.

Writing frames

Writing frames are a device for supporting some children, particularly in the context of non-fiction writing. Lewis and Wray explain the notion of writing frames:

> Writing frames are outline structures, enabling children to produce non-fiction writing in the different generic forms. Given these structures or skeleton outlines of starters, connectives ☞ and sentence modifiers, children can concentrate on communicating what they want to say. As they practise building their writing around the frames, they become increasingly familiar with the generic forms.
>
> (Lewis and Wray, 1995: 53)

One of the important ideas behind writing frames is that they are intended to support writing done in meaningful contexts; the sort of contexts where appropriate audiences and purposes have been identified. We would also point out that children need to experience the extensive reading of any genre that they are trying to write themselves. Prior to using writing frames, teacher modelling ☞ and shared construction of texts are important.

Lewis and Wray are quite clear that 'using the frames for the direct teaching of generic structures in skills-centred lessons' is inappropriate. There are six writing frames: recount, instruction, report, procedure, explanation, discussion, persuasion.

The following example shows how a child used the persuasive writing frame: the child's appears in italic within the frame text.

Although not everybody would agree, I want to argue that
Children should not wear school uniform.

I have several reasons for arguing for this point of view. My first reason is
That they feel more comfortable in clothes which they choose to wear. They would feel more relaxed and be able to work better and concentrate more on their work.

Another reason is
There wouldn't be the problem of parents not wanting to buy uniforms because they think they are too expensive.

Furthermore
Sometimes you might wake up and find your two lots of uniform in the wash.

Therefore, although some people argue that
Children might take it past the limits.

I think I have shown that
Children should be able to choose their clothing just as adults do, as long as they wear sensible clothes.

(ibid.: 85)

The writing frames are designed to be flexibly applied, and it is intended that children should move towards independence. This means that the form of the frame can be modified to offer a different level of support. If we return to persuasive writing, Figure 17.2 gives an example that includes a list of connectives:

I would like to persuade you that ...

There are several points I want to make to support my point of view. Firstly ...

> These words and phrases might help you:
> because
> therefore
> you can see
> a supporting argument
> this shows that
> another piece of evidence is

Figure 17.2 Part of writing frame with suggested connectives.
Source: Lewis and Wray (1995: 133).

Practice points

- Use a range of approaches to stimulate writing.
- Evaluate the extent to which children are motivated by writing and seek to improve their motivation.
- Do not underestimate the value of talk when preparing children for writing.

Glossary

Connectives – words and phrases whose main purpose is to connect phrases, sentences and other large units of text.
Genre – a form of writing such as newspaper, story, poem. In education can refer to spoken forms as well as written forms.
Teacher modelling – the teacher shows by demonstration and speaking their thoughts aloud how writing is composed.

References

Clegg, A. (1964) (ed.) *The Excitement of Writing*. London: Chatto & Windus.
Graham, L. and Johnson, A. (2003) *Children's Writing Journals*. Royston: United Kingdom Literacy Association.
Lambirth, A. and Goouch, C. (2006) 'Golden times of writing: the creative compliance of writing journals', *Literacy*, 40(3): 146–52.
Lewis, M. and Wray, D. (1995) *Developing Children's Non-Fiction Writing: Working with Writing Frames*. Leamington Spa: Scholastic.

Annotated bibliography

Bearne, E., Chamberlain, L., Cremin, T. and Mottram, M. (2011) *Teaching Writing Effectively: Reviewing Practice*. Leicester: UKLA.
Teaching for learning, planning for writing and how to offer choice and foster independence in writing.
L2 ★★

Fisher, R. (2006) 'Whose writing is it anyway? Issues of control in the teaching of writing', *Cambridge Journal of Education*, 36(2): 193–206.
Encouraging creative responses within the parameters of the writing curriculum.
L3 ★★

Graham, S. (2010) 'Facilitating writing development', in D. Wyse, R. Andrews and J. Hoffman (eds) *The Routledge International Handbook of English, Language and Literacy Teaching*. London: Routledge.
An excellent overview of research on effective writing teaching and recommendations for research-informed practice.
L3 ★★★

Lewis, M. and Wray, D. (1995) *Developing Children's Non-Fiction Writing: Working with Writing Frames*. Leamington Spa: Scholastic.
A thorough account that includes the rationale for the use of writing frames and examples of practice.
L2 ★★

Ministry of Stories http://www.ministryofstories.org/
An exciting initiative to engage disadvantaged young people and get them to write for pleasure.
L1 ★

Riley, J. and Reedy, D. (2000) *Developing Writing for Different Purposes: Teaching about Genre in the Early Years*. London: Paul Chapman.
A useful reminder of many of the main issues in the teaching of writing. Includes interesting six-point theory on the teaching of writing developed in New Zealand.
L2 ★★

Chapter 18

Spelling

Building on Peters' (1985) distinction between spelling being 'caught or taught', we show how children can be taught how to become competent and conventional spellers. A five-stage model of spelling development is presented, and the chapter concludes with reflections on the appropriate use of spelling tests and spelling homework.

Children's natural desire to make sense of the world can also be seen in their attempts to master English spelling, as the following examples of children's spelling attempts illustrate:

my klone

ches and unen

The first is a famous footballer originally from Liverpool; the second is a flavour of crisps. It is the irregularities of English that make it demanding for children to learn and for teachers to teach. Your ability to understand children's sophisticated attempts at spelling (that may at first glance seem incomprehensible), is one of the abilities you will acquire as part of your initial training. Not only will you learn to 'decode' their attempts, but you will also learn how to understand the child's thinking that lies behind their attempts to make meaning.

Spelling, particularly spelling in the English language, is dominated by history and convention. In many cases, non-standard English spelling communicates meaning without ambiguity. However, there are strong societal pressures for correct or standard spelling, and it is true that until children have mastered standard spelling they cannot be said to be fully competent writers. It is also the case that in order to write well in general, children need to be able to use standard spellings with fluency (Graham *et al.*, 2008).

An emphasis on *invented spelling* or the 'have a go' approach is one useful strategy for learners at the early stages of development. However, this emphasis should not be to the exclusion of other more direct teaching approaches because different children will respond better to different approaches dependent on their stages of development (Martello, 2004). Teaching spelling requires a clear focus on words and the letter patterns that words are built from. In the early stages, phonological knowledge is important but quite soon children need to learn that English spelling has complex patterns of sound–symbol correspondences. The ability to use standard spelling requires understanding of elements such as word stems, word functions and grammatical meanings supported by visual memory. One of the key elements of the educator's approach to spelling should be to encourage children to see patterns in related groups of words (Schlagel, 2007).

In her seminal book *Spelling: Caught or Taught?*, Peters (1985) argued that in the past spelling had not been taught effectively. She suggested that spelling is a particular skill, or set of skills, that requires direct instruction for the majority of school pupils. Children who are not taught to spell properly often develop a poor self-image as far as spelling is concerned and lack self-confidence in their writing as a whole. Crucially, she emphasised the significance of children acquiring visual strategies ☞ rather than auditory strategies ☞ in learning to spell, though she also acknowledged the usefulness of kinaesthetic strategies ☞. She strongly recommended the 'Look–Cover–Write–Check' approach:

1   Look carefully at the word, noting particular features such as familiar letter strings, suffixes, etc. and memorise it by saying the word silently, thinking of the meaning of the word and trying to picture it in the mind's eye.
2   Cover the word.
3   Write the word from memory.
4   Check that the word written is correct by matching it with the original. If the spelling is incorrect, the whole process should be repeated.

Peters' research also led her to believe that there is a direct correlation between confident, clear and carefully formed handwriting and the development of competent spelling (→ Chapter 19, 'Handwriting'). Her approach has since been extended to include the importance of saying the word out loud before writing it down: 'Look–Cover–Say–Write–Check.' When saying the word, children can segment it into their constituent phonemes.

Spelling development

Gentry (1982) suggested that there are five stages of development for spelling. His work is helpful when considering that children's spelling ability develops over a long period of time; it should always be acknowledged that children will make attempts to spell based on what they know and understand about the English language system. While these may not always be conventional attempts, what is produced is a helpful indicator for teachers about children's spelling knowledge.

The first stage is the *pre-communicative* stage, when young children are making their first attempts at communicating through writing. The writing may contain a mixture of actual letters, numerals and invented symbols and, as such, it will be unreadable although the writer might be able to explain what they intended to write.

When children are at the second stage, that is the *semi-phonetic* stage, they are beginning to understand that letters represent sounds and show some knowledge of the alphabet and of letter formation. Some words will be abbreviated or the initial letter might be used to indicate the whole word.

At the *phonetic* stage, children concentrate on the sound–symbol correspondences, their words become more complete and they gain an understanding of word division. They can cope with simple letter strings such as *-nd*, *-ing* and *-ed* but have trouble with less regular strings such as *-er*, *-ll* and *-gh*.

During the *transitional* stage, children become less dependent on sound–symbol strategies. With the experience of reading and direct spelling instruction, they become more aware of the visual aspects of words. They indicate an awareness of the accepted letter strings and basic writing conventions of the English writing system and have an increasing number of correctly spelled words to draw upon.

Finally, the fully competent speller emerges at the *conventional* (or *correct*) stage. Conventional spellings are being produced competently and confidently almost all the time and there is evidence of the effective use of visual strategies and knowledge of word structure. Children at this stage have an understanding of basic rules and patterns of English and a wide spelling vocabulary. They can distinguish homographs ☞, such as 'tear' and 'tear' and homophones ☞, such as 'pear' and 'pair' and they are increasingly able to cope with uncommon and irregular spelling patterns.

Teachers will be able to use the model to identify what stage individual pupils are at, what sort of expectations they might have of these individuals, what targets they might set for these children and what teaching strategies they might usefully employ.

Beard (1999) refers to Gentry's model as being very influential, but he does raise several notes of caution. He maintains that the different stages represent 'complex patterns of thinking and behaviour' and aspects of several stages might be evident in one piece of writing. The teacher therefore needs to evaluate the individual's progress through the stages on the basis of a wide sample of writing each time. He also points to the importance of parental support (making reference to the case study of Paul Bissex which was used as the basis for Gentry's stages: → Chapter 16, 'The development of writing') and the significance of effective teaching of spelling in school. The rate of children's progression through the stages will vary greatly depending on these factors and, of course, individual differences.

Developing strategies in spelling

Phonics plays a particular role in the early stages of learning to spell. Children learn that segmenting words into their constituent phonemes ☞ for spelling is the reverse of blending phonemes into words for reading. They also need to learn to spell words accurately by combining the use of their grapheme–phoneme correspondence knowledge. As their understanding progresses, morphological and etymological knowledge also play a role.

Consider what strategies you use when facing words you find hard to spell. Some general strategies that 'good' spellers use might be the following:

- sounding words out;
- drawing on a store of words they can spell, i.e. 'sight vocabulary';
- dividing words into syllables;
- knowing common prefixes and suffixes, for example, pre-; dis-; -ed; -ing;
- developing understanding of rules and their limitations;
- using dictionaries and spellcheckers;
- asking peers for help and/or confirmation.

O'Sullivan and Thomas (2000) found the following areas of spelling knowledge to be essential in the teaching and learning of spelling:

- extensive experience of written language;
- phonological awareness;
- letter names and alphabetic knowledge;
- known words which can form the basis for analogy making;
- visual awareness;
- awareness of common letter strings and word patterns, for example, -at, -ad, -ee, -ing, -one, -ough;
- knowledge of word structures and meanings, for example, prefixes, tenses, compound words, word roots and word origins;
- growing independence – where and how to get help; using dictionaries etc.
- making analogies and deducing rules.

We would add to this list the importance of extensive experience of spoken language, in line with recent research showing that children's early language experiences impact on later outcomes (Sylva *et al.*, 2010).

As children's spelling competence develops and they move from the phonetic to the transitional stage, teachers need to employ a variety of teaching approaches. These include:

- Visual strategies, where children are taught to recognise tricky or high frequency words, to use the 'Look–Cover–Say–Write–Check' procedure, to check critical features of the word such as shape and length and to ask questions such as 'Does it look right?'.

- A morphemic and word analogy approach using known spellings as a basis for correctly spelling other words with similar patterns or related meanings, and building words from awareness of the meaning or derivation of known words: here, there, everywhere; light, sight, bright.
- Knowing about and predicting the most likely order of letters in words, for example, what letter is likely to follow Q?
- Mnemonic approaches which involve inventing and using personal mnemonic devices for remembering difficult words, such as 'two ships on the sea', 'one collar and two sleeves' – necessary; 'there's an "e" for envelope in the middle of stationery'; or 'an "i" (eye) in the middle of "nose" makes a noise'.
- Thinking about and investigating spelling 'rules' and their exceptions.
- Games such as Scrabble, hangman, crosswords, word searches, Boggle, and Countdown can all be useful in stimulating and motivating children's interest in words and spelling.

Spelling tests and spelling homework

Weekly spelling tests are a common feature of primary classrooms. It is tempting to ask why this practice is so prevalent when there is very little evidence about its effectiveness. Historical tradition, and in particular the spelling test requirement in statutory tests, are the likely driving forces behind the practice. It is important to consider what the pros and cons of spelling tests are. A potentially positive feature of spelling tests is that lists of words are sent home to be learned. If this is carefully thought through, word lists can provide an activity that many parents feel confident to support their children with (although it is important to remember that some parents will not feel confident about this). These lists of words are often differentiated into ability levels. It is common for teachers to encourage children to put the words into a sentence context or even a paragraph context as part of the homework (see Figure 18.1 for a humorous response to using a particular set of words). Sometimes children are encouraged to identify problem words from the ones they have been writing as part of their lessons or words that are of particular interest.

The claim that spelling tests are used as an assessment tool is questionable. The biggest problem is that the true test of learning a spelling is whether it is written correctly in the course of normal writing. The most useful assessment of children's spellings will, arguably, take place at the time that the children are actually engaged in the writing process in the classroom; every piece of writing that a child carries out gives teachers an opportunity to assess their spelling, and it should be remembered that the kind of writing that the child is doing will affect the nature of their spelling mistakes. A diary, for example, will create different challenges from a piece of scientific writing. In addition, however

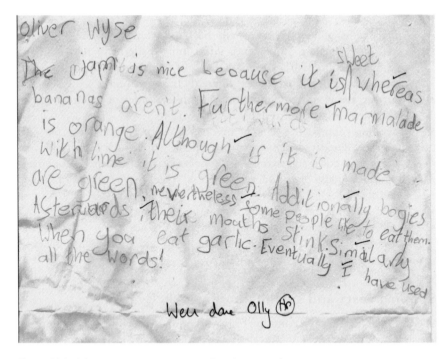

Figure 18.1 A humorous response to spelling homework.

sensitively tests are handled, there will always be children who are poor spellers whose self-esteem will be damaged each time they have to carry out a spelling test. Mudd (1994) points out that some children, often poor spellers, can have a visual memory deficit which requires remediation through multi-sensory techniques ☞ or mental linking by remembering sets of objects placed within their sight. One of the important issues addressed by Mudd concerns the teaching of spelling rules. Her view is that generalisations, not rules, should form the basis for instruction in school. Rules suggest immutability and correctness whereas generalisations allow for the possibility of exceptions.

When word lists and spelling tests represent the main approach to spelling and when the lists are sent home *every* week, some children can become demotivated. There is no reason why spelling homework cannot feature a wide range of activities such as the ones covered in this chapter; as pointed out in Chapter 17, teachers need to create meaningful contexts for children's learning; for example, one activity is the simple but potentially valuable one of bringing home a draft of writing and asking for help with proofreading.

Practice points

- In the early stages, the use of phonological understanding ☞ should be encouraged alongside visual strategies for conventional spelling.
- There needs to be a careful balance between encouraging invented spelling, which can aid composition, and standard spelling, which is the final goal.
- Every piece of writing provides an opportunity for the assessment of a child's spelling.

Glossary

Auditory strategies – the use of sounds to help spelling of unknown words.

Homographs – words with the same spelling as another but different meaning: 'a lead pencil/the dog's lead'.

Homophones – words which sound the same, but have different meanings or different spellings: 'read/reed'; 'right/write/rite'.

Kinaesthetic strategies – the use of the memory of physical actions to form words.

Multi-sensory techniques – the use of as many senses as possible through movement, vision, touch, and hearing in order to remember words.

Phoneme – the smallest unit of sound in a spoken word, e.g. /b/ in 'bat'.

Phonological understanding – understanding the way that letters represent speech sounds.

Visual strategies – the use of visual memory of words including common patterns of letters.

References

Beard, R. (1999) *National Literacy Strategy: Review of Research and Other Related Evidence*. London: DfEE.

Gentry, J. R. (1982) 'An analysis of developmental spelling in *GNYS AT WRK*', *Reading Teacher*, 36: 192–200.

Graham, S., Morphy, P., Harris, K., Fink-Chorzempa, B., Saddler, S. M. and Mason, L. (2008) 'Teaching spelling in the primary grades: A national survey of instructional practices and adaptations', *American Educational Research Journal*, 45(3): 796–825.

Martello, J. (2004) 'Precompetence and trying to learn: Beginning writers talk about spelling', *Journal of Early Childhood Literacy*, 4: 271–289.

Mudd, N. (1994) *Effective Spelling: A Practical Guide for Teachers*. London: Hodder & Stoughton.

O'Sullivan, O. and Thomas, A. (2000) *Understanding Spelling*. London: CLPE.

Peters, M. L. (1985) *Spelling: Caught or Taught: A New Look*. London: Routledge and Kegan Paul.

Schlagel, B. (2007) 'Best practices in spelling and handwriting', in S. Graham, C. A. MacArthur and J. Fitzgerald (eds) *Best Practices in Writing Instruction*. New York: The Guilford Press.

Sylva, K., Melhuish, E., Sammons, P., Siraj-Blatchford, I. and Taggart, B. (2010) *Early Childhood Matter: Evidence from the Effective Pre-school and Primary Education Project*. Oxford: Routledge.

Annotated bibliography

Brooks, P. and Weeks, S. (The Helen Arkell Dyslexia Centre) (1999) *Individual Styles in Learning to Spell: Improving Spelling in Children with Literacy Difficulties and All Children in Mainstream Schools*. London: DfEE.
In common with other research, demonstrates that important aspects of literacy learning need to be individualised. Includes fascinating ideas on 'neurolinguistic programming'.
L1 ★

Mudd, N. (1994) *Effective Spelling: A Practical Guide for Teachers*. London: Hodder & Stoughton.
As the title suggests, this book gives sensible, systematic and practical guidance to the effective teaching of spelling at Key Stages 1 and 2, as well as providing some interesting insights into the history of the English language and past and present approaches to spelling in school.
L2 ★★

Schlagel, B. (2007) 'Best practices in spelling and handwriting', in S. Graham, C. A. MacArthur and J. Fitzgerald (eds) *Best Practices in Writing Instruction*. New York: The Guilford Press.
A useful evidence-informed perspective from the US.
L2 ★★

Torgerson, C. J. and Elbourne, D. (2002) 'A systematic review and meta-analysis of the effectiveness of information and communication technology (ICT) on the teaching of spelling', *Journal of Research in Reading*, 25(2): 129–143.
Found only six studies addressing the issue of the benefits of ICT for spelling teaching that were randomised controlled trials. The evidence for use of dedicated spelling packages is not particularly convincing.
L3 ★★★

Chapter 19

Handwriting

The development of a fluent, comfortable and legible handwriting style helps children throughout their schooling, not least in exams. Basic principles of teaching handwriting are described in this chapter, along with suggestions for developing handwriting skills. We end with a section on handwriting problems.

Handwriting has always been taught; in England, for example, it has been a significant feature of the curriculum since the introduction of the 1870 Education Act. Increasingly, children have access to means of producing print without having to hand-write, which suggests that children should be taught how to use keyboards in the most efficient way. However, the teaching of handwriting is still an important part of the early years and primary curriculum. It is thought that the kinaesthetic movements that are part of forming letters help with visual memory of letter shapes. Also as you will see later, there is research showing that handwriting is linked with comprehension. Finally, it is interesting to note that there are a considerable number of professional writers, particularly writers of narrative and poetry, who find handwriting a better way to express themselves than the keyboard.

Learning to form the individual letters of the alphabet and produce legible handwriting at a reasonable speed, involves a complex perceptuo–motor skill ☞. The goal of handwriting teaching is a legible, fluent and comfortable style. Legibility will have different levels according to the purpose of the writing. Sassoon (1990) points out that children cannot be expected to produce their neatest handwriting all the time, so she advocates different levels of handwriting. While schools should have a handwriting policy in place which is shared with parents and which is adhered to when modelling writing and marking children's work, it is also important to acknowledge that handwriting needs to be fit for purpose. A calligraphic ☞ standard for special occasions, for example, might require a careful, deliberate approach which will be more time-consuming than a legible everyday hand. There will also be times when pupils are drafting text or making notes that they alone will read where a lower standard of legibility is appropriate. The importance of fluency is particularly important in tests and exams when time pressures are present.

A comfortable style requires an appropriate grip, appropriate seating and good posture. Posture and working space are important elements of hand-writing. For right-handed pupils, the paper is tilted to about 45 degrees anti-clockwise. It is important that the writing implement is not gripped too hard, as this can also lead to muscle tension in the shoulder and pain in the wrist and hand. It is important that you are aware of all the left-handed children in your class from the beginning of the year. As far as handwriting is concerned, left-handed children have particular needs. Their writing moves inwardly – that is, in towards their bodies – thus tending to make it difficult for them to read what they have just written. Left-handers should be encouraged to turn their paper *clockwise* (to about 45 degrees), not to hold their pen or pencil too near to the actual point and to sit on a chair that is high enough to allow them good visi-bility. Left-handers can be helped by ensuring that they sit to the left of a right-hander so that their elbows are not competing for space. Whatever your own writing orientation, you will need to ensure that these issues are made explicit and discussed when you model handwriting.

Basic handwriting concepts

Venerable Will played jazz sax 'til 3 o'clock in the morning before he quit.

The five boxing wizards jump quickly.

(Jarman, 1989: 101)

These examples that contain all the letters of the alphabet serve to remind us that quick brown foxes are not the only subjects for such sentences. They are of course quite a handy way to cover the formation of all the letters of the alphabet in one meaningful sentence.

Sassoon (1990) puts forward the concepts behind our writing system. Direction, movement and height are all crucial: left to right and top to bottom; the fact that letters have prescribed flowing movements with specific starting and exit points; the necessity to ensure that letters have particular height differences. In addition, the variance between upper and lower case must be recognised and correct spacing consistently applied. She also stresses the importance of taking particular care when teaching certain letters that have mirror images of each other, such as *b-d*, *m-w*, *n-u* and *p-q* to avoid confusion for young learners. She suggests that speed – but not too much speed – is important as this can lead to fluency and greater efficiency. Modern classroom situations do require pupils to think, work and write reasonably quickly.

There are a small number of technical terms that are useful when talking about handwriting. *Ascenders* are the vertical lines that rise above the mid-line (or x-line) on letters like 'd'; *descenders* are the vertical lines that hang below the baseline on letters like 'g'. Letters have an *entry stroke* where you start the letter and an *exit stroke*. The letter 't' is interesting in that its horizontal line is called a *crossbar* and the height of the letter should only be three-quarters. This means that the top of the letter finishes between the mid-line and the ascender line. There are four important horizontal lines: the *descender line*, the *baseline*, the *mid-line* and the *ascender line*. For adults, only the baseline is visible; for children, other lines have to be used carefully because there is a danger that they can measure the length of a stroke by the distance to the line not by understanding the differences in letter size. Children need to understand these concepts if they are to have legible and fluent handwriting.

Jarman (1989), like Sassoon, suggests that letters can be taught in families that are related by their patterns of movement. There are slight differences between their approaches, but both underline the importance of the idea of letter families. Jarman links specific patterns – which he regards as beneficial – with the families of letters. He also suggests that there are two kinds of join or 'ligature': horizontal joins and vertical joins. He points out that it is sensible to leave some letters unjoined – such as b g j p q and y – when joined to most vowels. Sassoon links together the following letters:

1   i l t u y j
2   r n m h b p k
3   c a d g q o e
4   s f
5   v w x z

Whilst we are outlining concepts and approaches here, it is important to be cognisant of the particular handwriting scheme that your school follows.

Handwriting and writing

Peters (1985) discussed perceptuo-motor ability and argued that carefulness in handwriting goes hand in hand with swift handwriting, which in turn influences spelling ability. Children who can fluently write letter-strings such as *-ing*, *-able*, *-est*, *-tion* and *-ous* are more likely to remember how to spell words containing these strings. It was also Peters' view that the teaching of 'joined up' (or 'cursive') writing, should begin long before the junior school, that is to say at Key Stage 1 rather than 2. The main advantages of this are:

1   the concept of 'a word' (and the spaces between words) is acquired from the outset as distinct from 'a letter' (and the spaces between letters);

2   correct letter formation with appropriate exit strokes is learned from the beginning;

3   the movement of joined-up writing assists successful spelling and is quicker than printing;

4   children do not have to cope with changing from one to the other at seven or eight years of age.

Sassoon (1990) suggests that with sufficient preparation in the 'movement' of letters and the different exit strokes required, pupils can begin to join up the simple letters by the end of the reception year or Year 1 at least.

More recent research has begun to show the importance of automaticity in handwriting in order to benefit composing processes. Medwell and Wray (2007) argue that handwriting has been taught in mainstream schooling based on the link between correct spelling and the use of fluent, joined-up handwriting, but with little emphasis placed on the connection between automaticity in handwriting and its impact on compositional skills. In Scheuer et al.'s (2006) study, children aged nine gave reflective accounts of learning to write. Their views represented writing as a developmental process which moves from early mark making to producing and understanding conventional writing over a relatively extended period of time.

Such research suggests that when teaching handwriting, we should focus on developing children's fine motor skills so that they are first and foremost able to hold a writing implement comfortably, and hand-eye co-ordination to support the 'uniform' formation of letters. Development of these early skills will support automaticity and fluency in handwriting. which will impact on their future success as writers. Some activities to develop early handwriting skills are:

- **Hand control:** jigsaws, gluing, cutting, threading, painting, using a variety of implements to mark make and draw.
- **Learning to form letter-shapes (large-scale):** 'skywriting' the letters in the air, using a large brush and bucket of water to 'paint' a wall or shapes on the ground, writing with a stick or finger in a sand tray or in shaving foam, writing letters with chalk on the playground, writing with big pens at an easel.
- **Learning to write letter-shapes on paper:** use blank paper, sometimes draw a line on the paper, encourage a comfortable grip. As the child becomes more competent, they can think about spacing letters and words, using consistent letter sizes.

As children progress through primary school, handwriting can be taught through whole class sessions, guided writing sessions and one-to-one support. It can be taught on a weekly basis and according to need.

Diagnosis of problems

Pupils entering the later phase of primary schooling sometimes arrive with handwriting problems. These might have been caused by indifferent teaching or they might, according to Sassoon (1990), be symptomatic of pupils' particular condition or set of circumstances. They might be considered 'dyspraxic', that is, prone to particular motor coordination problems. For example, they might not be able to catch a large ball, or cope easily with gymnastics or play games using the simplest of equipment. For these children, neat, regulation handwriting might be impossible. Teachers need to acknowledge this, not continually chastise them and help them to develop handwriting that is reasonably swift and legible.

Sassoon argues that handwriting can be regarded as a diagnostic tool in itself, indicating certain problems that pupils have and teachers need to address. Hesitancy and a lack of confidence in spelling will interrupt the flow of handwriting. If this is accompanied by frequent attempts at correcting mistakes, the result is 'messy' handwriting that many teachers find unacceptable. This may well bring to their attention that these children need help in spelling as well as handwriting. Occasionally, children have psychological problems to cope with too, such as bullying, bereavement, divorce and so on, which, in addition to a range of behavioural changes, can become evident in their handwriting. Often the writing becomes very variable and sometimes illegible, when previously it was conventional.

Some children with poor handwriting skills are found to have weak auditory, perceptual and memory skills and are not able to remember sequences of movements or sequences of verbal instructions. Difficulties with handwriting might indicate poor eyesight or a squint and perhaps the need for spectacles for an individual child. Children suffering from fatigue due to the after-effects of an illness, a physical disability or just insufficient sleep at night might also reflect this in their handwriting. Finally, poor handwriting might bring the teacher's attention to the poor posture of some children when writing or even generally. Thus alerted and made aware of any of these cognitive, psychological or physical problems, teachers will be able to take steps, possibly with support from other professionals, to remedy them and aim to improve not just children's handwriting, but other important features of their pupils' learning and development in school.

It is clear that children experiencing handwriting difficulties need to be identified and supported as these difficulties are likely to impact upon their ability to compose written language. Medwell and Wray (2007) suggest that there is evidence that intervention to teach handwriting to these children can improve not only their handwriting, but also their writing more generally.

Practice points

- Familiarise yourself with school's handwriting policies and schemes and ensure that you and other adults working with you model this when working with children.
- Handwriting should be taught on a weekly basis through whole group and small group sessions and supplemented by individual support during the writing process.
- A balance needs to be found between emphasis on standard letter formation and encouraging legibility and fluency.

Glossary

Calligraphic – description of a particularly skilled way of writing. Handwritten italic script is often seen as calligraphy.

Perceptuo–motor skill – skills that rely on use of the senses, the brain and learned physical movement.

References

Jarman, C. (1989) *The Development of Handwriting Skills: A Resource Book for Teachers*. Oxford: Basil Blackwell.

Medwell, J. and Wray, D. (2007) 'Handwriting: what do we know and what do we need to know?', *Literacy*, 41(1): 10–15.

Peters, M. L. (1985) *Spelling: Caught or Taught: A New Look*. London: Routledge and Kegan Paul.

Sassoon, R. (1990) *Handwriting: A New Perspective*. Leckhampton: Stanley Thornes.

Scheuer, N., de la Cruz., M., Pozo, J. and Neira, S. (2006) 'Children's autobiographies of learning to write', *British Journal of Educational Psychology*, 76: 709–725.

Annotated bibliography

The British Institute of Graphologists (2007) http://www.britishgraphology. org/
   Intriguing site that shows how seriously handwriting can be taken. Its media section includes various articles of interest to a general readership. **L1 ★**

Jarman, C. (1989) *The Development of Handwriting Skills: A Resource Book for Teachers*. Oxford: Basil Blackwell.
   Jarman makes a strong case for the teaching of eight specific patterns which he suggests account for all lower case letters. The book includes fascinating information about a range of handwriting-related topics. The main part of the book consists of photocopiable handwriting sheets. **L1 ★**

Medwell, J. and Wray, D. (2010) 'Handwriting and writing', in D. Wyse, R. Andrews and J. Hoffman (eds) *The Routledge International Handbook of English, Language and Literacy Teaching* London: Routledge.
A timely and very useful overview of research in an area that receives limited attention.
L3 ★★★

Sassoon, R. (1999) *Handwriting of the Twentieth Century*. London: Routledge.
Rosemary Sassoon made an important contribution to our understanding of the practice of handwriting. This book gives a historical perspective on the teaching of handwriting. Her book *Handwriting: The Way to Teach It* (Sassoon, 1990b; revised edition published in 2003 by Sage) focuses more on classroom practice.
L1 ★

Chapter 20

Punctuation

Two key ideas that underpin this chapter are linguistic and non-linguistic punctuation. The examples of punctuation that are given reveal that the communication of unambiguous meaning is central to punctuation, just as it is to writing more generally. Information about how punctuation works is linked with how best to help children learn to punctuate their writing.

Hall (1998) was one of the first researchers to look in depth at the teaching and learning of punctuation. His book includes an overview of the history of punctuation. For example, in 1700, Richard Browne said: 'What is the use of stops or points in reading and writing? To distinguish sense; by resting so long as the stop you meet with doth permit.' (Hall, 1998: 2) In Roman times, it was the readers who inserted the punctuation into texts, not the writers: this was related to the need to declaim texts orally. Since that time the function of punctuation has changed. However, the idea that punctuation is primarily designed to support oral reading – through pauses – still persists. Hall reiterates that punctuation is no different to writing in general in that the generation of *meaning is* the primary function of written language: one of the main points that he makes is that punctuation is learned most successfully in the context of 'rich and meaningful writing experiences' (1998: 9).

He usefully differentiates between 'non-linguistic punctuation' and 'linguistic punctuation'. An example of non-linguistic punctuation is where a child puts full stops at the end of every line of a piece of writing rather than at the end of the sentences. This illustrates the child's belief that punctuation is to do with position and space rather than to indicate meaning and structure. With regard to non-linguistic punctuation, the idea of 'resistance to punctuation' is discussed. One of the reasons that children can remain resistant to using punctuation appropriately is exacerbated by teachers whose comments are often directed to naming and procedures rather than explanation:

As already indicated, teacher comments which are simply directed to the placing of punctuation rather than to explaining its function can leave the child with no sense of purpose. Yet research suggests that teacher practices are, probably quite unconsciously, dominated by procedure rather than explanation.

(ibid.: 5)

Standard punctuation is linked with grammar and sentence structure. The necessary understanding of these complex concepts does not happen suddenly. Children gradually begin to realise that spatial concepts either do not work or do not match what they see in their reading material. Hall illustrates this with an example from his research:

> three children who were jointly composing a piece of text which was being scribed for them . . . After two lines, one child insisted on having a full stop at the end of each line. The rest of the piece was written with no more punctuation. Then there was a scramble for the pen and one child wanted to put a full stop after 'lot' on line three.

Derek: You're not supposed to put full stops in the middle.
Rachel: You are!
Derek: No, they're supposed to be at the end, Ooh!
Rachel: You are, Derek.
Fatima: Yeah. So that's how you know that (meaning the 'and' at the end of line 3) goes with that (meaning line 4).

(ibid.: 12)

An early piece of punctuation research was carried out by Hutchinson (1987) who worked closely with a child, Danny, on a piece of writing that was a retelling of *Come Away from the Water, Shirley* by John Burningham (1977). Danny wrote as he would speak:

> shirley and her mum and dad were going to the seaside and her dad told her to go and play with the other children and her dad didn no she went saling with a dog and a pirate ship was foiling and the pirates corght her.

An important aspect of teachers' knowledge is recognising the significant differences between speech and writing. Hutchinson made the point that Danny's reliance on speech in this extract resulted in the use of conjunctions ☞ where full stops would be more appropriate in writing. However, he also pointed out that an analysis based on one text in one context is not sufficient for assessing understanding. The following day when they revisited the writing, Danny added some full stops to his work. Another point to make here is that the process of redrafting can enable children to reconsider their use of punctuation.

One of the main uses of punctuation is to avoid ambiguity. The following example shows how completely different meanings can be created by different punctuation:

PRIVATE. NO SWIMMING ALLOWED.

PRIVATE? NO! SWIMMING ALLOWED.

Part of the intrigue of punctuation is spotting the frequent 'errors' that occur. The apostrophe is a bit of a classic in this regard. The following professionally printed banner appeared on a pub wall:

Qs monster meals won't scare you but the portion's might

One apostrophe is missing, one is correct, and one is incorrect. It is worth reminding ourselves of the common types of apostrophe:

1   contraction: didn't = did not;
2   possession singular: the cat's tail, the child's book;
3   possession plural: the cats' tails, the children's books (as 'children' is an irregular plural form, the apostrophe comes before the 's');
4   possession with name ending in 's': Donald Graves's book. Common errors include: this first happened in the 60's. – 60s is plural not a contraction; was that it's name? – because of the confusion with *it's* (as in: It's (it is) my party and I'll cry if I want to). This possessive form is irregular and does *not* have an apostrophe (was that its name?).

Here are further examples of some punctuation marks that children will need to learn.

- **Full stops** (.) are commonly placed at the end of a sentence.
- **Commas** (,) are used to separate items in a list or items in sentences which have list-like structures. They indicate a slight pause in the flow of the sentence when reading aloud.
- **Speech marks** ('. . .') can be used to show actual words spoken or written. Comic strips and speech bubbles are a useful way of teaching the use of speech marks.
- **Semicolons** (;) semicolon separate main clauses that are not joined by a coordinator ☞ which the semicolon replaces. The two parts of the sentence feel equally important. This represents a break in the flow of the sentence which is stronger than a comma but weaker than a full stop, e.g. the students in the first study were hard working; those in the second were lazy.

- **Colons** (:) separate a first clause, which could stand as a sentence, from a final phrase or clause that extends or illustrates the first clause. They are most commonly used to introduce things, like lists or an example.

Note that the use of colons and the semi-colons can also be particularly problematic so it is important to be as clear as one can be about their use.

Punctuation can be taught through shared and guided reading and writing sessions, during the process of writing, and as discrete mini lessons. Children should be encouraged to self and peer-assess their work. Waugh (1998), for example, looks at some practical approaches to teaching punctuation in the primary school and he makes an important point about 'response partners'. One of the most effective ways of improving punctuation is to work with someone who is proficient at proofreading. All professionally published materials pass through a proofreading stage: this book will be passed to a copy-editor and a proofreader; newspaper articles go to sub-editors who work on style and presentation, etc. This is in part a recognition that proofreading is often more efficient if it is not carried out solely by the author, who often is primarily concerned with the composition. This also reflects the idea that it is sensible to separate composition and transcription in the various stages of the writing process.

Practice points

- Use real texts (electronic and printed) to draw children's attention to the range of punctuation and the ways in which it is used
- Help children to understand that one of the main reasons for punctuation is to improve clarity and avoid ambiguity
- Encourage the use of response partners to help with proofreading

Glossary

Conjunction – a type of word that is used mainly to link clauses in a sentence, e.g. She was very happy *because* John asked for help with his maths.

Coordinator – a word that links parts of a sentence. The most common coordinators are 'and', 'or' and 'but'. Some people call these conjunctions.

References

Burningham, J. (1977) *Come Away from the Water, Shirley*. London: Cape.

Hall, N. (1998) *Punctuation in the Primary School*. Reading: University of Reading, Reading and Language Information Centre.

Hutchinson, D. (1987) 'Developing concepts of sentence structure and punctuation', *Curriculum*, 8(3): 13–16.

Truss, L. (2003) *Eats, Shoots and Leaves: The Zero Tolerance Approach to Punctuation*. London: Profile Books.
Waugh, D. (1998) 'Practical approaches to teaching punctuation in the primary school', *Reading*, 32(2): 14–17.

Annotated bibliography

Hall, N. and Robinson, A. (1996) *Learning About Punctuation*. Clevedon: Multilingual Matters.
A range of contributors offer their thoughts on the teaching of punctuation. Includes a study that looked at the development of a group of eight- and nine-year-old children.
L2 ★★
Kress, G. (1982) *Learning to Write*. London: Routledge and Kegan Paul.
An important text that looks closely at the differences between speech and writing. Also contains well-thought-out views on children's 'errors'.
L3 ★★
Wyse, D. and Shelbourne, H. (2005) 'Marks that make meaning (1)', *Primary English Magazine*, 11(1): 24–27.
The first of three articles (see volumes 11(2) and 11(3)) that expand some of the ideas touched on in this chapter.
L1 ★

Chapter 21

Grammar

The value of many forms of grammar teaching continues to be in doubt. This chapter reminds us that questions about grammar teaching have been around for some time. We outline the difference between 'descriptive' grammar and 'prescriptive' grammar. An examination of the important idea of 'knowledge about language' is followed by reflections on the approach adopted in the PNS Framework.

The word 'grammar' itself is used in two very distinct ways: prescriptively and descriptively. Prescriptively, the term is used to prescribe how language should be used; descriptively, the term is used to describe how the language actually is used. Prescriptive grammarians ☞ believe that English grammar is a fixed and unchanging series of rules which should be applied to the language. For prescriptive grammarians expressions such as *I ain't done nothing wrong* or *We was going to the supermarket* are quite simply wrong. To understand this rather better, it is necessary to consider two other related questions that often get muddled up with grammar in the public discourse ☞: the question of style and the question of Standard English.

Many complaints about incorrect grammar are actually complaints about style. Split infinitives ☞ are a case in point. There is nothing *grammatically* wrong with a sentence like: *I am hoping to quickly finish writing this paragraph.* It makes perfect sense, but it might be thought stylistically preferable to write: *I am hoping to finish writing this paragraph quickly*, or even to write: *I am hoping quickly to finish writing this paragraph.* However, if I were to write: *Hoping writing I paragraph finish to quickly am*, there would be something grammatically wrong with that!

So far as Standard English is concerned, an accident of history meant that, when printing developed, it was the Anglian regional dialect that was written down (→ Chapter 1, 'The history of English, language and literacy'). Because it was written, it became the 'standard'. It would thus be more accurate to describe Standard English as the standard *dialect*. Other dialects are then described as 'non-standard'. Standard English is distinguished from non-standard dialects by features of vocabulary and features of grammar. In addition, middle-class speech tends to keep some of the grammatical features of the written form, particularly with regard to the use of negatives and the use of some verb forms. Thus matters of class and matters of dialect have come to be linked.

From the point of view of *prescriptive* grammarians, the grammar of Standard English is 'good' or 'correct' grammar, and the grammar of non-standard dialects is 'bad' or 'incorrect' grammar. So, for example, children who say *I ain't done nothing* often have their language 'corrected' by their teachers, and even by their own parents, on the ground that it is 'bad' grammar, or indeed, more generally, that it is just 'bad' English.

Descriptive grammarians are interested in describing how the language actually is used rather than how it ought to be used. Thus a descriptive grammarian will note that a middle-class speaker, using the standard dialect known as Standard English, may say: *We were pleased to see you*, and that a working-class speaker using a working-class Cockney dialect may say: *We was pleased to see you*. Both examples are grammatical within their own dialects, both examples make perfect sense, and in neither example is there any ambiguity. The idea that a plural subject takes a plural verb is true only of the middle-class standard dialect, not of the working-class Cockney dialect. To put it another way, the plural form of the verb in middle-class Standard English is *were*, while the plural form of the verb in working-class Cockney is *was*.

Let us now offer this simple working definition: *grammar is an account of the relationship between words in a sentence.* In the light of this definition, what the grammarian has to do is to look for regular patterns of word use in the language and give labels to them. However, some of the relationships are pretty complicated and describing them is not easy. The definitions many of us half-remember from our own primary school days – 'a noun is a naming word', 'a verb is a doing word' – are at best unhelpful and at worst downright misleading. Though meaning has a part to play in determining the relationship between words, parts of speech are not defined in terms of word meaning, they are defined, rather, in terms of the function of the words within the sentence. To illustrate, think about the word *present*.

Present can be a verb:

I **present** you with this tennis racket as a reward for your services.

or a noun:

Thank you for my birthday **present**, I've always wanted socks!

or an adjective:

In the **present** circumstances I feel unable to proceed.

It will be clear, then, that teaching grammar has its problems. Confusion can occur at a number of levels: between prescriptive and descriptive approaches, between questions of grammar proper and questions of style, and around issues of variation between standard and non-standard dialects.

Grammar. For Writing?

One of the most long running debates about grammar has been whether the teaching of grammar has a positive impact on pupils' writing. Wyse (2001) concluded:

> The findings from international research clearly indicate that the teaching of grammar (using a range of models) has negligible positive effects on improving secondary pupils' writing (p. 422) . . . The one area where research has indicated that there may be some specific benefit for syntactic maturity is in sentence combining (p. 423).

This finding was independently verified by Andrews *et al.* (2004) in their study that used systematic review methodology developed by the EPPI systematic review centre at the Institute for Education (IOE), University of London:

> The results of the present in-depth review point to one clear conclusion: that there is no high quality evidence to counter the prevailing belief that the teaching of the principles underlying and informing word order or 'syntax' has virtually no influence on the writing quality or accuracy of 5 to 16 year-olds. This conclusion remains the case whether the syntax teaching is based on the 'traditional' approach of emphasising word order and parts of speech, or on the 'transformational' approach, which is based on generative-transformational grammar. (p. 4)

The study also cited Wyse (2001) as one of only three extensive reviews of the subject in a 100-year period (and the first for about 30 years).

Although it has been established that grammar teaching does not impact positively on pupils' writing, it is clear that pupils do need to learn to control language as one part of learning to write. Building on his earlier work from 2001, Wyse's (2006) research that used in-depth analysis of pupils' word choices during the process of writing proposed a pedagogical theory of contextualised teaching of language for writing:

> Although the notion that grammar teaching should be contextualized at text-level is common, such theories have not hitherto had a strong empirical base. The research reported in this paper begins to offer empirical evidence to support such theory. (p. 44)

One of the key findings was the idea that pupils' text-level thinking interacted with sentence-level and word-level thinking sometimes resulting in unconventional language use (or what would be called 'errors' by some).

As part of a large scale study, Myhill *et al.* (2011) claimed they had 'robust evidence from the data in favour of the use of grammar in an embedded way within the teaching of writing' but also that 'the study certainly does not suggest that this would be of universal benefit' (p. 162). This caveat was included because the study found larger gains for pupils with higher attainment. The idea of use of grammar in an embedded way can clearly be linked to the idea of grammar teaching contextualised at text-level that Wyse (2006) had theorised some five years earlier.

In spite of the interesting finding about embedded teaching in Myhill *et al.*, the study (and its reporting) does have some weaknesses. The attack on Andrews *et al.*'s (2004) systematic review seems unduly strident and unwarranted. For example, the suggestion that the Andrews *et al.* review 'takes an over-simplified view of causal relationships' is not borne out by an objective reading of the full report. The allegation that the research question which informs the review ignores the multifaceted nature of learning is weak because it fails to account for the process of limiting the research questions that is required in order that a systematic review can be methodologically rigorous. The criticism that some of the studies analysed by the review were 'at least 25 years old' is irrelevant if the methodology in such studies was sufficiently robust to ensure their continuing relevance, as was the case with the Elley *et al.* (1976) study (see below). Nor does it matter if these studies were carried out in another English-speaking country when the primary analytic focus was the teaching of the English language rather than the socio-cultural elements of the schooling system. The polemical allegation that Wyse (2001, but incorrectly cited as '2004' in Myhill *et al.*) used research 'selectively to justify a pre-determined position or to support a particular stance' is erroneous and entirely unwarranted. The suggestion that the Wyse paper shares this characteristic of selectivity with Hudson's work is also assertion. Wyse's (2001) account was written several years earlier than Hudson's, was much more extensive, and was preceded by an analysis of Hudson's views through a critical synthesis of every citation featuring in Hudson's (2000) online document. It is somewhat surprising to see such polemical (and personal) attacks, particularly ones that are so out of place in a research journal.

The Myhill *et al.* study also raises some methodological issues. The attribution of positive effects on the pupils' writing to grammar teaching is open to question because the intervention did not sufficiently isolate the effect of grammar, rather than other aspects of the teaching, nor is it clear what the control classes did instead of the grammar elements. The difficulty of disentangling the grammar effect is abundantly clear in the paradox of the pedagogical principles that underpinned the intervention contrasting with the claims about the positive effects for grammar more generally. The principles reveal a rich, and admirable, contextualised approach to writing:

- The grammatical metalanguage is used but it is always explained through examples and patterns.
- Links are always made between the feature introduced and how it might enhance the writing being tackled.
- The use of 'imitation': offering model patterns for students to play with and then use in their own writing.
- The inclusion of activities which encourage talking about language and effects.
- The use of authentic examples from authentic texts.
- The use of activities which support students in making choices and being designers of writing.
- The encouragement of language play, experimentation and games (Myhill et al., 2011: 148).

but these do not reflect grammar teaching in the tradition of the field which Myhill et al. are attempting to contradict.

Another potential weakness is that the effects of the intervention were assessed using a Key Stage 3 mark scheme format. This had three components, including the component of sentence structure and punctuation. So the intervention taught the pupils using grammar teaching, then tested the intervention through an assessment of grammar. A much tougher test would have been to report the outcomes for the composition and effect component of the pupils' writing alone.

The authors argue too strongly that their evidence contradicts the long-held view about the place of grammar in relation to the teaching of writing. In making their case, they too quickly dismiss a study (that is generally regarded as the most rigorous study on the teaching of grammar) as a comparison of 'discrete grammar instruction' versus no grammar instruction. In fact, the experimental group in the Elley et al. study (1976) were taught using a contextualised approach. The approach was called The Transformational Grammar Course and was based on Jerome Bruner's concept of the spiral curriculum. In this experimental group, all the activities 'were related to the central core of each strand of the curriculum, thus giving it [the teaching approach] a clear and consistent unity of purpose' (p. 8).

The Elley et al. study is regarded so highly because of its rigorous methodology. At the start of the study, each comparison group had about 80 pupils, giving roughly 250 in total. By the end of the study, there were about 50 pupils per group. The study also included the much sought-for longitudinal dimension, as it was carried out over three years (with different teachers teaching each of the groups over the course of the study in order to minimise teacher effects), and covered '574 periods of English' (p. 10).

The Elley et al. study took place in one large co-educational high school on the outskirts of Auckland city. It involved 248 pupils in eight matched classes of average ability who were taught, observed and regularly assessed from beginning of third-form year (February 1970) to latter part of fifth-form year in November 1972. The results of the reading test; of the assessment of the distribution of fathers' incomes; the secondary certificate of education exam results, and the inclusion of 15 per cent Polynesian pupils indicated a 'normal' sample. One 'bright' and three 'slow learning' classes were excluded.

Data was collected in the form of a series of set essays at the end of each year marked by teachers from neighbouring schools. The battery of tests included 'PAT' reading comprehension and vocabulary tests, '(NZCER, 1969)'; sentence combining; error correction tests; literature appreciation tests and anonymous questionnaires to assess attitudes to work.

The intervention transformational grammar (TG) and 'Let's Learn English' (LLE) grammar groups found English more 'repetitive' and 'useless' than the control group. However the semantic differential analysis found that 'writing' and 'literature' were viewed more positively by the TG groups than the LLE groups. The reading/writing (RW) group showed more positive attitudes to reading. The TG group were particularly negative about 'sentence-study'. Overall transformation and traditional grammar teaching showed no measurable benefits. The RW group, who studied no formal grammar for three years, demonstrated competence in writing and related language skills fully equal to that shown by the two grammar groups. Elley *et al.* dismissed the idea of the introduction of grammar at primary level mainly based on developmental theory: 'it seems most unlikely that such training would be readily applied by children in their own writing. Furthermore the researchers' empirical findings do not support the early introduction of grammar.' (p. 18)

Another point not explained in Myhill *et al.* is that in spite of an explicit focus on grammar as part of the National Literacy Strategy (including the Grammar for Writing resources that seems in significant ways similar to the approach in the Myhill *et al.* study) implemented in England between 1998 and 2010, the gains for writing shown in statutory test score were negligible, nor was there any evidence of significant gains compared to earlier periods that did not include explicit grammar teaching. It is also important to remember that the NLS grammar approach was mainly focused on primary schools. Contrary to their claims, Myhill *et al.* have not provided evidence to contradict the well-established view that grammar teaching (apart from sentence combining) has minimal positive impacts on pupils' writing. As the research was carried out in secondary schools it is also important that it is not cited in support of more grammar teaching in primary and early years settings.

Knowledge about language

The proposal to teach children explicitly about language raises some questions:

- What are the reasons for teaching primary children about language?
- What are the benefits to be gained?
- What should be taught, and at what ages?
- How should it be taught?

- What is the place of terminology?
- Where does grammar fit into all of this?

Cox (1991) suggested that there are two justifications for teaching children explicitly about language. The first is that it will be beneficial to their language use in general. The second is that it is essential to children's understanding of their social and cultural environment, given the role language plays in society. A third suggestion, related to the second, is that 'language should be studied in its own right as a rich and fascinating example of human behaviour' (LINC, 1992: 1).

Although the Language in the National Curriculum (LINC) project was carried out many years ago now, its recommendations about teaching knowledge about language are still valid. The starting point is that children should be encouraged to discuss language use in meaningful contexts that engage their interest. Here are some examples of work done in primary schools under the auspices of the LINC project all of which were extremely productive in getting children to think and talk about language itself (all examples from Bain et al., 1992):

- Making word lists.
- Compiling dictionaries including slang and dialect dictionaries.
- Discussing language variation and social context. For example, how does a mobile phone text message compare with a formal letter?
- Discussing accent and Standard English.
- Compiling personal language histories and language profiles.
- Capitalising on the language resource of the multilingual classroom beginning with in-depth knowledge of languages spoken, read, written and their social contexts including religious ones.
- Role play and drama particularly to explore levels of formality and their links with language.
- The history and use of language in the local environment.
- Collecting and writing jokes.
- Collaborative writing which involves discussion about features of writing and language.
- Media work including the language of adverts.
- Book-making.

One of the aspects of language variation is the way that spoken language differs from written language, as Table 21.1 shows.

Many of the examples in the list above could be, and indeed were, done with the youngest children, and terminology was learned in context as and when the children needed it in their work.

Effective grammar teaching will involve pupils playing with language, and exploring language in ways that are meaningful and fun. Teachers will need both to understand the issues and to be confident in naming terms themselves, so that they can then use them with confidence in everyday discussion with pupils. If teachers use the terms correctly with the children all the time, the children will learn what the terms refer to, even if they are not able to define them to the satisfaction of a linguistics expert until they are older. Dry as dust, decontextualised, old-fashioned grammar exercises of the *underline the noun* variety do not work and put more children off than they help. In addition, textbooks that do not discuss dialect variation, that confuse matters of style with matters of grammar and that take a prescriptive 'correct English' approach throughout are to be avoided.

Table 21.1 Differences between speech and print

Speech	Print
Requires other speakers to be present at time of speech (unless recorded)	Readers are not present at the time of writing
Speakers take turns	Primary writer works alone
Instant and cannot be changed	Can be composed and reworked
Can be incomplete and make sense because of shared understanding of conversation	Writing usually doesn't make sense if it is not complete
Intonation, pitch and body language used to support meaning	Font effects such as italics used to support meaning
Organised in communicative units	Organised in sentences
Separated by pauses in flow of sounds	Separated by communication
Words integrated within streams of words	Words demarcated by spaces
Consists of phonemes (sounds)	Consists of graphemes (letters)
Accent and dialect recognisable features of speakers	Accent and dialect not features unless used as a deliberate device in fiction or poetry
Tends to be informal	Tends to be formal

Practice points

- Plan grammar teaching to enthuse children about the way that language works.
- Engage children's curiosity about language through work on, for example, accent and dialect.
- Use metalanguage only if it actually helps learning not simply to teach technical terms.

Glossary

Grammarian – someone who studies grammar.
Infinitive – part of a verb that is used with 'to': e.g. to *go* boldly.
Public discourse – discussions and debates in the public domain particularly seen through the media.

References

Andrews, R., Torgerson, C., Beverton, S., Locke, T., Low, G., Robinson, A. and Zhu, D. (2004) 'The effect of grammar teaching (syntax) in English on 5 to 16 year olds' accuracy and quality in written composition', *Research Evidence in Education Library* Retrieved 5 February 2007, from http://eppi. ioe.ac.uk/cms/.

Bain, R., Fitzgerald, B. and Taylor, M. (1992) *Looking into Language: Classroom Approaches to Knowledge about Language.* Sevenoaks: Hodder & Stoughton.

Carter, R. (ed.) (1990) *Knowledge about Language and the Curriculum: The LINC Reader.* London: Hodder & Stoughton.

Cox, B. (1991) *Cox on Cox: An English Curriculum for the 1990s.* London: Hodder & Stoughton.

Department for Education and Employment (DfEE) (2000) *The National Literacy Strategy: Grammar for Writing.* London: DfEE Publications.

Elley, W. B., Barham, I. H., Lamb, H. and Wyllie, M. (1976) 'The role of grammar in a secondary school English curriculum', *Research in the Teaching of English*, 10: 5–21.

Hudson, R. (2000) *Grammar Teaching and Writing Skills: the research evidence.* Department of Phonetics and Linguistics, UCL, Gower Street, London. Accessed August 2000 from: http://www.phon.ucl.ac.uk/home/dick/writing.htm

Language in the National Curriculum (LINC) (1992) 'Materials for professional development', unpublished.

Myhill, D., Jones, S., Lines, H. and Watson, A. (2011) 'Re-thinking grammar: the impact of embedded grammar teaching on students' writing and students' metalinguistic understanding', *Research Papers in Education*, 27(2): 139–166.

Wyse, D. (2001) 'Grammar. For Writing?: A critical review of empirical evidence', *British Journal of Educational Studies*, 49(4): 411–427.

Wyse, D. (2006) 'Pupils' word choices and the teaching of grammar', *Cambridge Journal of Education*, 36(1): 31–47.

Annotated bibliography

Bain, R., Fitzgerald, B. and Taylor, M. (1992) *Looking into Language: Classroom Approaches to Knowledge about Language.* Sevenoaks: Hodder & Stoughton.

This is the book that describes some of the classroom activities that arose out of the LINC project. There are lots of excellent ideas here, some of which could even be adapted for use within a literacy hour; others would be more suitable for extended language and literacy work.
L2 ★★

Carter, R. and McCarthy, M. (2006) *Cambridge Grammar of English*. Cambridge: Cambridge University Press.
A comprehensive account of English grammar that uses examples of oral and printed language in modern use (corpus data) in order to describe and explain the way the language works.
L3 ★★

Crystal, D. (1988) *Rediscover Grammar*. Harlow: Longman.
The best book of its kind if you want to learn about grammatical terms and concepts. Succinct and as straightforward as possible.
L1★

Wyse, D. (2006) 'Pupils' word choices and the teaching of grammar', *Cambridge Journal of Education*, 36(1): 31–47.
This paper shows what Year 5 and Year 6 pupils say about their reasons for selecting unconventional grammar. It is suggested that unconventional grammar is directly linked to text-level concerns.
L3 ★★★

Chapter 22

Assessing writing

Assessment of children's writing is built on an understanding of writing development (→ Chapter 16), taking into account children's motivation to write and their understanding of genre. This chapter reviews formative assessment ☞ strategies applicable to working with children on a one-to-one basis and in guided group work. The chapter concludes with some reflections on Assessing Pupil Progress (APP) in writing and on statutory tests. This chapter should be read in conjunction with Chapter 15, 'Assessing reading' and Chapter 8, 'Assessing talk', as some strategies are applicable to all three modes.

Some of the most important assessment of children's writing is carried out orally during the process of writing when the teacher sits with the child and gives feedback. This kind of feedback is likely to be most effective if the teacher has a clear idea of how children's writing should develop (→ Chapter 16) and has a clear idea about each child as an individual, taking into account motivation to write and understanding of genre. Choices about when and how to give oral feedback are key in supporting a child to make progress as a writer.

It is helpful to give oral feedback to children in the immediacy of the writing moment. Information should be given to the child about the successes of their writing and the next steps to be taken, matched to the lesson objectives and the teacher's knowledge of the child's current writing ability. Clarke (2003) argues that oral feedback is the most natural and frequent feedback experience for children. At its best, it is tailor-made and powerful in meeting the immediate needs of the child. Teachers give oral feedback to children using a variety of strategies, sometimes offering specific prompts, but also using questions and engaging in dialogue about their work. At all times, key principles are that children's efforts should be valued and also that a level of challenge is offered to provide for new learning. Getting children to talk before writing in response to this feedback will increase their achievement.

Clarke (2003) advocates providing the child with specific ways to 'close the gap' using written feedback. It is important to give written feedback on both transcriptional and compositional features of writing, but if children are given too many criteria to focus on, they can be deterred from making adventurous choices in their writing. An appropriate balance of targeted feedback in relation to all elements of writing and across all genres is therefore necessary. 'Closing the gap' is a form of written feedback where the teacher provides such specific, targeted feedback in relation to lesson objectives and the child is given the opportunity – as soon after the piece as written and marked – to respond to the feedback. Clarke (2003) suggests that the time allowed to respond to this feedback is a maximum of five minutes.

The choice of pupils' writing for detailed feedback depends on the nature of the writing and the teacher's approach to assessment. One of the ways to select can be on the basis of range. So if on the last occasion you marked a story, a piece of non-fiction might be appropriate the next time. Or if on the previous occasion you had commented on the presentation of a final draft, you might want to comment on an early draft. It is worth remembering that appropriate written comments can be collected together to form the basis of an assessment profile for a child.

One of the difficult aspects of marking children's work relates to the range of choices that are available for your response. One possible way to think about these choices can be to have a system for responding:

1   A specific positive comment about the writing.
2   A specific point about improving something that is individual to the child's writing.
3   A specific point about improving something that relates to a more general target for writing.

Using marking techniques such as ticks, stars, smiley faces, scores out of 10, etc., need to be thought about carefully. These give no information to the child about what in particular they did well or specifically how they could improve next time. However, for young children the extrinsic rewards such as stickers, smiley faces or merit awards can be an important way of rewarding hard work. As a teacher you need to be clear about the pros and cons of the different strategies. A tick at the end of a piece of work should perhaps be used only to indicate that you have checked that the child completed the work and it indicates that you have read the piece. A reward such as a sticker could be used to indicate that the child has worked particularly hard and ideally should accompany more detailed feedback which could be oral and/or written.

Black and William's (1998) review of the literature about formative assessment established self-evaluation and peer-evaluation as key strategies in enabling children to make progress in their learning. Self- and peer-evaluation involves the child as an active learner engaged in thinking and articulating their thinking throughout a lesson. Children should therefore be given opportunities to assess their writing by themselves, for example, in relation to the oral and written feedback they have been given, or the success criteria. They should also be given opportunities to work collaboratively with a peer, evaluating each other's writing and making constructive suggestions for improvements. Russell's work in Sweden and Finland has enabled him to see the ways that pupils set their own targets, as equal partners in the process, for example, creating their own language priorities for the short and medium term. Assessment becomes more than a judgement and is a genuinely negotiated process which appears to be quite different from standard practice in English classrooms.

As discussed in Chapter 17, small group writing is often called 'guided writing', where children are grouped on the basis of ability and need. The aim of guided writing sessions is to encourage, practice and extend independent writing skills. The teacher leads the session, guiding the children to focus in on objectives from the Primary Framework and the Assessment Focuses (AFs) for Writing. While working with the group, the teacher gives focused attention to individuals. Based on identified needs at any stage of the writing process (planning, drafting, editing), the teacher selects a relevant targeted objective for the session and assesses the children's work throughout. Decisions about which AF(s) to focus on in any one session will depend on the teacher's knowledge of where the children are now and what they need to learn. Strategies which can be used to assess during guided writing include observing, questioning, discussing and marking writing alongside the child/children. Feedback should be oral and written and children should have the opportunity to self-assess and develop peer-assessment.

Assessing writing and APP

Assessing Pupils' Progress (APP) is the national approach in England to periodic assessment. APP materials are available for reading, writing and speaking and listening. It is a tool used to refine judgements made using assessment for learning and combines a range of outcomes (written, oral and observed) to inform a level judgement. In relation to writing APP was developed to help teachers make judgements about children's writing achievement as a whole, rather than being informed by only individual pieces of writing. The process supports judgements about the progress of all children in the class over a range of writing samples during a specific period of time.

The Assessment Focuses (AFs) for Writing are:

* **AF1:** write imaginative, interesting and thoughtful texts.
* **AF2:** produce texts which are appropriate to task, reader and purpose.
* **AF3:** organise and present whole texts effectively, sequencing and structuring information, ideas and events.

- **AF4:** construct paragraphs and use cohesion within and between paragraphs.
- **AF5:** vary sentences for clarity, purpose and effect.
- **AF6:** write with technical accuracy of syntax and punctuation in phrases, clauses and sentences.
- **AF7:** select appropriate and effective vocabulary.
- **AF8:** use correct spelling.

The APP process involves teachers selecting a sample of pupils (usually six, two from each ability group). Each term, they review the full range of evidence for each Assessment Focus (AF), usually about six pieces of written work in different genres and curriculum areas. They then refer to the APP assessment criteria and arrive at judgements using the *assessment guidelines* sheet. You may find further information created during the development of APP at http://webarchive.nationalarchives.gov.uk. One of the intentions of APP is to be able to identify which AFs children are struggling with and to modify planning accordingly. It also enables teachers to establish where there is insufficient evidence to make a judgement and therefore to again modify planning accordingly. From the outset, guidance has been given about how to moderate ☞ APP judgements within and across school settings.

Statutory tests

Statutory tests for writing have been in place in England since 1991. For those children in Key Stage 1, teachers have to make judgements on children's attainment in relation to National Curriculum level descriptions ☞ for each eligible child. The aim is to reach a rounded judgement of a child's writing based on knowledge of how the child has performed over time and across a range of contexts. Test materials are available but should form only one part of the evidence. Details about assessing and reporting arrangements are produced annually for both Key Stage 1 and Key Stage 2. Since 2003, the Key Stage 2 writing test has involved a short and long writing task and a spelling test. Handwriting has been assessed through the long writing task. Following Lord Bew's Independent Review of Key Stage 2 (2012) testing, a new statutory Key Stage 2 grammar, punctuation and spelling test will be introduced for the 2013 test cycle.

Practice points
- Ensure your classroom promotes a rich writing environment.
- Response to writing should be focused on specific guidance to help the developing writer (Bearne *et al.*, 2011).

- Keep a balance between day-to-day formative assessment and high-quality in-depth assessment where you use the moderation process with other teachers to help secure your judgements.

Glossary

Formative assessment – ongoing assessment that is used to inform teaching, interaction and planning.

Level descriptions – short paragraphs in the National Curriculum which describe the understanding that children should have gained in order to attain a particular level.

Moderation – the process of agreeing assessment judgements with other people.

Summative assessment – assessment that sums up progress at a particular point in time.

References

Bearne, E., Chamberlain, L., Cremin, T. and Mottram, M. (2011) *Teaching Writing Effectively: Reviewing Practice*. Leicester: UKLA.

Black, P. and William, D. (1998) *Inside the Black Box: Raising Standards Through Classroom Assessment*. London: King's College.

Clarke, S. (2003) *Enriching Feedback in the Primary Classroom*. Abingdon: Hodder Murray.

Annotated bibliography

Assessment of Pupil Progress
   The national archive has examples of APP speaking and listening collections.
   http://webarchive.nationalarchives.gov.uk/20090707073355/http://
   nationalstrategies.standards.dcsf.gov.uk/node/20005
   L1 *

Bearne, E., Chamberlain, L., Cremin, T. and Mottram, M. (2011) *Teaching Writing Effectively: Reviewing Practice*. Leicester: UKLA.
   Succinct yet comprehensive overview of the purposes for writing in the curriculum as a whole, including guidance on assessing writing.
   L2 **

Gipps, C., McCallum, B. and Hargreaves, E. (2000) *What Makes a Good Primary School Teacher?* London: RoutledgeFalmer.
   The assessment chapter in this book covers the whole curriculum but many of the suggestions are relevant to the assessment of writing.
   L2 **

Harlen, W. and Deakin Crick, R. (2002) 'A systematic review of the impact of summative assessment ☞ and tests on students' motivation for learning (eppi-centre review, version 1.1*)', *Research Evidence in Education Library*.

Issue 1. Retrieved 9 January 2007, from http://eppi.ioe.ac.uk/cms/Default.aspx?tabid=108.
This review clearly shows the negative aspects of high stakes testing systems.
L3 ★★★

Johnson, S. (2011) *Assessing Learning in the Primary Classroom*. Abingdon: Routledge.
Comprehensive guide to assessment in primary schools covering assessment of pupils' learning, statutory assessment, international surveys like PISA and PIRLS and much more.
L2 ★★★

Part V

General issues

Chapter 23

Planning

How to plan creatively within the parameters of the curriculum is the main concern of this chapter. The premise is that good planning is enabling and should not be seen as a constraint.

Planning is commonly described in three levels: long-term, medium-term and short-term. Long-term planning tends to mean planning for a year or more and provides a broad framework of curricular provision for each year of each primary school year, to ensure progression, balance, coherence and continuity. Medium-term planning refers to planning for terms and half-terms. Short-term planning is usually weekly or daily and includes detailed lesson plans, including objectives, procedures, differentiation, resources and assessment considerations. Within this overall structure, teachers need to provide high-quality, responsive literacy experiences for the pupils in their class. Key questions to be asked include:

- Does the planning take account of prior knowledge of pupils?
- Are you clear about what you intend the children to learn?
- Is the planning underpinned by secure subject knowledge and subject pedagogy?
- Does the planning take account of potential barriers to learning?
- Does this planning encourage creative and innovative responses to the task?
- Are children likely to be motivated by the suggested activities?
- Across a sequence of lessons, does the planning demonstrate progression?

A critical question you should ask about any planning is to what extent are children's choices taken into account?

There are many ways to find ideas for activities. The best way is for you to think about what you want your children to learn and then to create a suitable activity. When you create activities and resources yourself, you go through a process of development which includes having teaching objectives that are closely matched with the needs of your class. This creative process can, of course, involve you using ideas from all kinds of sources: colleagues; the internet; published materials, etc. While it can be tempting to use published schemes and material, these must always be tailored for the specific learning needs of your class.

Approaches to planning

Until recently, many schools in England have used the Primary National Strategy (PNS) Literacy Framework to guide their planning. This website has now been archived, but many teachers still use the resources as the basis for literacy planning. The main features of this extensive set of materials are:

- a separate link to information about communication, language and literacy in the early years framework;
- guidance papers on issues such as phonics;
- specific information about early reading including phonics;
- the learning objectives which can be viewed by strand or by year group;
- general statements about assessment;
- planning.

The planning link starts with general advice on how to use the planning guidance. Each year group is detailed separately and features sections on narrative, non-fiction, poetry and planning guidance.

The suggested teaching approach is the model developed from the Raising Boys' Achievement in Writing research (UKLA, 2004). The first part of the teaching process involves reading, viewing and exploring and discussing the features of the text types covered by the unit. The idea is that pupils should become confidently familiar with the features of the chosen text type. Ideas for writing will then be captured in a variety of ways. This part of the process is where the class is likely to benefit from talk, drama or role-play activities to support their grasp of the whole text structure. Once there has been extensive experience of the text features, the process of teacher demonstrating, modelling and guiding writing is used to support successful, sustained and independent writing. This sequence can be planned on a piece of A4 paper using three interlocking circles.

Units of work in the framework are divided into phases which follow the above sequence. These units however do not provide specific suggestions for areas that you will need to plan for such as guided reading, phonics, and spelling. As a starting point when constructing a medium-term plan, it is useful to annotate this sheet with possible ideas and activities leading to a learning outcome at the end of the unit. These ideas then need to be transposed onto a medium-term plan. We include the following suggested proforma:

Table 23.1 Proforma for planning sessions

Session	Whole class teaching and learning	Link to objectives and success criteria	Activities/ independent learning	Plenary	Guided work
1					
2					
3					
Etc . . .					

The following detailed example is taken from a Year 5 four-week unit on narrative which covers traditional stories, fables, myths and legends. Here is the unit overview:

• Read wide range of myths, legends, fables and traditional stories. Discuss common themes. Identify features of particular fiction genres.
• Read several different versions of same story, for example retellings from different times or countries, film versions. Draw out evidence of changing context and audience.
• Discuss and look for evidence of narrative viewpoint in particular stories, for example looking at the way that characters are presented. Infer the perspective of the author from what is written and implied.
• Plan and tell stories orally. Show awareness of audience and use techniques such as humour or repetition.
• Plan and write a new version of a myth/legend/fable/traditional tale. Identify audience and adapt writing accordingly. Revise to produce polished version of at least one story.

The guidance highlights an approach in which there is an initial emphasis on analysis of genre. All units are further divided into phases: in this unit there are four, as follows:

Phase 1
Read and analyse features of the text-type. Make comparisons between different versions of the same legend.

Phase 2

Children continue familiarisation with the text-type. Discuss and investigate the effect of different techniques used by the author. Work in a group to explore and empathise with characters through drama activities. Children use a reading journal to record inferences and demonstrate understanding of characters by writing in the first person.

Phase 3

Make comparisons between oral and written narratives. The teacher demonstrates effective note-taking techniques. Children make notes on visual and oral performances before working in small groups to prepare and present an oral retelling of the legend of Robin Hood for an audio or digital video file.

Phase 4

Children evaluate their oral performances against agreed success criteria. The teacher demonstrates how to write a legend, transferring oral storytelling skills into writing. Children work collaboratively to write the legend, exploring how to transfer the visual and oral text to a written narrative.

> (Year 5, Narrative Unit 2 – Traditional stories, fables, myths, legends, http://webarchive.nationalarchives,gov.uk)

Even more detailed specification is then offered for each of these phases. However, the teacher, with their knowledge of the class and interests of the children should adapt planning to reflect these. The legend of Robin Hood is suggested as a possible topic for analysis, for example, but is not a topic that will necessarily be engaging for your children. Note how speaking and listening is embedded within the unit ($\rightarrow$ Chapter 6) and also that use of film and interactive whiteboards is recommended ($\rightarrow$ Chapter 25).

In Phase 4 of this unit, after a suggested 15 days of text study and exploration (we have some significant reservations about the length of time before children begin writing properly), the children are encouraged to do some extended writing: collaborative writing for a tourist leaflet based on the legend. Throughout the phases of this unit, there are many other good ideas such as activities on empathising with characters, the use of drama to explore texts and comparison of oral and printed versions. The teacher who uses such resources flexibly will be able to follow their interests and enthusiasms, adapting and innovating the suggested sequence in the light of their children's responses.

Long-term and medium-term planning leads to lesson planning. New teachers often need to devise individual lesson plans. These provide structure and security but should not be seen as completely inflexible; it is important to be responsive to the children during the session. Elements of a lesson plan are likely to include:

1 administrative details (date and length of session, number and age of children, supporting adults, etc.);
2 curriculum links (links to appropriate documentation, e.g. the Primary Framework or published schemes of work);
3 learning objectives;
4 success criteria;
5 assessment opportunities;
6 key vocabulary;
7 resources;
8 phases of the lesson (introduction, activities, plenary);
9 roles of others.

Lesson plans should be annotated after teaching with evaluations and comments about children's learning.

Practice points

- Consider your children's interests and enthusiasms as you think about planning.
- Be confident in your ability to develop your own pedagogical approaches in the classroom.
- Carefully critique any suggested planning, including that from government.

References

Department for Education and Skills (DfES) (2007) *Primary National Strategy: Primary Framework for Literacy and Mathematics*. http://webarchive. nationalarchives.gov.uk
UKLA (2004) *Raising Boys' Achievements in Writing*. Royston: UKLA.

Annotated bibliography

Bearne, E. (1998) *Making Progress in English*. London: Routledge.
Helpful text which includes sections on planning for reading, writing, talk and grammar.
L ★★
Department for Education and Skills (DfES) (2007) *Primary National Strategy: Primary Framework for Literacy and Mathematics*. http://webarchive. nationalarchives.gov.uk
Useful for finding ideas for activities and resources.
L1 ★

Medwell, J. (2006) 'Approaching short-term planning', in J. Arthur, T. Grainger and D. Wray (eds) *Learning to Teach in the Primary School*. London: Routledge.
Further support for short-term planning.
L2 ★★

Chapter 24

Home–school links

Research shows that children learn in different ways at home and at school. The importance of developing a partnership with parents/carers in order to build bridges between home and school environments is addressed. We also explore issues surrounding the setting of homework and home-reading. The chapter includes some ideas from research on working with families.

It is common practice in education settings to develop home–school links. By this we mean parents/carers acting as partners with educational professionals as part of their child's education. There is of course much more to children's education than the school curriculum. Having an understanding of learning at home and learning at school will enrich teaching and outcomes for children. Throughout the history of education in England there has been a tendency by some to think that children are like 'empty vessels' who know nothing until they are filled with knowledge by schools. This attitude resulted in parents/carers and children feeling powerless to engage in ways that would benefit their schools and their communities. Research now supports the notion of children learning from birth. It therefore follows that children will be learning in their home environments both before, and alongside, educational settings. As early as 1975, the Bullock Report signalled that a change in attitude was necessary (→ chapter 1 for the historical sequence that led to this report):

No child should be expected to cast off the language and culture of the home as he [sic] crosses the school threshold, nor to live and act as though home and school represent two totally separate and different cultures which have to be kept firmly apart. The curriculum should reflect many elements of that part of his life which a child lives outside school.

(DES, 1975: S20.5)

In order to turn the words of the Bullock Report into practice, many schools work hard to involve parents/carers more in their children's education. Indeed, in England there is a premise of parents as partners in their children's education. However, the ever-increasing documentation that accompanies the school curriculum runs many risks, one of which is the alienation of parents/ carers who may feel that they have nothing to offer in such a complex world. Nothing could be further from the truth.

Learning at home and at school

Direct evidence of the importance of the home environment in supporting children's learning comes from a range of research. Tizard and Hughes's early work looked at the differences between talking and thinking at home and at school. They argued forcefully that the home was a 'very powerful learning environment' (1984: 249) and that school nurseries were not aware of this:

> Our observations of children at home showed them displaying a range of interests and linguistic skills which enabled them to be powerful learners. Yet observations of the same children at school showed a fundamental lack of awareness by the nursery staff of these skills and interests. There is no doubt that, in the world of the school, the child appears to be a much less active thinker than is the case at home. We do not believe that the schools can possibly be meeting their goals in the most efficient manner if they are unable to make use of so many of the children's skills.
>
> (ibid.: 264)

Later work by Hughes looked again at some of the issues. Greenhough and Hughes (1999) suggested that the 'conversing' ☞ of parents may be weaker than the conversing of teachers. They tentatively suggested that there might be a link between the amount of meaningful conversation about books at home, and the child's reading progress at school. One part of their research was an illustration of the different ways that four schools tried to improve the level of conversing in the home: (1) a workshop for parents; (2) a modified version of the home–school reading diary; (3) introductory talk by the class teacher and a modified diary; (4) use of a 'visitors' comments' book for each reading. They concluded that these strategies only had limited success and argued that changing parents' approaches with their children may be similar to changing teachers' practice; often a gradual and sophisticated process. One aspect that Greenhough and Hughes did not seem to address was the child's own perspective. It is possible that some children might have wanted a different kind of reading experience at home – such as 'just' listening to a story – after a day at school that was full of a high level of conversing.

As far as reading is concerned, there are two particularly powerful seminal studies that showed the positive influence of parents. Prior to 1966, Durkin carried out some research in the US and published it in a book called *Children Who Read Early* (Durkin, 1966). These were the things that were common to the children's experiences:

- Parents had read to their children frequently, and had also found time to talk with them and answer their questions.
- Real books were more commonly read by the children than typical school textbooks or reading scheme books.
- Whole-word learning had been used more than letter-sounds for reading, although letter-sounds had been used to help writing.
- Print in their everyday surroundings was of interest to the children.
- Many of the children had been interested in writing as well as reading.

A decade later, Clark (1976) published a very similar study in England. She said that although the child's natural abilities were important, 'the crucial role of the environment, the experiences which the child obtained, their relevance to his interest and the readiness of adults to encourage and to build upon these, should not be underestimated' (1976: 106).

And here are the factors that were common to the children in Clark's study:

- At least one parent, often the mother, had a deep involvement with their child and their progress.
- Parents welcomed the opportunity to talk to their children.
- Non-fiction and print in the home and local environment were mentioned as much as the reading of storybooks.
- Most of the children used the public library.
- Parents would happily break off from other activities and tell their child what words said if the child couldn't work them out independently from the context.
- Very few parents taught their children the letter-sounds. If they did, this was to help with writing more than reading. More children learned the letter names first.
- The children had a range of strategies for working out difficult words if their parent wasn't available to supply the word.
- Many of the children were interested in writing as well as reading.

There was very little evidence that systematic instruction in reading, including phonics, was part of these children's pre-school experiences, yet they all learned to read before they started school. Socio-economic differences were not a significant factor in the research which showed that children from a range of family backgrounds learned to read. The implications for teachers are: (1) a range of approaches to reading is beneficial; (2) support for children should be based on understanding of home experiences; (3) other parents/carers may benefit from guidance in the kinds of approaches that the parents in the two studies used. Wyse (2007) offers guidance to parents/carers on supporting their children, not just in reading but also in writing because of the mutual benefits that occur from looking at both.

More recent research by Marsh (2003), Maddock (2006) and Levy (2011), drawing on Bhaba's (1994) 'third space theory', reiterates the case for children's home literacy experiences to be valued. 'Third space theory' is a metaphor for the space in which cultures of home and school meet and explores how these diverse worlds can be brought together in educational settings. Millard (2003: 6) refers to this process as a 'transformative pedagogy of literacy fusion' suggesting that children's out-of-school interests can be fused with schooled literacy in classroom practice that pays attention to what happens when the two textual worlds collide.

Home–school agreements

Since September 1999, all schools have had to have 'home–school agreements'. Bastiani and Wyse (1999) looked beyond the legal requirement (that such an agreement must be in place) to the hard work that is involved in setting up a meaningful home–school agreement. One of the interesting points they make is that parents/carers are not obliged to sign such agreements nor should there by any punitive consequence if they do not. It is suggested that if parents/carers have reservations, these should be used as a basis for discussion and a possibility for greater understanding of families' needs. They also stress the vital importance of genuine consultation:

> A key ingredient in the process of consultation with parents/carers, which is a formal requirement in the introduction of agreements, is genuineness. Unfortunately educational practice is littered with the debris of glossy rhetoric ☞, phoney consultation and unfilled promises. Schools may, for example, consult but only hear what they want to hear; they may listen to some parents/carers and ignore others; they may hear, but do nothing.
>
> (ibid.: 10)

The Department for Education in England requires governing bodies in educational settings to provide a home–school agreement explaining the school's aims and values, the school's responsibilities towards its pupils, the responsibility of each pupil's parents, and what the school expects of its pupils.

Homework

Most home–school agreements include statements about homework. Findings from the *Cambridge Primary Review* (Alexander, 2010) show that in general, parents want schools to set homework and other outside-of-school activities for their children. The government recommendation is that children as young as six (Years 1 and 2) should do one hour a week of homework, ages 7–9 (Years 3 and 4) should do 1.5 hours a week, and those aged 10 and 11 (Years 5 and 6) should do 30 minutes a day.

As schools are required to set homework, it is important that they encourage children to engage in interesting activities. For example, one of our children's teachers suggested that they phone up a grandparent and ask them about the time when they were children. This activity inspired Esther to write one of her longest pieces of writing at home:

> My grabad [grandad] and gramar didn't have a tely. they did hav a rabyo [radio]. they had a metul Ian [iron]. they had sum bens [beans] and vegtbuls. thee wa lots ov boms in the war. the shoos were brawn and blac Thay had long dresis. Thay had shun trawsis and long socs.

There is always the danger that the pressures of time for teachers can result in photocopied homework sheets that are uninteresting and of questionable value. As is the case with many things in teaching, it is better to organise a limited number of really exciting homework tasks that are genuinely built on in the classroom, than to set too many tasks where it is difficult for the teacher to monitor them all.

One of the most common strategies to support home–school links has been through book bags. Each child has a durable bag that contains books, often a reading scheme book and a free choice book, and the child takes this home on a regular basis. A reading diary generally accompanies the books, and parents/ carers are encouraged to note the date, title of the book and to make a comment about their child's reading. Table 24.1 shows an example of a parent's comments.

The idea of book bags was extended by the Basic Skills Agency (and subsequently build on by BookTrust) who set up a National Support Project to promote 'story sacks' throughout England and Wales. These have proved

Table 24.1 A parent's comments on a child's reading

Date	Book	Comments
7/5	Roll over	Well read.
14/5	Better than you	Fluent reading.
17/5	Big fish	Well read. Why no punctuation, i.e. question marks, speech marks? Esther commented on this.
		[Teacher: I don't know. I will check.]
21/5	Sam's book	Well read.
28/5	Lion is ill	Well read.

very popular and are widely used. Story sacks, containing a good children's book and supporting materials, are designed to stimulate reading activities. The sacks and the artefacts associated with the book can be made by parents/carers and other volunteers. This can be a good way to involve parents/carers in the school community. Other related items such as an audio recording of the text, language game and other activities, can be used by parents/carers at home to bring reading to life and develop the child's language skills.

Working with parents/carers in the classroom

As a teacher, you are likely to have the opportunity to work with parents/carers who have volunteered to help in the classroom. These parents/carers volunteer to support schools in their own time and are a precious resource. Teachers have responsibility for managing other adults who work with them.

One of the most important things to remember is that schools and teachers need to offer guidance to people who are supporting literacy in the classroom. Parental help is often invaluable in the group work section of the literacy sessions. They can also support struggling readers either individually or in groups, but it should be remembered that this is a skilled task and they will require the chance to discuss how things are going and how they can best help the children.

Knowsley Local Education Authority carried out a project that included the recruitment and training of large numbers of adult volunteers who helped primary pupils with their reading on a regular basis. An evaluation by Brooks et al. (1996: 3) concluded that the training for parents/carers and other volunteers was one of the most important components of the project and 'it seemed to make the most significant difference to raising reading standards'. The idea of training parents/carers is one that the Basic Skills Agency has also been involved in. The main purpose of their family literacy initiatives was to raise the basic skills of both parents/carers and children together. For parents/carers, the emphasis was mainly on helping them to understand more about what happened in schools and how they could support this. The children's sessions involved hands-on motivational activities. Joint sessions were also held where parents/carers were encouraged to enjoy a natural interaction with their children during joint tasks. Brooks et al. (1999) found that these family literacy programmes – with some modifications – worked as well for ethnic minority families as for other families.

Practice points
- Genuinely seek information from parents/carers about their children.
- Think out about how to incorporate children's learning outside the classroom with the school curriculum.

- Involve and support parents/carers who work in your classroom as much as possible.

Glossary

Conversing – a broad range and high quality of talk related to a book or other text.
Rhetoric – literally the skills of speech used for particular effects, but in this case fine-sounding words not reflected by the day-to-day reality.

References

Alexander, R. (ed.) (2010) *Children, Their World, Their Education: Final Report and Recommendations of the* Cambridge Primary Review. London: Routledge.
Bastiani, J. and Wyse, B. (1999) *Introducing Your Home–School Agreement.* London: Royal Society of Arts (RSA).
Bhaba, H. K. (1994) *The Location of Culture.* New York: Routledge.
Brooks, G., Cato, V., Fernandes, C. and Tregenza, A. (1996) *The Knowsley Reading Project: Using Trained Reading Helpers Effectively.* Slough: The National Foundation for Educational Research (NFER).
Brooks, G., Harman, J., Hutchison, D., Kendall, S. and Wilkin, A. (1999) *Family Literacy for New Groups.* London: The Basic Skills Agency.
Clark, M. M. (1976) *Young Fluent Readers.* London: Heinemann Educational Books.
DES (Department of Education and Science) (1975) *A Language for Life (The Bullock Report).* London: HMSO.
Durkin, D. (1966) *Children Who Read Early.* New York: Teachers College Press.
Greenhough, P. and Hughes, M. (1999) 'Encouraging conversing: trying to change what parents/carers do when their children read with them', *Reading*, 24(4): 98–105.
Levy, R. (2011) *Young Children Reading at Home and at School.* London: Sage.
Maddock, M. (2006) 'Children's personal learning agendas at home', *Cambridge Journal of Education*, 36(2): 153–169.
Marsh, J. (2003) 'Connections between literacy practices at home and in the nursery', *British Educational Research Journal*, 29(3): 369–382.
Millard, E. (2003) 'Transformative pedagogy: Towards a literacy of fusion', *Reading, Literacy and Language*, 37(1): 3–9.
Tizard, B. and Hughes, M. (1984) *Young Children Learning: Talking and Thinking at Home and at School.* London: Fontana Press.
Wyse, D. (2007) *How to Help Your Child Read and Write.* London: Pearson/BBC Active.

Annotated bibliography

Bastiani, J. and Wyse, B. (1999) *Introducing Your Home–School Agreement*. London: RSA.
A useful guide to introducing home–school agreements. Informed by good practice in secondary schools but relevant to all phases.
L1 ★

Greenhough, P. and Hughes, M. (1998) 'Parents/carers' and teachers' interventions in children's reading', *British Educational Research Journal*, 24(4): 283–398.
A fuller version of the research that we refer to in this section. This was included in a special edition of the journal where all the articles are concerned with 'families and education'.
L3 ★★★

Levy, R. (2008) ' "Third spaces" are interesting places: Applying "third space theory" to nursery-aged children's constructions of themselves as readers', *Journal of Early Childhood Literacy*, 8(1): 43–66.
A study of how third space theory can be applied to nursery children's home–school experiences in relation to reading.
L3 ★★★

Shah-Wundenburg, M., Wyse, D. and Chaplain, R. (2012) 'Parents helping their children learn to read: The effectiveness of paired reading and hearing reading in a developing country context', *Journal of Early Childhood Literacy*, Vol. 13. DOI: 10.1177/1468798412438067.
Includes useful overview of research in the field of home–school reading. Reveals that challenges that are part of working with poorer communities in India.
L3 ★★★

Wyse, D. (2007). *How to Help Your Child Read and Write*. London: Pearson/ BBC Active.
As this book was written for parents/carers, it may offer a useful source of information to support your discussions with parents/carers who often ask how they can help their child with reading and writing.
L1 ★

Chapter 25

Multimodality and ICTs

Information and Communications Technologies (ICTs) should be viewed as useful tools which, with the appropriate pedagogy, can enhance learning and teaching. This chapter includes a focus on multimodality including the use of film to enhance children's learning.

The prime importance of the role of the teacher and their pedagogy, more than the technology, has been understood for a long time. Miller and Olson's (1994) research found that the personal pedagogy of teachers could not be easily separated from the use they made of ICT and that ICT did not seem to drive practice; if anything, previous practice determined the nature of ICT use.

There is a vast and growing range of technologies available for teachers and children to engage with to support learning. However, the possibilities of these technologies for learning are defined not just by device or functionality but by what both teachers and children see as the affordances and constraints of particular hardware and software. While it is impossible for any teacher to have a complete grasp of the functionality of all the hardware and software available to them, the important point is to regard technology as a tool and to see the wide range of possibilities it can offer to promote learning.

Traditional constructions of what is meant by reading and writing have focused on linear printed texts. Bearne (2003: xvii) argues for broader constructions of reading to include digital and multi-literacies. She notes: 'children now have available to them many forms of text which include sound, voices, intonation, stance, gesture, movement, as well as print and image. These have changed the way young readers expect to read.' These many forms of text have also changed the way teachers should expect children to write. As far as classroom writing is concerned, although handwriting will not disappear, there will be much more on-screen writing. It is also likely that the process of composing, editing and revising will expand to include screen-based presentations as well as writing.

Examples of multimodal texts include picture books, graphic novels, films, comics, slide presentations, computer games, podcasts, etc. To this end, there are four modes of communication that we all rely on and use.

1   **Written mode:** meaning and design of the words – font, size, layout, spacing, colour.
2   **Visual mode:** composition, movement, colour, light, space.
3   **Sound mode:** tone, pitch, pauses, choice of instrument.
4   **Gestural mode:** facial expression, holding of posture or expression, spacing of people.

In multimodal texts, meaning is constructed through the combination of these four modes. Many of the texts that children experience and enjoy at home are multimodal and research has shown that they respond enthusiastically to texts and activities which involve the visual (Essex Writing Project, 2003).

Multimodal texts can be examined with regard to their design and layout and how different combinations of representations convey meaning. Activities involving reading complex picture books in which word and image interact are very helpful in developing children's reading comprehension. Here, a visualiser is an extremely helpful tool to enable the whole class to engage with a text. Children can then apply the observed relationship between words, image, gesture and sound to their own constructions on paper and on screen. Hardware and software such as digital cameras, PowerPoint and Photo Story can be used by children to create multimodal texts.

Moving image work

Research into underperformance in writing has shown that work on moving image media can raise attainment (Marsh and Bearne, 2008). These studies point to a range of positive effects including sustaining commitment, showing greater independence, enthusiasm, confidence and motivation and improved attitudes and attainment in writing;

> We live in a world of moving images. To participate fully in our society and its culture means to be as confident in the use and understanding of moving images as of the printed word. Both are essential aspects of literacy in the twenty-first century.
>
> (Film: 21st Century Literacy, 2010)

Just as we teach children to read written words, so we need to teach them to 'read' moving images. Film texts convey meaning through multiple modes: spoken language, music, performance, costume, lighting, editing, sound effects, etc. A very helpful resource to go to is the Film Education website, www.filmeducation.org. It has a wide range of curriculum-focused resources to use with ages 4 to 19, most of which are free. There is a library of films and clips, stills, trailers, interviews and suggestions for activities related to current releases.

When analysing film sequences with children, some helpful questions to think about are:

- What is the purpose of this sequence – what is it trying to do or say?
- Does it have a narrative?
- What does it look like?
- What does it remind me of?
- Why does it look the way it does?
- Why was it produced, how, and who by?
- Who is it for?
- What effects does it have on the viewer and how does it achieve these?

The British Film Institute (BFI) strongly advocates film work and has produced some suggestions for structured teaching. Pilot work for the teaching resource *Story Shorts* (British Film Institute, 2001) involved teachers and others from Birmingham LEA, Bristol and Lambeth EAZ (Education Action Zone), Bristol Watershed Media Centre and Warwickshire Arts Zone. Some of the teachers' comments show their excitement about the work: 'I have been more surprised by the children's reactions to the films than anything else I have ever seen'; 'Using the film *Growing* stimulated the strongest poetry ever written by the children.' The resource consists of a series of films which are about five minutes long. The films are all interesting and the length means that they can be used more easily in literacy lesson than a feature film. However, this does raise some issues. Some of the best work with film can come from using films that are current and that relate closely to children's interests. Although these are feature-length films, DVD technology means that they can be viewed in short sections (called 'chapters'). This means that teachers can design activities which do not require children to see the whole film each time.

Story Shorts suggests a set of opening questions that can be used to stimulate discussion: the '3 Cs' are Camera; Colour; Character; and the '3 Ss' are Story; Sound; Setting. So, for example, with regard to *Lord of the Rings* you might ask: What is the motion of the *camera* just before we see an Orc being born from the filth of the earth? Or, what kinds of *colours* do you see after Gandalf's death as the fellowship emerges from the Mines of Moria? Or, what kinds of *sounds* make the black riders so terrifying? Following whole group discussion supported by the Cs and Ss questions, there are suggestions for how the films can be used to stimulate other more extended activities which take speaking and listening into writing and drawing.

Story Shorts is more about using film as a stimulus for reflection than actually getting involved with creating films, but there are many examples where the skills learned could be applied to such work. Although it steers an uneasy path through the competing demands of the objectives in the NLS Framework for Teaching and the institute's own agenda for greater knowledge about the techniques of film-making, it was an important development in the context of working with film to support the teaching of English at primary level.

Parker (1999) showed that there can be positive links between moving image media and literacy development. His research featured a project that involved Year 3 children adapting Roald Dahl's story *Fantastic Mr Fox* into an animated film. One aspect of the programme of study involved some children working towards a simplified version of the book for younger children, and others were getting ready to use the animation package on the computer. Parker felt that some of the children's first-person writing to support the script had particularly strong visual characteristics:

1   'I saw some metal in the moonlight night.'
2   'All I can see is the 4 walls. Brown, dim and muddy like a pison.' [prison].
3   'I can see the opening to our den. Its daytime the light is coming in.'

(ibid.: 31)

David Buckingham has done much work on the influence of television, and more recently has written about multimedia ☞ technologies. He suggests that society – and ironically the media – tend to take up two main positions: either that new technologies are a very good thing or that they are dangerous. He points out that neither position is satisfactory as the real picture is much more complex. Buckingham's (1999) research has included a focus on computer games and creative use of multimedia. In contrast to public concerns, he found that gaming was very much a social activity. Although games were played alone, they were also played collaboratively. The games also provided a topic for much discussion that included swapping games, sharing cheats and hints and discussion about the wider world of games playing such as TV programmes about the subject, games shops, games arcades and magazines. Buckingham also added a cautionary note that a great deal of the discussion was influenced by consumerism. This perhaps adds further justification for helping children to become critical consumers of media messages so they are not unfairly influenced by advertising messages.

In another piece of research, Parker (1999) tried to find out 'to what extent, and how, were children using computers for digital animation, design work, sound or video editing, or for what is sometimes called "multi-media authoring" ' (p. 31). Some of this survey's results mirrored the previous piece of research; for example, overall he found that 'boys were generally more interested and involved' in the area than girls. He also found that although many of the children claimed to be involved in multimedia authoring, it was rarely a creative process. For example, although some of the children thought that they had made animations, they confused their own input with examples that were already available on the computer. The lack of creativity was caused by parents' lack of skill and therefore ability to help their children, the children's view that computers were mainly to be used for 'messing about' when they were bored, and the lack of meaningful audiences for their work. This kind of work at home is an area that teachers can actively address.

Applications software

As a teacher, your emphasis in relation to ICT should be on *composing* and *creating* using a range of application packages, not on the overuse of skills-building software. The scope for the 'spiral' development of knowledge, skills and understanding using applications packages is vast. Applications are tools that allow us to carry out various jobs quicker and more efficiently. Examples include: word processing, desktop publishing, spreadsheets, Web authoring packages, databases and a range of multimedia packages.

The biggest area of expansion in recent years has been in multimedia applications. Children can now make films by filming moving image sequences, editing them with packages like Apple iMovie, composing music for soundtracks, inserting editing effects and 'burning' DVDs. This kind of project requires extended regular periods of time to bring together the different sources to create a satisfying outcome. We feel that the learning that is possible through such projects is very promising indeed.

Word processing software continues to become more and more sophisticated. It offers the chance to compose from first draft (but how often does this happen in early years and primary settings?) and to go through several editing stages. Spell checkers are particularly useful, grammar checkers less so because they are very poor at understanding the context for the words and phrases being used. Documents created in word processors can easily be saved as Web pages and published on school websites. Integration of images is straightforward, helped by the use of tables to organise documents. One of the biggest limitations of word processing software is that use of the keyboard is slow if you do not learn to type. Given that voice recognition software is still slower than fluent typing, and because of the difficulties you find if not in a quiet environment, the keyboard is likely to be used for the foreseeable future. For that reason, children should be taught how to type properly. We found a very inexpensive but good-quality typing package, called *Master Key*, online.

The software that enables children to design Web pages has the added facility to include moving images and sound. The other significant difference that this software has is the ability to link different texts by clicking on an icon, picture or piece of text using hyperlinks. These packages challenge us to think about what a 'text' really is. If children are encouraged to record their own sounds, create their own images, develop their own writing and establish their own links, this really can lead to exciting learning outcomes.

Practice points

- Use ICTs as tools that naturally extend your pedagogy.
- Critically evaluate all software and ask tough questions about its effectiveness for helping pupils learn more.
- Emphasise active creation and composition more than the more passive aspects of ICTs.

Glossary

Multimedia – texts that use a range of media in their production including text, pictures, links, moving images, sounds.

References

Andrews, R., Dan, H., Freeman, A., McGuinn, N., Robinson, A. and Zhu, D. (2005) *The Effectiveness of Different ICTs in the Teaching and Learning of English (Written Composition), 5–16.* London: EPPI-Centre, Social Science Research Unit, Institute of Education, University of London.

Bearne, E. (1998) *Making Progress in English.* London: Routledge.

Becta (2007) 'What are the main benefits of a learning platform?' Retrieved 24 January 2007, from http://schools.becta.org.uk/index.php?section= re&-rid=12889.

British Film Institute (2001) *Story Shorts: A Resource for Key Stage 2 Literacy.* London: British Film Institute.

Buckingham, D. (1999) 'Superhighway or road to Nowhere? Children's relationships with digital technology', *English in Education*, 33(1): 3–12.

Department for Education and Skills (DfES) and Primary National Strategy (PNS) (2006) *Multimodal – Ict Digital Texts.* Retrieved 26 January 2007, from http://www.standards.dfes.gov.uk/primaryframeworks/literacy/ Papers/learningandteaching/.

Essex Writing Project (2003) *Visually Speaking: Using Multimedia Texts to Improve Boys' Writing.* Chelmsford: Essex Education Authority.

Film: 21st Century (2010) Film 21st Century Literacy Project. London: Film 21st Century. Retrieved 5 July 2012 from http://industry.bfi.org.uk/ media/pdf/g/t/Film-21st_Century_Literacy.pdf.

Marsh, J. and Bearne, E. (2008) *Moving Literacy On. Evaluation of the BFI Lead Practitioner Scheme for moving image media.* Leicester: UKLA.

Miller, L. and Olson, J. (1994) 'Putting the computer in its place: a study of teaching with technology', *Journal of Curriculum Studies*, 26(2): 121–141.

Parker, D. (1999) 'You've read the book, now make the film: moving image media, print literacy and narrative', *English in Education*, 33(1): 24–35.

Annotated bibliography

Burn, A. and Leach, J. (2004) *A Systematic Review of the Impact of ICT on the Learning of Literacies Associated with Moving Image Texts in English, 5–16.* London: EPPI-Centre, Social Science Research Unit, Institute of Education, University of London.
Makes the important point that pupils should *produce* moving image texts. This kind of work should be regarded as a form of 'writing' and should not just be a feature of the reading curriculum. There are also cross-curricular benefits for use of moving image texts.
L3 ★★★

Jewitt, C. and Kress, G. (2010) 'Multimodality, literacy and school English', in D. Wyse, R. Andrews and J. Hoffman (eds) *The Routledge International Handbook of English, Language and Literacy Teaching* London: Routledge.
Gunther Kress and Carey Jewitt have devoted their academic careers to the study of multimodality and have developed theories based on semiotics.
L3 ★★★

Marsh, J. (2004) 'The primary canon: a critical review', *British Journal of Educational Studies,* 52(3): 249–362.
Marsh's work on popular culture including multimedia is excellent. This paper offers further evidence of the marginalisation of multimedia.
L3 ★★★

Teachers Evaluate Educational Multimedia (TEEM) http://teemeducation. org.uk.
Very useful site that includes teacher evaluations of packages to support the teaching of English and literacy and most areas of the curriculum.
L1 ★

Chapter 26

Supporting black and multilingual learners

The importance of supporting all languages at children's disposal is emphasised in this chapter. It is argued that in schools it is important to celebrate the cultural and linguistic diversity of the children we teach. Classroom practices that are part of multicultural literacy teaching are suggested.

Teaching can be an exhilarating experience because of the tremendous diversity within the classroom. Because the diversity of language is a reality in the classroom, all children's language use should be viewed as a powerful resource. Over two hundred languages are spoken by children in British schools and the number of young bilingual speakers continues to rise.

Bilingual learners ☞ in England face two main tasks in school: they need to learn English and they need to learn the content of the curriculum, tasks which should proceed hand in hand. Nearly all children learn their first language successfully at home. Children learning an additional language in a classroom are learning under conditions that are significantly different. Learning a language is more than just learning vocabulary, grammar and pronunciation. Children need to use all these appropriately for a whole range of real purposes or functions, functions they will need to perform in order to 'do' Maths, Science, History etc. such as questioning, analysing and hypothesising, which are clearly linked to thinking and learning skills.

Cummins (1996) adapted the metaphor of an iceberg to distinguish between basic interpersonal communicative skills and cognitive and academic language proficiency (BICS and CALP respectively for short). All children develop communicative skills first, in face-to-face highly contextualised situations, but take longer to develop the cognitive and academic language proficiency that contributes to educational success. Cummins acknowledged that some interpersonal communication can impose considerable cognitive demands on a speaker and that academic situations may also require social communication skills. Generally speaking, children learning an additional language can become conversationally fluent in the new language in two to three years but may take five years or longer to catch up with monolingual peers on the development of CALP.

A large-scale study of emergent bilingual pupils in the US clearly showed the importance of supporting all pupils' languages:

> Non-English speaking student success in learning to read in English does not rest exclusively on primary language input and development, nor is it solely the result of rapid acquisition of English. Both apparently contribute to students' subsequent English reading achievement ... early literacy experiences support subsequent literacy development, regardless of language; time spent on literacy activity in the native language – whether it takes place at home or at school – is not time lost with respect to English reading acquisition.
>
> (Reese *et al.*, 2000: 633)

Multilingual children are experts in handling language because they become adept at 'code switching' (switching between languages). This is not a sign of confusion, but has cognitive, metalinguistic, and communicative advantages. Indeed, bilingual children outperform monolinguals in cognitive flexibility tasks (Bialystok, 2007) because they work constantly with two linguistic systems. These children have considerable language skills on which the teacher can build, and they are likely to have much to offer others, particularly with regard to the subject of language study. Having said this, even if the child may be skilled in language use, they may still need particular support and guidance to develop greater proficiency in the use of English at school, especially in terms of written English.

As we argued previously in Chapter 24, children's home literacies, including their language, need to be valued. This means that the use of mother tongues/community languages should be positively encouraged in the classroom, both for children who are new to English and also as they become more fluent. Bilingual children are hearing two languages – or two distinct systems – to which they have to internalise and respond. At an early age, neither language is likely to interfere with the other, so young children can acquire two languages easily (Kuhl, 2004).

It is important therefore for teachers to be aware of what children know with regard to English. In terms of assessing proficiency in English language development, Hester (1990) developed the following categories:

Stage 1	**New to English:** Bilingual English learners who might be able to engage in classroom activities using their own mother tongue, but need support to operate in English.

Stage 2	**Becoming familiar with English:** Bilingual English learners who can engage in all learning activities but whose spoken and/or written English clearly shows that English is not their first language. Their oral English is well developed but their literacy development in English in such that they need considerable support to operate successfully in written activities in the classroom.
Stage 3	**Becoming confident as a user of English:** Bilingual pupils whose oral and written English is progressing well and who can engage successfully in both oral and written activities, but need further support for a variety of possible reasons, for example pupils who are achieving considerable success in subjects such as Mathematics and Science but much less in others such as English or in Humanities, which are more dependent upon a greater command of English.
Stage 4	**Fully fluent in English:** Bilingual pupils whose use of English and engagement with the curriculum are considered successful and who do not require additional language support.

In a study carried out with 2,300 11-year-olds in London, Strand (2005) found that:

> EAL pupils at the early stages (1–3) of developing fluency had significantly lower KS2 test scores in all subjects than their monolingual peers. However, EAL pupils who were fully fluent in English achieved significantly higher scores in all KS2 tests than their monolingual peers.
>
> (ibid.: 275)

Consequently, the teacher needs to be aware of the need to apply greater sensitivity to these children. On the one hand, the child should be encouraged to use spoken English at every possible opportunity; on the other, the teacher needs to employ teaching strategies which ensure that the same child does not begin to lose confidence in their language use because they perceive themselves as failed readers and writers.

Language use is closely linked with a person's identity so requires sensitivity and perception by all who work with children. Teachers need to understand that it is unhelpful to conceive of 'multilingual children' as some kind of homogeneous group. Some children will have been born in this country and their parents may have insisted on a different first language in order to retain the child's sense of ethnic identity and community. It is important to acknowledge that there are social and cultural differences which have direct relevance for the teacher of English. British Black and Asian parents may have different perceptions of their relationship to and role within the 'host' white community. Some will encourage their children to embrace British customs, language, codes, etc., as fully and as unproblematically as possible; others will seek to resist such moves and instead promote and defend their own cultural beliefs, languages and practices in order to maintain their cultural identity as distinct within British society. It would be unwise to begin to enter into a debate which meant that one side or another would be seen as preferable; it is more important to acknowledge that the child's own role within this can be difficult to negotiate. It is professionally important, therefore, to be aware of the child's and their community's set of cultural beliefs, to make every effort to understand and respect the position of the parents and to ensure that the child is not placed in a position whereby he or she is required to make unhelpful comparisons between the school and the home. The teacher will also need to be sensitive to the fact that some children prefer to be seen as similar to everyone else and not to be made to stand apart because of their 'difference'. As Blackledge (1994: 46) pointed out:

> If English is to replace rather than add to the languages of the children we teach, we must ask what will be the effect of such a programme on their cultural identity, their self-esteem and sense of place in the community?

Classroom approaches

There is evidence to show that the least successful way to deliver English teaching to a multilingual child at the early stages of English acquisition is to remove them from the classroom setting and provide short sharp bursts of tuition in isolation, or to group them with children who are struggling, or with SEN. More effective is the practice of resourcing the multilingual classroom with, for example, bilingual texts (including big books), dual-language CD-Roms, and stories recorded (often by parents) in other languages. Teachers who develop practices which ignore or exclude the needs of bilingual pupils in order to serve a perceived need of the white majority in the class should be aware of research into this area which reported the success of 204 'two-way bilingual' schools, demonstrating through achievement data that all pupils benefited from such approaches and not, as might be expected, only the bilingual children themselves (Thomas and Collier, 1998). It can also be helpful for teachers in England to be aware that full bilingualism is a daily reality in schools in Wales, and Scotland includes fully bilingual elements in its curriculum for excellence.

Many teachers find themselves developing their own resources in response to the challenge of multilingual children. While this may initially stem from a lack of suitable resources, more positively it stems from the teacher's overt recognition of the child's needs, and the production of such materials helps to consolidate the early support for multilingual children. Such materials also communicate a positive message to parents, who can be encouraged to use them either in the school or at home.

It has been pointed out that dual-language books are not always as immediately helpful as may be presumed (Gravelle, 1996). One language may be given greater status than another, cultural subtleties in translation are not always successful and there are difficulties when written languages which are read from right to left are placed next to English as the starting points for the child could become confusing. However, the construction of dual-language books are a popular way forward in many multilingual classrooms, as children often find the process supportive and beneficial. Language issues should be less problematic when children are allowed to create dual-language books for themselves, and when parents are encouraged to take part in this process. Walker *et al.* (1998: 18) offers particularly interesting and intricate designs for dual-language book-making, and it should be remembered that once these books are made, they can serve the purpose of recording the child's personal development and later provide an immediate and personal starting point for other children who need similar support (for further book-based resources → Chapter 3).

Cross-curricular and thematic approaches in primary classrooms often offer opportunities to acknowledge multicultural dimensions to study. Teachers can acknowledge consciously the monocultural way in which many primary school themes are conceived, and open this planning up to more accurately reflect a multicultural society. Themes such as 'Ourselves', 'Food', 'Shelter', 'Sacred Places' and 'Journeys' all offer the potential for links across the curriculum and possibilities for multicultural work to emerge (Hix, 1992).

Story telling can be another particularly successful method of encouraging the multilingual child to negotiate more than one language. There is evidence that story telling has been a particularly important strategy with bilingual learners in the early years (MacLean, 1996). All cultures have their own histories, myths, legends and stories which are passed on through generations of children. These stories cross cultural boundaries; some are recognisably similar with subtle shades of difference, others will be particular within a specific cultural context. In either case, the story itself becomes a powerful, shared experience and the telling, the retelling, the writing and reading of the range of possible stories open a rich vein of language study for the teacher to exploit. Again, parents should be seen as a valuable and authoritative resource in this area.

As far as the potential for ICT to support children with EAL, Low and Beverton (2004) found that there need to be sufficient computers for children to work on and that the work should be part of normal classroom teaching but tailored to the specific needs of the children. There were indications that collaborative computer work could be valuable and that although computer work could be motivational, it should not be done to extremes as, for example, in the case of word processing, some pupils composed better on the computer and some composed better with pen and paper.

A range of recommendations relating to successful practices and strategies for the support of black and multilingual children in British schools, including the important need to combat racism, has been published to guide teachers in these areas (Blair and Bourne, 1998; Jones, 1999). These are a summary of our suggestions for supporting bilingual and multilingual learners ☞ new to English in your classroom:

- Include the child in activities/lessons right from the start.
- Make a point of speaking to the child every session even if they do not respond at first.
- Set up a buddy system.
- Give children longer to respond. Repeat what was said if necessary. Only re-phrase if this does not appear to work.
- Use pictures, photographs and picture dictionaries.
- Organise scribing of writing in first language.
- Picture books are an ideal support for language learning.
- A collection of independent 'respite' activities can be helpful for the child to consolidate and work at a less demanding pace.
- Gradually include the child in group discussion starting with answers which require single words that the child knows.
- Be aware of the difficulties of idiomatic expressions.

(adapted from Haslam, Wilkin and Kellet, 2005)

Practice points

- Be particularly aware of the bilingual child's first few weeks in the classroom. Look for opportunities to display your respect for their language through dual-language notices and opportunities to share new words and phrases together.
- Consider and plan how you can help bilingual and multilingual children to access learning at every stage of teaching.
- Acknowledge that you are unlikely to know everything about every child's culture, but in so doing acknowledge also that it is your responsibility to understand the lives of *all* the children in your class, not just those who share your own cultural background.

Glossary

Bilingual learners – children who speak two languages.
Multilingual learners – children who speak more than two languages.

References

Bialystok, E. (2007) 'Cognitive effects of bilingualism: How linguistic experience leads to cognitive change', *International Journal of Bilingual Education and Bilingualism*, 10(3): 210–223.

Blackledge, A. (ed.) (1994) *Teaching Bilingual Children*. Stoke-on-Trent: Trentham Books.

Blair, M. and Bourne, J. (1998) *Making the Difference: Teaching and Learning Strategies in Successful Multi-Ethnic Schools*. London: Department for Education and Employment (DfEE).

Cummins, J. (1996) *Negotiating Identities: Education for Empowerment in a Diverse Society*. Los Angeles: California Association for Bilingual Education (CABE).

DES (Department of Education and Science) (1975) *A Language for Life (The Bullock Report)*. London: HMSO.

Gravelle, M. (1996) *Supporting Bilingual Learners in Schools*. Stoke-on-Trent: Trentham Books.

Haslam, L., Wilkin, Y. and Kellet, E. (2005) *English as an Additional Language: Meeting the Challenge in the Classroom*. London: David Fulton.

Hester, H. (1990) *Patterns of Learning*. London: CLPE.

Hix, P. (1992) *Kaleidoscope: Themes and Activities for Developing the Multicultural Dimension in the Primary School*. Crediton: Southgate.

Jones, R. (1999) *Teaching Racism or Tackling It?* Stoke-on-Trent: Trentham Books.

Kuhl, P. (2004) 'Early language acquisition: cracking the speech code', *Nature Neuroscience*, 5: 831–843.

Low, G. and Beverton, S. (2004) *A Systematic Review of the Impact of ICT on Literacy Learning in English of Learners between 5 and 16, for whom English is a Second or Additional Language*. London: EPPI-Centre, Social Science Research Unit, Institute of Education.

MacLean, K. (1996) 'Supporting the literacy of bilingual learners: storytelling and bookmaking', *Multicultural Teaching*, 2: 26–29.

Reese, L., Garnier, H., Gallimore, R. and Goldenberg, C. (2000) 'Longitudinal analysis of the antecedents of emergent Spanish literacy and middle-school English reading achievement of Spanish-speaking students', *American Educational Research Journal*, 37(3): 622–633.

Strand, S. (2005) 'English language acquisition and educational attainment at the end of primary school', *Educational Studies*, 13(3): 275–391.

Thomas, W. and Collier, V. (1998) *School Effectiveness for Language Minority Students*. Alexandria, VA: National Clearinghouse for Bilingual Education.

Thomas, W. P. and Collier, V. P. (1998) 'Two languages are better than one', *Educational Leadership*, 55: 23–26.

Walker, S., Edwards, V. and Leonard, H. (1998) *Write Around the World: Producing Bilingual Resources in the Primary Classroom*. Reading: University of Reading, Reading and Language Information Centre.

Annotated bibliography

Edwards, V. (1998) *The Power of Babel: Teaching and Learning in Multilingual Classrooms*. Stoke-on-Trent: Trentham Books.
A particularly helpful text in terms of its sensitivity to new arrivals in school and its guidance for teachers with limited experience of children from a range of cultures. Practical advice for the production of dual-language cassettes, books, displays, etc.
L1 ★★

Ethnicity, Social Class, and Gender Achievement – examples from the primary frameworks in the government archive. http://webarchive.nationalarchives.gov.uk
Range of resources including on black pupils and English as an additional language.
L1 ★

Jones, R. (1999) *Teaching Racism or Tackling It?* Stoke-on-Trent: Trentham Books.
A book aimed in particular at white teachers working in predominantly or exclusively white classrooms.
L3 ★★★

Kennedy, E. (2006) 'Literacy development of linguistically diverse first graders in a mainstream English classroom: connecting speaking and writing', *Journal of Early Childhood Literacy*, 6(2): 163–189.
Argues that teachers' understanding of home and school languages is still an issue and that this understanding has an impact on multilingual children's learning.
L3 ★★★

Chapter 27

Gender and the teaching of English

Following some general introductory remarks about gender and education, this chapter focuses on the issue of boys and attainment in literacy. We conclude with a look at an insightful study of the work of one school.

Exploration of issues such as gender is fraught with difficulties for teachers, particularly because stereotypes and preconceptions are rife in society. The danger of preconceptions is that they can lead to low expectations of children's capabilities. It is very difficult to collect 'objective' evidence because characteristics of gender are shared across men and women in subtly different ways. One example of a gender characteristic is preference for reading fiction as opposed to non-fiction. In general, it is argued that women and girls tend to prefer fiction whereas men and boys prefer non-fiction. However, there are many qualifications that need to be made to such an idea. The characteristic does not mean that *all* boys prefer non-fiction or *all* girls prefer fiction. Therefore, in every class of children while it may be true that the characteristic is generally accurate, there will still be boys and girls who do not conform to the stereotype.

There is also a developmental angle. The youngest children tend to have a particularly strong relationship with story, nursery rhymes and songs. There is less of a distinction for them between fiction and non-fiction. As pupils get older, non-fiction forms tend to take on more importance as part of school work but the texts that children select themselves to read at home will not necessarily follow this pattern. It is probably also true to say that most people read a wide variety of texts, hence it may be difficult to classify someone as mainly a fiction reader or mainly a non-fiction reader. So, the statement about boys' and girls' reading habits needs to be carefully qualified by the factors raised above. Before a judgement could be made about your class, you would have to analyse the reading habits of all the children. If you involve the children and parents in such a survey, it could provide helpful information for teaching and provide an opportunity for children to learn more about gender. This strategy of opening up investigation and discussion is one very good way to practically address gender issues in the classroom.

Even if there is evidence to show gender differences there is still the question of how the knowledge should affect our teaching. For example, if we accept that girls prefer fiction, then we could look at this in at least two ways: (1) there is a potential problem that they are not accessing non-fiction texts which becomes increasingly important in secondary schooling and later life, therefore we should take steps to encourage them to access non-fiction; or (2) we want to relate our teaching to girls' interests and want to motivate them so we will expose them to even more fiction. We think that a combination of (1) and (2) is probably a sensible way forward. Another practical way to address gender differences is the use of in-class single sex groupings.

In a systematic review of studies on classroom practice Francis *et al.* (2002) concluded that different kinds of classroom groupings could be effective in helping to reduce children's stereotypical gender constructions. For example, the use of some in-class single sex grouping could do the following:

- increase the self-confidence of girls and/or encourage their experimentation with non-gender-traditional activities; or
- provide a setting for boys to tackle aspects of traditional forms of masculine attitudes and behaviours.

(ibid.: 2)

But overall the authors were struck by how little research had been carried out in the area, the predominance of small-scale studies, and how the issue of boys' attainment had become an area of concern.

Boys and attainment

There has been concern about boys' attainment in the statutory English tests for some years. Raising boys' attainment, particularly that of white, working-class boys, is an important goal (Moss, 2010). Many boys do less well than girls in reading and the difference is even more marked in writing, however as stressed above, it is important to consider *which* boys we are talking about when looking at disparities in achievement between the genders.

Strategies to consider to encourage boys' reading include:

- a holistic approach to the reading curriculum which assimilates opportunities for reading, writing, speaking and listening into an integrated whole;
- concentration on the need to encourage boys to become successful and motivated readers as well as decoders of texts (the difference between learning to read and choosing to read);

- offering a wide range of texts in a variety of media to stimulate and sustain interest;
- giving children space to talk and reflect on their reading;
- offering male as well as female role models who show that reading is a pleasurable activity.

In 2004, the United Kingdom Literacy Association (UKLA) and the Primary National Strategy (PNS) launched some research to look at the issue of attainment in writing. Working with teachers in three different areas of the United Kingdom, they designed and taught three-week integrated teaching units for literacy designed to raise boys' engagement, motivation and achievements in writing using either visual stimuli (including integrated technologies) or drama and other speaking and listening activities. Their research found that this approach to teaching writing impacted not only on standards of boys' achievements, but also on teachers'/practitioners' professional development and capacity.

A survey which measured pupils' perceptions about writing, carried out as part of the research, included the question: 'Is there anything you don't like about writing?' Although there is a lack of clarity about the number of pupils who answered this question in relation to the number of statements they made, before and after the project the pupils' main dislike was, 'Technical: spelling, handwriting, use of grammatical devices, particular text types' (UKLA, 2004:14). The first three items in this list are consistent with other research which has shown the demotivating effects of an undue emphasis on the transcription elements of the writing process (→ Chapter 16). The fourth item is particularly interesting in that the technical analysis of text types has not previously been mentioned as a demotivating factor. An emphasis on analysis of text types was a key feature of literacy teaching from 1997 to 2010 as part of the NLS.

Overall, the research makes very strong claims in favour of the approach to writing that was adopted, but it is possible to critique the methodological design of the study. It has a number of factors which mean we have to be cautious about accepting the findings at face value. It is possible that the impact on standards of writing in the project could have been a result of the emphasis on a new approach rather than the specific teaching methods that were tried. No control groups were used. The teaching methods used were not the only aspect of the change in practice: for example, the projects involved a series of review and evaluation meetings. This opportunity to reflect and discuss could have been a key factor in attainment gains.

The claimed gains in writing standards were unusually large. On average the boys progressed one-third of a National Curriculum level in one term. However, the validity of this assessment needs some investigation. Teachers assessed their target pupils using local authority guidance that sub-divided National Curriculum levels into assessment statements. No examples are included in the report of the different scales that the three different authorities used. Although we are informed that moderation meetings were held, there is very little detail about the ways that pupils' writing was assessed, the nature of the samples that were collected or how attainment across different text types was accounted for.

Despite the caveats about the methodology of the research, the practices used by the teachers are interesting. The teaching was generally planned in three-week blocks concentrating on one type of text. Electronic and print-based forms of texts were used. Reading, writing and speaking and listening were integrated. Drama techniques were used to enhance understanding of texts. Although these approaches are interesting, the report does not explain why they might benefit boys in particular. It is probable that girls would benefit from such an approach as well. The approach used in the research seemed to anticipate the methods of the PNS Framework in 2006, and was similar to a DfES study which found the following:

> We would suggest that gains can be made in primary literacy, particularly in the levels achieved by apparently under-achieving boys, when:
>
> - a variety of interactive classroom activities are adopted, with a 'fitness for purpose', so that both short, specific focused activities and more sustained, ongoing activities are used, as and when appropriate
> - acknowledgement is given to the central importance of talk, to speaking and listening as a means of supporting writing
> - the advantages to be gained through companionable writing with response partners and through group work are recognised
> - teachers are prepared to risk-take to bring more creativity and variety to literacy
> - more integrated use is made of ICT so that quality presentation can be more easily achieved, and drafts amended with more ease.
>
> (Younger *et al.*, 2004: 10)

The work of one school

Trisha Maynard's study looked at the issue of gender from the perspective of one school who decided to address the problem of boys' underachievement. Very early on in her book, Maynard makes it clear that despite renewed concerns about boys' achievements, it was not a new phenomenon. As long ago as 1868 girls outperformed boys and had more positive attitudes to learning. At that time, the issue was defined as a problem for *girls* because they were in danger of 'overstrain':

> Girls' excessive conscientiousness and their almost morbid obsession with learning were castigated as unhealthy and contrasted with boys' 'breezy

attitude' towards life. Cohen comments that boys' poor academic performance and their negative attitudes towards school and school-work were
tolerated – even admired – as natural expressions of their rebellious and
superior intellect.

(Maynard, 2002: 17)

Maynard also raises the issue of narrative versus non-narrative texts. As we
show in Chapter 16, in the 1980s claims were made that there was too much
story writing going on in primary schools. Maynard says that her data showed
that boys were particularly reluctant to write stories. Some of the teachers at the
school claimed that this was due to the attitude of the boys rather than their
ability. The teachers felt that the boys often had very imaginative ideas during
whole class discussion but were reluctant to put their ideas down on paper.
Other chapters in the book shed more light on boys' motivation for writing.
One of the teachers describes a child who was usually motivated by practical
science work but when asked to write up the results would say: 'Why do I have
to write it down? . . . There's no need . . . I know it.' There is also convincing
evidence in the book that boys preferred action in their stories and tended to
include more violence, which is often regarded by teachers as inappropriate.

This does present a dilemma. Schools do not want to encourage violence in
any way. But it should not be the inclusion of violence in stories *per se* that is
the problem. If violence is included, one of the questions should be, is it
written about in a way that is powerful, meaningful, consequential, etc.? In
other words, is it good writing whatever the subject? Maynard observes:

> What is so wrong with the inclusion of ideas gained from the visual
> medium of television and computer games? . . . Should we take more
> account of boys' popular cultural interests when planning children's
> literacy work . . . And are we clear why the development of narrative
> through dialogue and passages of description is considered preferable to a
> more episodic, visual narrative style?

(Maynard, 2002: 66)

The most powerful chapter in the book features the children's own thoughts.
The children identified issues that transcended the gender question. The
monotonous use of story planning sheets received short shrift:

G: The planning sheet . . . that's the worst part of the story.
TM: Why?
G: Because it takes up too much time.
B: I write it and then I forgets it.
B: It worns you out.
B: I don't reckon there's any point in doing it because we only rush
       through it . . . and then don't even look at it . . . I bet you any money

that everybody who uses a planning sheet they don't even look at it . . . they just write it to keep the teacher happy and then put it in the bin.

B: That's what I does. I writes on it then puts it to one side and carries on . . . I don't bother with the planning sheets . . .

G: It's a waste of time.

B: Say Miss gives us an hour to do it all, it takes us nearly an hour to fill in the planning sheet and we don't have time to write the story.

B: He's exaggerating.

G: I would prefer to use a rough book . . . just jot things down.

(Maynard, 2002: 101)

The children also didn't like other techniques that teachers used to help them structure their writing. This was powerful evidence and not surprising. The mantra of 'shared reading; teacher demonstration; scribing; supported composition'; . . . finally followed by *independent* writing can so easily become an inflexible model. It can also signal low expectations based on the idea that all children are incapable of writing unless their writing is scaffolded; children will have interesting ideas for their writing and they are able to write well given appropriate support. If they are unable to, for whatever reason, then you can offer them more structured support.

I hate writing stories in school. If we were allowed to choose our own titles it would be all right. When I go to bed I don't go to bed . . . I put my lamp on and writes stories.

I prefer writing my own stories because you've got a free mind . . . You don't have to put down what Mrs G says.

(ibid.: 99)

At the end of the period of study, the teachers in the school had tried out a number of strategies to tackle the gender problem and had been encouraged to reflect on these. The teachers realised in the main that there were no easy solutions but some were frustrated that they couldn't 'solve the problem'.

As this chapter has shown, there are no simple solutions to addressing gender and attainment. First and foremost teachers need to collect evidence about boys' and girls' learning rather than rely unduly on anecdotal evidence. Involving children in discussion about their opinions is both a necessary part of education and a good way to start to address gender in the classroom. The use of single gender groups as a regular part of classroom organisation can help girls and boys access curricula that are more closely tailored to their needs. Teachers also need to find out about boys' and girls' interests and use this information to provide a curriculum that is relevant to their different needs. Giving pupils opportunities to make choices, for example, over reading material and writing topics is also an important way to support the preferences of girls and boys and gives the sensitive teacher a deeper understanding of the pupils that they teach.

Practice points

- Use evidence about your class as the basis for decisions in terms of the needs of girls and boys.
- Organise your classroom for occasional use of single gender groups. This can work well in collaboration with another colleague.
- Give opportunities for pupils to make choices as part of their English learning.

References

Francis, B., Skelton, C. and Archer, L. (2002) 'A systematic review of classroom strategies for reducing stereotypical gender constructions among girls and boys in mixed-sex UK primary schools', *Research Evidence in Education Library*. Retrieved 28 January, 2007, from http://eppi.ioe.ac.uk/cms/.

Maynard, T. (2002) *Boys and Literacy: Exploring the Issues*. London: RoutledgeFalmer.

Moss, G. (2010) 'Gender and the teaching of English', in D. Wyse, R. Andrews and J. Hoffman (eds) *The Routlege International Handbook of English, Language and Literacy Teaching*. London: Routledge.

United Kingdom Literacy Association (UKLA) and Primary National Strategy (2004) *Raising Boys' Achievements in Writing*. Royston: UKLA.

Younger, M., Warrington, M., Gray, J., Ruddock, J., McClellan, R., Bearne, E. *et al.* (2004) *Raising Boys' Achievement*. London: Department for Education and Skills.

Annotated bibliography

Barrs, M. and Pidgeon, S. (eds) (1998) *Boys and Reading*. London: The Centre for Language in Primary Education.
An early examination of boys' underachievement which features case studies of teachers showing the strategies they use to address the issues.
L1 *

Jackson, S. and Gee, S. (2005) ' "Look, Janet", "No, you look, John" ': constructions of gender in early school reader illustrations across 50 years, *Gender and Education*, 17(2): 115–128.
Shows that gender stereotypes are still a feature of reading schemes.
L3 **

Maynard, T. (2002) *Boys and Literacy: Exploring the Issues*. London: RoutledgeFalmer.
A powerful and in-depth exploration of the issues relating to boys and literacy.
L2 **

Moss, G. (2010) 'Gender and the teaching of English', in D. Wyse, R. Andrews and J. Hoffman (eds) *The Routlege International Handbook of English, Language and Literacy Teaching*. London: Routledge.

Gemma Moss has done some particularly thoughtful work on the experiences of white boys from disadvantaged backgrounds.
L3 ★★★

Teacher Training Resource Bank (TTRB). Now an archived site, but resources are still available; see a review of the United Kingdom Literacy Association/Primary National Strategy (2004) project on Raising Boys' Achievement in Writing.
L2 ★★

Index